PERSONNEL MANAGEMENT

PERSONNEL MANAGEMENT

Jyotsana Singh

CENTRUM PRESS
NEW DELHI-110002 (INDIA)

CENTRUM PRESS
H.O.: 4360/4, Ansari Road, Daryaganj,
New Delhi-110002 (India)
Tel: 23278000, 23261597, 23255577, 23286875
B.O.: No. 1015, Ist Main Road, BSK IIIrd Stage,
IIIrd Phase, IIIrd Block, Bangalore-560085 (INDIA)
Tel: 080-41723429
Email: centrumpress@gmail.com
Visit us at: www.centrumpress.com

Personnel Management

First Edition, 2011

ISBN 978-93-80921-01-3

PRINTED IN INDIA

Printed at Balaji Offset, Delhi.

Contents

Preface *vii*

1. Concept of Personnel Management 1
2. Functions, Policies and Roles 15
3. Organizing the Human Resource Management Department 44
4. Human Resource Management in India 64
5. Human Resource and Audit 72
6. Human Resource Planning 82
7. Training and Development 115
8. Work Life, Job Satisfaction and Morale 132
9. Worker Participation 156
10. Counseling for Effective Human Resource Development 165
11. Human Relations 182
12. Collective Bargaining 191
13. Personnel Management and Industrial Relations 233
14. Employee Training and Development: Reasons and Benefit 275

Index 310

Preface

Personnel management is concerned with the effective use of the skills of people. They may be salespeople in a store, clerks in an office, operators in a factory, or technicians in a research laboratory. In business, personnel management starts with the recruiting and hiring of qualified people and continues with directing and encouraging their growth as they encounter problems and tensions that arise in working towards established goals.

Personnel management works to achieve practical solutions to such problems. It generally provides support to line management. In this staff capacity, the personnel department has the responsibility to develop and implement policies, procedures, and programmes for recruitment, selection, training, placement, safety, employee benefits and services, compensation, labour relations, organization planning, and employee development.

Author

1

Concept of Personnel Management

INTRODUCTION

People of a country are an important asset for it, so is the case with organisations. The successful functioning of an organisation depends on its manpower and quality of leadership. The manpower by itself does not contribute to the development of an organisation, it has to be converted into human resources through systematic planning, adequate training and proper education.

Without the growth of human resources called the human capital, goals and objectives of an organisation can never be achieved. Human capital can be defined as the sum total of knowledge, skills and aptitudes of the people in the society development human resources poses a major of challenge for the developing countries like India. Manpower planning is an important tool for developing human resources. Investments in manpower planning whether made by government or a, private organisation belong to the individual and do not depreciate.

In fact they increase with the passage of time. Thus human resources are an important part of the total resources of an organisation. Though financial resources, physical resources and technological resources are also very important, it is the human resources which are most vital as they generate the other resources. Adequate utilisation of human resources would automatically lead to optimum utilisation of financial, physical and: Technological resources. Organisation can achieve the desired goals without effective management of all its resources, but human capital is the most essential element of an organisation. As, personnel administration deals with the management of the human resources, the study of its concept, nature, scope and development assumes importance.

CONCEPT OF PERSONNEL ADMINISTRATION

The tasks of government are increasing everyday. Development and welfare orientations have led to the expansion of government and its administrative machinery. As the tasks, responsibilities and activities of organisations whether public or private multiply, the demands on personnel, at every level, in terms of efficient discharge of their duties also rise.

Thus the task of personnel administration is to, assure a steady source of people who can contribute to the success of an organisation and meet the growing demands of development. To understand the concept of personnel administration, it is very essential to first understand the meaning and nature of the term.

Personnel Administration: Meaning

Personnel administration is that part of administration which is concerned with people at work and with their relationships within an organisation. It refers to the entire spectrum of an organisation's interaction with its human resources from recruitment activity to retirement process. It involves personnel planning and forecasting, appraising human performance, selection and staffing, training and development and maintenance and improvement of performance and productivity.

There is no standard definition of the term 'personnel administration': Still there is a widespread unaniaity among writers on its meaning, scope and purpose. Flippo, personnel function is concerned with the procurement, development, compensation, integration and maintenance of the personnel of an organisation for the purpose of contributing toward the accomplishment of that organisation's major goals and objectives. Dale Yoder uses the term "manpower management" instead of "personnel management" and includes both labour relations and personnel administration within its ambit.

According to him, "the term effectively describes the processes of planning and directing the application, development and utilisation of human resources in employment. Employers, employees, unions and public agencies all have important roles to play in these processes).

Thomas G. Spates, "personnel administration is a code of the ways of organising and treating individuals at work so that they will each get the greatest possible realisation of their Mrinsic abilities, thus attaining maximum efficiency for themselves and their group and thereby giving to the enterprise of which they are a part, its'determi~in~ competitive advantage and optimum results."

Michael Juciqk defines personnel administration as "the field of management which has to do with planning, organising, and controlling various operative functions of procuring, developing, maintaining and utilising a labour force such that the: "objectives for which the company is established are attained economically and effectively: "objectives of all levels of personnel are served to the highest possible degree; "objectives of the community are duly considered and served."

The Institute of Personnel Management in U.K. defines personnel management as "that part of the management function which is primarily concerned with the human relationships within the organisation. Its objective is the maintenance of those relationships on a basis which, by consideration of the well-being of the individual, enables all those engaged in the undertaking to make their maximum personnel contribution to the effective working of that undertaking." The Indian Institute of Personnel Management has also adopted this definition.

It reads, "Personnel management is that part of the management function which is concerned with people at work and with their relationships within an enterprise. Its aim is to bring together and develop into an effective organisation the men and women who make up an enterprise and, having regard to the well-being of an individual and of working groups, to enable to make their best contribution to its success. In particular, personnel management is concerned with the development of policies

CONCEPT, NATURE AND SCOPE OF PERSONNEL ADMINISTRATION

Governing: Manpower planning, recruitment, selection, placement and termination. Education and training, career development. Terms of employment, methods and standards of remuneration Working conditions and employees' services. Formal and informal communication and consultation both through the representatives of employers and employees and at all levels throughout the organisation.

Negotiation and application of agreements on wages and working conditions, procedures for the avoidance and settlement of disputes. Personnel management is also, concerned with the "human and social implications of change in internal organisation and methods of working and of economic and social changes in the community:' Thus we can say that personnel administration deals with the recruitment, placement, training, disciplinary measures, monetary and non-monetary incentives and retirement benefits of the human beings or the personnel within an organisation. It also deals with the nature of human relationships in an organisation, interaction between the human beings within an organisation and interaction of human beings the organisation.

Personnel administration includes all activities and functions. Relating to policy formulation, planning, policy implementation, social change and modernisation, administrative reforms and public relations in an organisation. It aims at optimum utilisation of human resources in order to achieve maximum results with minimum wastage of funds and technology. Personnel administration is variously known as 'personnel management', 'labour relations', 'manpower management', labour welfare management', etc. But the term 'personnel administration' connotes a wider meaning, it includes both personnel management and industrial relations. Many a times the terms labour relations and industrial relations are used interchangeably with personnel administration but it is always better to distinguish between them. The term 'labour relations' refers primarily to the relation between management and organised labour.

It-kcluaes negotiations of contracts with unions. It deals with handling of differences with unions and business agents. Some organisations have a labour relations officer or director whose primary task is to advise and assist top management in their dealing with union representatives. This official may or may not reject to personnel administrator. In an unionised organisation, where there is no labour relations officer or director, the personnel administrate or performs the task of labour relations officer.

Thus personnel administration aims at:

- Effective utilisation of human resources
- Desirable working relations among all members of the organisation
- Maximum development
- Meeting the organisation's social and legal responsibilities.

Michael J. Jucius, personnel management should aim at: attaining economically and effectively the organisationa, goals;

- Serving to the highest possible degree the individual goals: and
- Preserving and advancing the general welfare of the community.
- To obtain these objectives, personnel administration is concerned with planning, organising, directing, coordinating and controlling the cooperative efforts- of individuals within an organisation.

Nature of Personnel Administration

Personnel Administration

Personnel function is crucial in any administrative organisation. The organisation cannot afford to ignore it.

Hence it becomes a basic responsibility of the management, be in the government or in semi or non-government organisations. The-changes in the socio-economic environment has its effect on management.

The management environment keeps changing due to the changes that occur in the total socio-economic environment. The political environment also affects the work environment in an organisation. Such changes get reflected in personnel administration.

These changes can be: Changing mix of the personnel entering government service organisation changing values of personnel increasing expectations of the government from their employees, and increasing expectations of the people from the government at different levels.

Thus management is affected by the changes in the social, economic and political scenario. In fact it has to keep up with these changes. A higher number from schedule castes, tribes and other economically backward classes are joining the government service. A greater number of people with higher education, more women, more technically skilled workers are also joining the government service.

'This has really changed the ratios of working force. With the proliferation of activities under 'development' and 'welfare' programmes, the employees are now expected to be more competent and efficient. People at large expect the administration to be efficient, effective and sympathetic. People's involvement in administrative activities is increasing. Due to the constant demands oh administration, the role of personnel administration is also changing.

Personnel are required to perform 'line' and 'staff' functions. Activities directly related to the primary objective of an organisation are called as 'line' functions. The staff functions are those which facilitate and assist the performance of line work.

They are in the nature of secondary activities and enhance the effectiveness of the line agencies. For example, assistance in processing and supplying the required number of personnel and training and development of personnel are essentially staff functions. An organisation cannot function without the assistance of line and staff personnel. At the same time, personnel function cannot be isolated from the rest of the administrative functions. Personnel functions include both line and staff activities in an organisation.

Personnel administration does not always function in a formal organisation. No organisation can solely run on the basis of formal rules and regulations, it comprises human beings who are structured in an authority and responsibility network in order to carry out the tasks and activities for the fulfillment of organisational objectives.

This formal structure is supplemented, supported or sometimes obstructed and on occasions taken over by the informal organisation. Informal organisation grows within the formal organisation. It is a natural phenomenon and is based on social and cultural relations among the personnel of formal groups. Political, economic and psychological factors also contribute to the growth of informal organisation.

The functions of personnel administration are becoming more complicated day by day. The problems of personnel administration differ from one organisation to the other. Big organisations have more tasks to perform, they employ more people.

The task of personnel administration in such organisations becomes more intricate. As personnel administration deals with human beings all the time, the crucial functions of motivation and morale of employees have to be performed by it. It has to meet the growing needs of the people as well as satisfy the increasing expectations of its employees.

EVOLUTION AND DEVELOPMENT

While the evolution and development of personnel administration in U.K. and U.S.A. was largely voluntary, in India, the growth of personnel administration can be attributed to the efforts made by the government. Hile in the West, the pioneering work in the field of personnel management was motivated by the managerial preoccupation with the concept of welfare, in India, unsystematic recruitment practices, growing labour unrest, loss of production etc., initiated some interest in personnel management. In U.K., personnel administration had its origin in the concept of welfare as propounded and practised by some of the enlightened entrepreneurs, who sought the establishment of modern personnel administration. The term personnel management actually originated in the U.S.A.

It was F.W. Taylor's scientific management which laid the foundation for the development of personnel administration. Taylor laid emphasis on scientific selection and systematic training and development of the individual worker. H.L. Gantt, a close associate of Taylor, in scientific management movements, foresaw the need for obtaining the willing cooperation of the worker.

He maintained that it was not enough to tell the worker how to do a job, but it was also necessary to promote the ability and willingness to do a job. Mary Parker Follet also laid stress on training and development aspects of management. The pioneers of scientific management, apart from increasing efficiency, aimed at fighting fatigue and monotony among the workers. Most important breakthrough for personnel administration was Elton Mayo's Hawthorne experiments and the human relations movement. These experiments paved the way for using the disciplines of sociology, psychology, industrial psychology, social psychology etc., with a view to understanding employees and organisational behaviour and influencing them through a motivational approach. All this led to the gradual evolution and development of a theory and practice of personnel management.

There were also other events and influences which led to the growth of personnel management. Various revolutionary concepts like mass production, mass distribution and mass financing were evolved by industrial and business empires. The labour shortages during the world wars and various labour problems posed a challenge to management. With the Great Depression in 1929, big business suffered a severe setback. The State, the public and the trade unions, aimed at efficient professional management. Their demands were, elimination of waste and maximum utilisation of resources, particularly human resources.

Personnel Administration

All these developments in America emphasised the fact that management of people or personnel management is just as important as the management of production. Thus the entrepreneurial interest, apart from other events in the sphere of worker welfare provided the source of inspiration for the evolution of modem dynamic personnel administration.

The history of the evolution and growth of personnel management in our country is not very old. It was the Royal Commission on Labour which recommended in 1931 the appointments of Labour Officers to deal with the recruitment of labour to settle their grievances. The industrial disputes of 1920s forced the government and businessmen to think in terms of labour problems and promotion of personnel management.

The recognition of trade unions in India gave a new perspective to the employer and employee relationship. Entrepreneurs like the Tatas, Calico Mills, British India Corporation etc. had appointed Welfare Officers as early as 1920. These Labour Welfare Officers performed the functions of employee grievances and promotion of industrial harmony.

In 1937 in Bengal, on the suggestion of the Government, the Indian Jute Mills Owners' Association appointed a Labour Officer to bring about a settlement of employee grievances with the mills and by 1939 five more Labour Officers were appointed. Other Employers' Associations like Indian Engineering Association, Indian Tea Association, the Engineering Association of India etc., also followed the example of Indian Jute Owners' Association in appointing labour officers.

In 1941, the Government of India initiated the Tripartite Labour Conference with the representatives of Government, labour and employees in order to promote uniform labour legislation, determine a procedure to settle industrial disputes, and promote consultations on industrial matters affecting the country. Now they have become permanent and regular features of labour policy. In 1948, the Factories Act laid down the appointment, duties and qualifications of a new statutory officer in industry called the Welfare Officer.

The following years saw the emergence of yet another officer called the Personnel Officer. The Personnel Officer deals with labour welfare, industrial relations and personnel administration. Many companies in India now have specialised personnel departments and a full-time Personnel Officer in charge. Now the number of personnel is increasing at a very fast rate, expenditure on personnel is also correspondingly increasing.

There has also been a trend in regard to the diversification in the personnel as more and more specialists, experts and technicians are being appointed in government departments, public and private organisations. Contemporary personnel does not just deal with welfare of employees but also aim at achieving profits for the organisation. The motive is to earn profits as well as benefits for the organisation and its employees.

SCOPE OF PERSONNEL ADMINISTRATION

Personnel administration in corporates all aspects of management of persons in organisation. The primary objective of personnel administration, as we have read earlier in the unit is to ensure effective utilisation of human resources in pursuit of organisational goals.

The personnel administration departments should design and establish an effective working relationship among all the members of an organisation by division of organisational tasks into jobs defining clearly the responsibility and authority for each job and its relation with other jobs in the organisation.

Personnel administration must try to enthuse among the employees feelings of commitment, involvement and loyalty to the organization, unfavourable practices like favouritism and nepotism in an organization Concept, Nature and Scope Personnel administration has to concentrate on various aspects of management like Personnel Administration recruitment, training, promotion, conditions of service, employees welfare, employer-employee relations and processes of morale and motivation. It has to develop links with immediate, intermediate and external environment to make itself effective and efficient. As the tasks of organisation increase, the responsibilities of personnel administration also increase accordingly. It is not possible to solve the problems with a one-time and one-stroke decision. Larger the system more are the complexities.

Take for example, the Government of India, it is divided into ministries, departments, divisions, units etc. It is spread over the entire length and breadth of the country. Lakhs of people work in it, they operate at different hierarchical levels and carry out a large variety of functions. A number of services and their division into groups constitute the entire workforce of the Central government. Almost similar is the situation in each state.

Personnel administration has to cater to all these aspects. It requires continuous managerial input. Planning and providing for the regular supply of the needed manpower for different positions and in different numbers is an important task of the government. The process of recruitment and utilisation of each micro-unit of human resource calls for effective personnel administration, similarly, creating and maintaining desirable working relationships also call for a series of continuous efforts on the part of the personnel.

Those responsible for personnel administration have to work for it constantly. The achievement of these two objectives becomes easier if the organisation provides appropriate opportunities for individual development. These opportunities can be in the form of training internal and external mobility, promotion, recognition and reward.

They act as strong motivators and satisfier. Besides, salary structuring of lakhs of employees is a wholesome task because each category has to be adequately and equitably compensated for the contribution it is expected to make towards organisation's objectives. This is also a work of personnel administration. The working force also has to be subjected to certain discipline in order to regulate .proper performance of duty. Framing of conduct rules, laying down procedures of disciplinary action, enforcement of those rules and appropriate procedures are also a part of personnel administration.

Employer-employee relations, provision for Joint Consultative Machinery, establishment of public service tribunals for adjudication, adoption of welfare measures and payment of retirement benefits etc. to the employees are the added responsibilities of personnel' administration. Trade unionism among government employees, has increased during the past few decades. Both employer and employee unions have come up. There is now a dire need for expert skills to foresee personnel needs and problems 2nd to plan for their satisfaction and rectification. All this requires systematic personnel administration. Thus the scope of personnel administration is wide and varied, moreover it is continuously expanding with the changes in environment.

CEASE

Thus we can say that it is the personnel which more than anything else determines the quantity and quality of the performance and output of an organisation. Even the contribution of money and material to the performance of an organisation depends substantially upon their manipulation by the human beings in an organisation. Even the poorly devised machinery may be made to work if it is manned with well-trained, intelligent and imaginative staff. On the other hand, the best planned organisation may produce unsatisfactory results if it is operated by disorganised staff.

Personnel constitute an integral part of the organisation. Personnel administration with its ever increasing responsibilities has become an indispensable part of management. There is a need for making personnel administration responsible for bringing about innovative changes in the structure of organisation, undertaking personnel research and conducting attitude surveys. There is also a need for making personnel administration accountable for formulating cost effective policies and programmes and establishing positive relationship between the organisation and environment.

A constantly changing scenario calls for better recruitment procedures, newer training techniques, retraining methods, mid-career training, more coordination between private and public welfare programmes, effective organisational development, better performance appraisal devices and more useful leadership methods.

DIFFERENCE BETWEEN PERSONNEL AND HR?

Some experts assert that there is no difference between human resources and personnel management. They state that the two terms can be used interchangeably, with no difference in meaning. In fact, the terms are often used interchangeably in help-wanted ads and job descriptions.

For those who recognize a difference between personnel management and human resources, the difference can be described as philosophical. Personnel management is more administrative in nature, dealing with payroll, complying with employment law, and handling related tasks. Human resources, on the other hand, is responsible for managing a workforce as one of the primary resources that contributes to the success of an organization.

When a difference between personnel management and human resources is recognized, human resources is described as much broader in scope than personnel management. Human resources is said to incorporate and develop personnel management tasks, while seeking to create and develop teams of workers for the benefit of the organization. A primary goal of human resources is to enable employees to work to a maximum level of efficiency. Personnel management can include administrative tasks that are both traditional and routine. It can be described as reactive, providing a response to demands and concerns as they are presented. By contrast, human resources involves ongoing strategies to manage and develop an organization's workforce. It is proactive, as it involves the continuous development of functions and policies for the purposes of improving a company's workforce.

Personnel management is often considered an independent function of an organization.

Human resource management, on the other hand, tends to be an integral part of overall company function. Personnel management is typically the sole responsibility of an organization's personnel department. With human resources, all of an organization's managers are often involved in some manner, and a chief goal may be to have managers of various departments develop the skills necessary to handle personnel-related tasks. As far as motivators are concerned, personnel management typically seeks to motivate employees with such things as compensation, bonuses, rewards, and the simplification of work responsibilities.

From the personnel management point of view, employee satisfaction provides the motivation necessary to improve job performance. The opposite is true of human resources. Human resource management holds that improved performance leads to employee satisfaction. With human resources, work groups, effective strategies for meeting challenges, and job creativity are seen as the primary motivators. When looking for a job in personnel management or human resources, it is important to realise that many companies use the terms interchangeably. If you are offered a job as a personnel manager, you may be required to perform the same duties as a human resource manager, and vice versa. In some companies, a distinction is made, but the difference is very subtle

2

Functions, Policies and Roles

Historically, it was taken for granted that public services would be delivered by a staff of career civil service employees, working within the structure of centralized public agencies budgeted with appropriated funds.

Today, none of these are true - public programmes are more than likely performed by alternative organizations or mechanisms rather than by public agencies; and when public agencies are used, they are more likely to be staffed by contingent workers hired through flexible employment mechanisms rather than permanent employees protected by civil service regulations and collective bargaining agreements.

ALTERNATIVE MECHANISMS FOR DELIVERING PUBLIC SERVICES

Purchase-of-service agreements with other governmental agencies and non-governmental organizations have become commonplace. For example, Metropolitan Dade County, FL now provides fire and rescue services to almost every small- and medium-sized municipality in Dade County.

These arrangements were negotiated because they offer persuasive advantages for Dade County and municipalities. For Dade County, there is the opportunity to expand services within a given geographic area using economies of scale. For municipalities, the arrangement offers the opportunity to reduce capital costs, personnel costs, and legal liability risks. In addition, because fire fighters are heavily unionized, it offers the opportunity to avoid the immediate political and economic costs associated with collective bargaining. As another example, many local governments contract with individual consultants or private businesses to conduct personnel services such as employee development and training.

The use of outside consultants and businesses increases available expertise and managerial flexibility by reducing the range of qualified technical and professional employees that the agency must otherwise hire to provide training. The costs of service purchase agreements may actually be lower than the same function performed by in-house personnel, in that the government agency pays no personnel costs or associated employment taxes and reduces its own legal liability risks. Privatization is the performance of a formerly public function by a private contractor.

It differs from service purchase agreements primarily in philosophy and scope. While service purchase agreements contract for delivery of a particular service to a public agency, privatization means abolition of the entire public agency, replacing the infrastructure with an outside contractor who then provides all services formerly provided by the public agency. Privatization has become commonplace over the past 15 years because it offers all the advantages of service purchase agreements, but on a larger scale. Privatization has become commonplace in areas such as solid waste disposal, where there is an easily identifiable "benchmark" and where public agency costs tend to be higher because of higher pay and benefits.

But privatization is spreading rapidly in other areas that have previously been almost entirely the prerogative of the public sector: schools and prisons. In 1994, the school board of a working-class Pittsburgh suburb was facing desperate problems. It had the highest tax rate in the county; only one of 40 students who took the Scholastic Achievement Test in the year from June 1993 to June 1994 scored above the national average of 950 on math and verbal test results; and the number of high school graduates plummeted from 225 in 1978 to 60 in 1994. It sent layoff notices to teachers at one of four schools and hired a Tennessee company to pick its own teachers and run the school. Not surprisingly, it made this decision over strong opposition from unionized teachers and school administrators, who intimated that the purpose was union-busting rather than educational reform. A state court issued an injunction forbidding the contact; the district is considering an appeal.

In 1990 a record of over one million people were incarcerated in federal and state prisons. Despite heavy increases in prison construction, most states have been at capacity for the past five years. Privatization is one option for increasing government performance while attempting to hold down costs. During the past five years, a number of private corporations have gotten in to the business of managing prisons, halfway houses, boot camps, and detention facilities. These organizations offer elected officials an alternative to public construction and management of prison facilities, which is a soaring cost for most state governments.

Franchise Agreements often allow private business to monopolize a previously public function within a geographic area, charge competitive rates for it, and then pay the appropriate government a fee for the privilege. Examples are private shuttle bus companies in many major cities using vans instead of buses. The vans frequently duplicate public transportation services by "skimming" riders off of popular bus routes; but municipalities often encourage the procedure because it reduces their own costs, provides some revenue in return, and results in a continuation of a desirable public service. Subsidy Arrangements enable private businesses to perform public services, funded either by user fees to clients or cost reimbursement from public agencies.

Examples include airport security operations (provided by private contractors and paid for both by passengers and airlines), some types of hospital care (for example, emergency medical services provided by private hospitals and reimbursed by public health systems), and some higher education programmes. For example, a state may choose to subsidize a private university by paying it to operate a specialized programme, rather than to assign responsibility and resources for it to a public institution. It is because of subsidy arrangements that the University of Miami, a private institution with a prestigious (and expensive) medical centre, receives more appropriated funds from the state of Florida than does Florida International University, the state university in Miami. Or, local housing authorities may choose to subsidize rent in public housing projects based on tenant income to encourage occupancy by low-income residents. Vouchers enable individual recipients of public goods or services to purchase them from competing providers on the open market.

Recent public opinion has focused on educational vouchers as a possible alternative to public school monopolies. Under this system, parents receive a voucher that could be applied to the cost of education for their child at a number of competing institutions - public schools, private schools, etc. Another variant is housing vouchers as a substitute for publicly constructed and managed housing. These vouchers allow public housing recipients to purchase the best possible housing on a competitive basis from available private landlords.

Volunteers are widely used by a range of public agencies to provide services that might otherwise be performed by paid employees. These include community crime watch programmes, which work in cooperation with local police departments. Volunteer teachers' aides provide tutoring and individual assistance in many public schools.

Self-help is common in community development programmes and correctional facilities. Community development programmes frequently use residents on a volunteer basis to provide recreation, counseling, and other support services for a community. Frequently, such contributions are required to "leverage" a federal or state grant of appropriated funds. Contrary to the popular image of prisons as vacation resorts, prison inmates are usually responsible for laundry, food service and facilities maintenance.

Regulatory and Tax Incentives are typically used to encourage the private sector to perform functions that might otherwise be performed by public agencies with appropriated funds. The Job Partnership Training Act (JPTA), for example, was a tax incentive-based national system for manpower training that replaced CETA.

CETA (the Comprehensive Education and Training Act, was a federally-funded programme that passed money through to state and local governments for assessment, training and job placement activities. Its successor, the Job Training Partnership Act, offered income tax deductions for corporations that hired, trained and retained disadvantaged employees. The intended effect - human resource development and employment - was the same as with CETA, only the mechanism was different. Regulatory incentives include the zoning variances granted to condominium associations. Frequently, construction requires variances for roads, parking, waste collection and disposal. In return for these variances, the condominium association agrees to provide many services normally performed by local government.

These include security (if the condominium has a gated entrance), waste disposal, public works (maintenance of common areas), etc. This may seem an unfair arrangement to the residents, who pay both maintenance fees to the condominium association and local property taxes for the same services (which are not provided by the municipality).

But it does explain the increasing popularity among builders and residents of condominiums - their lower unit cost often makes them the only low or moderate housing available; and they would not be approved by local planning councils or zoning boards unless the contractor agreed in advance to require the condominium association to be responsible for services that otherwise would be the municipality's responsibility.

FLEXIBLE EMPLOYMENT RELATIONSHIPS FOR REMAINING PUBLIC EMPLOYEES

All of these mechanisms are used for providing public services without using public employees, and in many cases through other funding sources besides appropriated funds. Yet even in those cases where public services continue to be provided by public employees working in public agencies funded by appropriations, massive changes have occurred in employment practices. Chief among these are increased use of temporary, part-time, and-seasonal employment; and increased hiring of exempt employees (those outside the classified civil service) through employment contracts.

These two devices, along with the increased use of outside contractors, have markedly changed the face of the public work force. Increasingly, employers reduce costs and enhance flexibility by meeting minimal staffing requirements through "permanent" employees, and by hiring "contingent" (temporary, part-time or seasonal) workers to meet peak workload demands. These positions usually offer lower salaries and benefits than career positions.

And employees can be hired and fired "at will" (without reference to due process entitlements of civil service employees, or collective bargaining agreements). Skill requirement of these jobs are reduced by job-redesign or work simplification. Where commitment and high skills are required on a temporary basis, employers may seek to save money or maintain flexibility by using contract or leased employees to positions exempt from civil service protections.

Exempt positions are classified, in that positions must be created and funded before they can be filled. But they are not classified within civil service systems, so their incumbents are not "permanent" (at least, not in the sense of having a property interest in their positions).

Instead, the terms and conditions of these positions are specified through performance contracts specifying pay and benefits, and limiting the term of employment. While contracts may be routinely renewed with the approval of the employee and the employer, employees may also be discharged "at will" in the event of a personality conflict, a change in managerial objectives, or a budget shortfall.

Frequently, once employees become exempt, they lose their "bumping rights" back into a classified position in the event of a reduction in force (RIF). Increasingly, managerial and technical employees are hired into these types of contracts. They increase the salary and benefits that can be offered to highly qualified employees, and they enhance managerial flexibility to trim personnel costs quickly, should this be necessary, without having to resort to the bureaucratic chaos precipitated by the exercise of "bumping rights" during an RIF situation.

The impact of these two devices is accelerated by retirement "buyouts," which offer employees close to retirement age an incentive to retire early within a limited period of eligibility ("window"). In a typical example, employees with 17-20 years of service (in a jurisdiction with a 20-year eligibility requirement for retirement) may be offered, for a limited time period of two months, the opportunity to resign and receive retirement benefits equal to those they would have received with three additional years' service.

And the employer may even "sweeten the pot" by offering to pay its share of the cost of employee and family health benefits during the early retirement period (before the employee is eligible for Medicare). If the plan is designed properly so that enough employees retire to save substantially, but enough stay to provide for organizational continuity and skills, both employer and employee benefit. The employee gets an option to retire early at close to current salary; the employer gets to fill the vacant position with an entry-level employee at a much lower salary.

The major drawback for the municipality is unexpectedly large lump-sum payments for accrued annual leave or sick leave. For example, the City of Miami, FL estimates that it will need to find $10 million to compensate 339 employees who elected early retirement. The highest payout is $87,000; the average is $20,000.

Managerial Functions of Personnel Management

- *Planning*: Plan and research about wage trends, labour market conditions, union demands and other personnel benefits. Forecasting manpower needs etc.
- *Organizing*: Organizing manpower and material

resources by creating authorities and responsibilities for the achievement of organizational goals and objectives.

- *Staffing*: Recruitment & Selection
- *Directing*: Issuance of orders and instructions, providing guidance and motivation of employees to follow the path laid-down.
- *Controlling*: Regulating personnel activities and policies according to plans. Observations and comparisons of deviations

Operational Functions of Personnel Management

- *Procurement*: Planning, Recruitment and Selection, Induction and Placement
- *Development*: Training, Development, Career planning and counseling.
- *Compensation*: Wage and Salary determination and administration
- *Integration*: Integration of human resources with organization.
- *Maintenance*: Sustaining and improving working conditions, retentions, employee communication
- Separations: Managing separations caused by resignations, terminations, layoffs, death, medical sickness etc.

CHALLENGES OF HRM IN INDIAN ECONOMY

- *Globalization*: Growing internationalization of business has its impact on HRM in terms of problems of unfamiliar laws, languages, practices, competitions, attitudes, management styles, work ethics and more. HR managers have a challenge to deal with more functions, more heterogeneous functions and more involvement in employee's personal life.
- *Corporate reorganizations*: Reorganization relates to mergers and acquisitions, joint ventures, take over, internal restructuring of organizations. In these situations, it is difficult to imagine circumstances that

pose a greater challenge for HRM than reorganizations itself. It is a challenge to manage employees' anxiety, uncertainties, insecurities and fears during these dynamic trends.

- *New organizational forms*: The basic challenge to HRM comes from the changing character of competitions. The competition is not between individual firms but between constellations of firm. Major companies are operating through a complex web of strategic alliances with local suppliers, etc. These relationships give birth to completely new forms of organizational structure, which highly depend upon a regular exchange of people and information. The challenge for HRM is to cope with the implications of these newly networked relations more and more, in place of more comfortable hierarchical relationships that existed within the organizations for ages in the past.
- *Changing demographics of workforce*: Changes in workforce are largely reflected by dual career couples, large chunk of young blood between age old superannuating employees, working mothers, more educated and aware workers etc. These dynamic workforces have their own implications for HR managers and from HRM point of view is a true challenge to handle.
- *Changed employee expectations*: With the changes in workforce demographics, employee expectations and attitudes have also transformed. Traditional allurements like job security, house, and remunerations are not much attractive today, rather employees are demanding empowerment and equality with management. Hence it is a challenge for HRM to redesign the profile of workers, and discover new methods of hiring, training, remunerating and motivating employees.
- *New industrial relations approach*: In today's dynamic world, even unions have understood that strikes and militancy have lost their relevance and unions are

greatly affected by it. The trade union membership has fallen drastically worldwide and the future of labour movement is in danger. The challenge before HRM is to adopt a proactive industrial relations approach which should enable HR specialist to look into challenges unfolding in the future and to be prepared to convert them into opportunities.

- *Renewed people focus*: The need of today's world and business is the people's approach. The structure, strategy, systems approach which worked in post war era is no more relevant in today's economic environment which is characterized by over capacities and intense competition. The challenge of HR manager is to focus on people and make them justifiable and sustainable.
- *Managing the Managers*: Managers are unique tribe in any society, they believe they are class apart. They demand decision-making, bossism, and operational freedom. However in the post liberalization era, freedom given to managers is grossly misused to get rid of talented and hard working juniors. The challenge of HRM is how to manage this tribe? How to make them realise that the freedom given to them is to enable them make quick decisions in the interest of the organization and not to resort to witch-hunting.
- *Weaker society interests*: Another challenge for HRM is to protect the interest of weaker parts of society. The dramatic increase of women workers, minorities and other backward communities in the workforce has resulted in the need for organizations to reexamine their policies, practices and values. In the name of global competition, productivity and quality the interests of the society around should not be sacrificed. It is a challenge of today's HR managers to see that these weaker parts are neither denied their rightful jobs nor are discriminated against while in service.

- *Contribution to the success of organizations*: -The biggest challenge to an HR manager is to make all employees contribute to the success of the organization in an ethical and socially responsible way. Because society's well being to a large extent depends on its organizations.

IMPACT ON THE ROLE OF THE PUBLIC PERSONNEL MANAGER

The emergence of alternative personnel systems has meant changes in the role of the public personnel manager, and the comparative importance of personnel functions. First, historical traditions emphasize the technical side of personnel management, with less emphasis on policy-related analytical work, relationships with outside organizations and conflicting values. In addition, both employees and line management are seen as clients, and are perceived as being served through the merit system. The traditional department's work includes record keeping and the processing of personnel transactions, especially in smaller government agencies or units. A more contemporary view emphasizes different activities and relationships.

While the traditional functions continue to be important, they are relatively less important than the "brokering" or mediating of conflicts among competing personnel systems. For example, the modern personnel director might be called upon to prepare cost-benefit analyses of alternative pay and benefit proposals related to collective bargaining with employees in the solid waste department. At the same time, he or she might also be asked to evaluate the comparative feasibility, productivity and cost of privatizing or contracting this entire function out (thus making the collective bargaining analysis obsolete).

Or, since the majority of employees in the department are minorities, the director might be asked to assess the impact of contracting out on the city's overall level of affirmative action compliance. Modern personnel directors do not work in isolation; rather, they work closely with other officials within their own agency (budget directors, attorneys, collective bargaining negotiators, affirmative action compliance officers, and supervisors) and outside it (legislative staff, union officials, affirmative action agencies, civil service boards, health and life insurance benefit representatives, pension boards, ethics commissions, and employee assistance programmes dealing with substance abuse and other personal problems).

Most public personnel departments have moved cautiously into the modern era because of their traditional reluctance to be identified with or become involved in "politics." Yet as their function is increasingly viewed as the development and management of human resource systems involving the reconciliation of value conflicts, they are overcoming this reluctance and working outside the confining environment of the civil service system.

And they are finding that this expanded role brings benefits as well as risks. They are able to bring their expertise to bear on a range of critical human resource issues in a variety of contexts - issues traditional personnel managers might define as falling outside their area of responsibility. For example, they can work with legislators on privatization and benefits issues, with labour negotiators on alternative pay and grievance procedures, and with affirmative action compliance agencies on affirmative action proposals or minority business contracting procedures.

By continuing to assert their central role in the most critical issues of agency management, they are developing not only their own professional status, but the status of their profession.

Changes in Job Duties

The use of non-governmental organizations reduces the absolute number of public employees, thereby diminishing human resource functions of the personnel department - especially those functions related to acquisition, development, and sanction of public employees.

However, it does increase the importance of planning, that is necessary to estimate the type and number of contract employees needed to provide a desired level of service; share in developing contract proposals for outside organizations; and evaluate responses to proposals by comparing costs and services. The use of volunteers and self-help means that personnel directors work increasingly with citizen volunteers and community-based organizations, much as personnel directors for not-for-profit organizations (community recreation programmes, hospitals, and schools) have traditionally used volunteers to supplement paid staff. In these cases, public personnel managers need to become more skilled in recruitment, selection, training, and motivation of volunteer workers.

Flexibility in employment relationships is achieved primarily by the increased use of temporary, part-time, and seasonal employment; and by increased hiring of exempt employees (those outside the classified civil service) through employment contracts. Use of contingent employment relationships generally means less emphasis on planning and employee development, at least for these employees. The organization is typically staffed at minimum workload levels, and additional employees are added as needed based on fluctuations in workload.

Development of employees (through training, performance evaluation, or motivation) is largely irrelevant. Contingent workers are hired with the skills needed to perform the job immediately. Performance evaluation is unnecessary - if they do their jobs adequately, they get paid; if not, they get fired. Their motivation is financial, perhaps augmented by the chance of being hired into a civil service position if any vacancies become available.

Nor is the sanction function particularly important for public personnel managers with respect to these workers. Of course, employers are required to maintain a safe and healthy workplace; but compliance with the Americans with Disabilities Act, the Family Medical Leave Act, and the Fair Labour Standards Act are not required for temporary, part time, or seasonal workers. Nor is it at all difficult, from the employers's perspective, to maintain the terms of the employment relationship - "at will" employment means just that. Like political appointments, but unlike their civil service counterparts, "at will" employees have no right to retain their jobs. They can be discharged for any reason, or for no reason, without management having to give a reason or to support it.

Changes in Job Objectives

The evolution of public personnel management values and systems has meant corresponding changes in the fundamental objectives of public personnel management. During the development of public personnel management as part of the transition from patronage to merit systems, public personnel management functioned as the champion of merit system principles.

The growth of public personnel management regulations and procedures occurred within the context of civil service systems whose development was characterized by a bipolar dynamic of competition between political patronage appointments (the "spoils system") and civil service appointments (the "merit system"). In this context, the public personnel manager was viewed as a moral guardian responsible for protecting employees, applicants and the public from the evils of the spoils system.

This required knowledge of civil service policies and procedures, and a willingness to apply them in the face of political pressure. During Stage Three, public personnel managers sought to maintain compliance with civil service rules and regulations and limit patronage appointments, and legislators and chief executives sought to maintain bureaucratic compliance, efficiency and accountability through budgetary controls and position management. Through such devices as personnel ceilings and average grade level restrictions, it became the role of public personnel management to control the behaviour of public managers and to help assure compliance with legislative authority.

In effect, it was the responsibility of public personnel managers to synthesize two distinct values (bureaucratic compliance as the operational definition of organizational efficiency, and civil service protections as the embodiment of employee rights). There was tension between them because they were both symbiotic and conflicting. Taken to extremes, either would diminish the other; in moderation, both supported the concept of a qualified and effective public service that was at the heart of bureaucratic theory and scientific management. During Stage Four, due to a variety of political and economic pressures, the focus of public personnel management shifted to work management as managers and public personnel specialists continued to demand flexibility and equitable reward allocation through such alterations to classification and pay systems as rank-in-person personnel systems, broad pay banding, and group performance evaluation and reward systems.

This trend coincided with employee needs for utilization, development, and recognition. In addition, because this period was characterized by a dynamic and self-correcting equilibrium among four competing values, the role of the public personnel manager involved political (mediating and conflict resolution) skills in addition to technical knowledge.

During this period, public personnel managers functioned as interpreters and mediators of four conflicting values. Intuitively, maintaining an acceptable balance among four conflicting pro-government values was difficult, yet it gave value to the profession because of the political, professional, and technical skills it demanded of personnel managers.

Because the current period (Stage Five) has emerged so recently, the ways in which it is changing the role of the public personnel manager are not yet entirely clear. But it is possible to predict their probable impact. Public personnel managers will still be required to be good managers under Stage Five, but the definition of "good management" is narrow by previous standards.

First, public personnel managers are required, more than ever, to manage government employees and programmes in compliance with legislative mandates for cost control. Given the common legislative presumption that the public bureaucracy is an enemy to be controlled rather than a tool to be used to accomplish public policy objectives, public personnel managers in the future may have less opportunity to exercise professional responsibilities in balancing conflicting values. The scope of their authority may be diminished by legislative micro-management, or the value of cost control may be so dominate as to preclude other considerations - even concern for employee rights, for organizational efficiency, or social equity. Second, "good management" may in time comprise skills that are more directed to minimizing maximum loss (such as risk management and contract compliance) than to maximizing human development and organizational performance for permanent employees. "People skills" will continue to be important.

For example, public personnel managers will increasingly be responsible for developing and managing a range of public employment systems for contract, temporary, and "at will" employees. They may be required to work increasingly with volunteers and community-based not-for-profit organizations that increasingly constitute the social safety net by which the value of community responsibility is carried out. Civil service and collective bargaining continue to be important, for many public employees (particularly school teachers and administrators, police and firefighters) are still covered by union contracts and collective bargaining agreements.

But risk management, cost control, and management of other types of employment contracts will become more important than ever. In this sense, substituting a calculating perspective for an optimistic view of the joint possibilities for organizational productivity and individual growth represents a narrowing of the public personnel manager's perspective. It is noteworthy that the search and screen process for the personnel director of a mid-sized Florida city resulted in the highest ranking being given to a person with no previous civil service personnel experience.

Instead, this person was a labour attorney with extensive private-sector experience negotiating and administering employment contracts with outside vendors and contractors. It is evident from this analysis that the field of public personnel management is turbulent and transitional. Some traditional public personnel departments continue to function as technical staff agencies within an environment characterized by agreement on values. This role is most common for personnel departments or civil service boards operating within civil service systems in homogeneous political environments.

More progressive departments might be called upon to take a more active role in designing, implementing, or evaluating human resource management systems within an agency that operates in an environment characterized by disagreement on personnel systems and values. A good example of this type of environment is the personnel systems found in some state court systems.

First, state judges are elected, and appoint their primary administrators. Second, some court administrators are appointed "at will" to exempt positions by the Chief Judge. However, these are not political appointments, in that applicants must meet stringent qualifications. Third, some court employees may be covered by county civil service systems (including probation officers).

Fourth, some court employees (such as process servers) are officers of the court because they discharge official functions, yet they are paid on commission by private attorneys. Fifth, family law cases are often assigned to court-appointed mediators selected at random and paid by the court as independent contractors. It is important to recognize that the court administrator is the chief administrative officer, responsible among other things for budget and personnel management. This means dealing with multiple levels of government, multiple funding sources, and multiple personnel systems simultaneously.

These activities usually require the use of analytical human resource management information systems. For example, they might conduct analyses like the cost of absenteeism, sick leave abuse, and fringe benefits for the agency. They might distribute and evaluate ratings on employee performance evaluation systems to measure their effect on productivity. They might experiment with new techniques for selecting employees (such as assessment centres), or new techniques of job design intended to meet employee needs and increase employee productivity (such as job sharing or flextime). They might be responsible for developing policies and procedures for substance abuse testing; for developing proposals for establishing EAPs (employee assistance programmes) to help employees maintain productivity while resolving personal problems; or for encouraging QCs (quality circles), groups of employees responsible for proposing and implementing changes in procedures to make the organization more productive.

They might be called upon to monitor the frequency of turnover in various departments, "cost out" proposed changes in pay and benefits, and monitor the compliance of benefits contractors with previously negotiated contracts.

Changes in Required Knowledge, Skills and Abilities

Traditional public personnel management requires that personnel directors know the laws and regulations that control practices within a particular system, as well as the techniques used to perform personnel functions within that system. For example, traditional civil-service-oriented personnel management requires knowledge of civil service rules and regulations (such as competitive examination procedures, or how to select from a list of eligible applicants), as well as how to develop and administer examinations, write job descriptions, administer pay and benefit programmes, and process personnel actions.

Contemporary public personnel management requires these skills and more. It requires a knowledge of public personnel management techniques, an understanding of historical developments in the field, and the ability to resolve ethical dilemmas among competing values under conditions of change and uncertainty.

Personnel rules and procedures are not value-neutral; rather, they are the implicit or explicit implementation of a particular public personnel system (or compromises among several such systems). This means that each selection or promotion decision must be viewed not merely as a technical exercise, but as a case that reflects and exemplifies this historical conflict over alternative values, power and public personnel systems.

Public personnel directors must be sensitive to the need for administrative systems to be responsive to legitimate political values and public participation in governance, especially in local government. These kinds of changes inevitably challenge the shield that the rhetoric of "merit" has provided the traditional manager.

Now there is no escaping the political pressure personnel managers must face. They work under consent decrees and with unions that traditionally have set barriers to hiring women and minorities. At the same time, they are expected to respond to their political leaders while maintaining the integrity of the civil service system they oversee. Yet they have no guidance from within the traditional civil service system for how to integrate these increasingly insistent and conflicting demands.

Given that the emergence of two new alternative public personnel systems has brought about changes in the duties, objectives, and skills required of personnel managers, it might be useful to assess how well prepared they consider themselves to function in this new environment. What follows is the results of a focus group discussion held among 19 public managers and officials, primarily public personnel managers, to discuss their use of alternative systems, their actual and desired extent of involvement in choosing these strategies and desired topics for further training.

Of the 19 participants, the typical participant was a local government personnel director with a graduate degree, working for an agency with over 500 employees. All of the participants' employers use some alternatives to traditional civil service systems, with purchase of services from outside vendors being universal. Most use purchase of service from other government agencies, privatization, volunteers, self-help, and regulatory and tax incentives. Some use franchise agreements and subsidy arrangements. Almost none use vouchers. In the future, most respondents predict about the same usage of part-time civil service and exempt employees, less usage of civil service employees, and more usage of full-time exempt and contract employees. The typical respondent reported that they had shared responsibility, though not primary responsibility, for choosing these alternatives to civil service. This was consistent with their expectations. Most reported that the most important decision-maker had been elected/appointed officials, followed in second place by managers and budget directors, with human resource directors ranked third.

Most participants reported that they needed some or much information on these alternatives to function effectively. Their main sources of information are professional associations and journals, classes and seminars, and other human resource professionals. This is as they think it should be. But a majority reported having received no formal training on the subject during the past two years. Those who reported receiving formal training indicated that it was for the most part self-initiated, and paid for by themselves rather than their employer.

When asked what topics should be covered, they responded as follows: Because civil service at some level will always be present, some comparison of benefits and costs with those of alternative personnel systems is necessary. Public personnel managers should be taught how to deal with political and union opposition to changing a civil service system, including getting rid of it as an option. Elected and appointed officials should also be trained on civil service systems and alternatives.

Civil service, personnel managers need training in how to select outside contractors and administer outside contracts. Training should include more detail on actual case examples. Closer to home, more attention should be given to alternatives for performing the human resource function itself. Outside vendors should be trained in how to prepare responses to RFPs (requests for proposals) developed by government agencies. Most importantly, this issue should be looked at from all angles with a view toward long term objectives for a viable system, not a banded or quick fix. These findings are quite preliminary, consisting as they do of the results of one focus group in one locality. However, some ceases seem evident, at least as working hypotheses for further study. First, local governments' use of alternatives to civil service delivery of public programmes is already widespread, and expected to become more prevalent in the future.

Second, as they expect, public personnel managers have considerable involvement in the choice of these alternatives. Third, because formal training in public personnel management is usually based around civil service systems and collective bargaining, public personnel managers do not consider themselves adequately trained in this area.

Fourth, existing organizations and mechanisms (particularly other human resource managers, professional associations, training, and professional journals) are considered sufficient for this training, though most have not had training in this area.

It is clear that public personnel managers themselves are aware that the change to alternative personnel systems is a significant choice for public agencies. They wish that elected and appointed officials, those they consider as having the primary role in making these decisions, had more training and insight into the comparative advantages and disadvantages of alternative public personnel systems, including civil service.

STRATEGIC HUMAN RESOURCE MANAGEMENT

Strategy

"Strategy is a way of doing something. It includes the formulation of goals and set of action plans for accomplishment of that goal."

Strategic Management

"A Process of formulating, implementing and evaluating business strategies to achieve organizational objectives is called Strategic Management"

Definition of Strategic Management

"Strategic Management is that set of managerial decisions and actions that determine the long-term performance of a corporation. It includes environmental scanning, strategy formulation, strategy implementation and evaluation and control."

The study of strategic management therefore emphasizes monitoring and evaluating environmental opportunities and threats in the light of a corporation's strengths and weaknesses.

Steps in Strategic Management

- Environmental Scanning: Analyse the Opportunities and Threats in External Environment
- Strategy Formulation: Formulate Strategies to match Strengths and Weaknesses. It can be done at Corporate level, Business Unit Level and Functional Level.
- Strategy Implementation: Implement the Strategies
- Evaluation & Control: Ensure the organizational objectives are met.

IMPORTANCE & BENEFITS OF STRATEGIC MANAGEMENT

- Allows identification, prioritization and exploration of opportunities.
- Provides an objective view of management problems.
- Represents framework for improved coordination and control
- Minimizes the effects of adverse conditions and changes
- Allows major decisions to better support established objectives
- Allows more effective allocation of time and resources
- Allows fewer resources and lesser time devoted to correcting ad hoc decisions
- Creates framework for internal communication

- Helps to integrate the individual behaviours
- Provides basis for the clarification of responsibilities
- Encourages forward thinking
- Encourages favourable attitude towards change.

ROLE OF HRM IN STRATEGIC MANAGEMENT

Role in Strategy Formulation: HRM is in a unique position to supply competitive intelligence that may be useful in strategy formulation. Regarding advanced incentive plans used by competitors, opinion survey data from employees, elicit information about customer complaints, information about pending legislation etc. can be provided by HRM. Unique HR capabilities serve as a driving force in strategy formulation. Role in Strategy Implementation: HRM supplies the company with a competent and willing workforce for executing strategies. It is important to remember that linking strategy and HRM effectively requires more than selection from a series of practice choices. The challenge is to develop a configuration of HR practice choices that help implement the organization's strategy and enhance its competitiveness.

Human Resource Development

- *Definition* 1: *Organizing and enhancing capacities to produce.* HRD is a process of organizing and enhancing the physical, mental and emotional capacities of individuals for productive work.
- *Definition 2: Bring possibility of performance and growth.* HRD means to bring about the possibility of performance improvement and individual growth.

Human resource development is a process to help people to acquire competencies and to increase their knowledge, skills and capabilities for better performance and higher productivity.

PROACTIVE HRD STRATEGIES FOR LONG TERM PLANNING AND GROWTH

In today's fast changing, challenging and competitive environment HRD has to take a proactive approach that is to seek preventive care in human relations. Using HRD strategies maximizations of efficiency and productivity could be achieved through qualitative growth of people with capabilities and potentialities to grow and develop.

HRD is always a function of proper utilization of creative opportunities and available environment through acquisition of knowledge, skills and attitudes necessary for productive efforts. Long-term growth can also be planned by creating highly inspired groups of employees with high aspirations to diversify around core competencies and to build new organizational responses for coping with change.

A proactive HRD strategy can implement activities that are geared up and directed at improving personal competence and productive potentialities of human resources.

Following strategic choices can be considered which would help today's organizations to survive and grow:

- *Change Management*: Manage change properly and become an effective change agent rather than being a victim of change itself.
- *Values*: Adopt proactive HRD measures, which encourage values of openness, trust, autonomy, proactivity and experimentation.
- *Maximize productivity and efficiency*: Through qualitative growth of people with capabilities and potentialities to grow and develop thrive to maximize productivity and efficiency of the organization.
- *Activities directed to competence building*: HRD activities need to be geared up and directed at improving personal competence and productive potentialities of manpower resources.

Team Effectiveness

What is the definition of a team? A team is defined as a reasonably small group of people, who bring to the table a set of complementary and appropriate skills, and who hold themselves mutually accountable for achieving a clear and identifiable set of goals. Teams can be very effective. In many situations teams can achieve more than individuals working on their own. Teams can bring to bear a wider range of skills and experience to solve a problem. Teams also produce better quality decisions. When a team has been working on a problem, and they have a sense of commitment to the common solution.

What do we Mean by Team Effectiveness?

- A team can be considered to be effective if their output is judged to meet or exceed the expectations of the people who receive the output. Producing a quality output is not enough to judge the effectiveness of the team.
- The second criteria, is that the team should still be able function effectively after they have completed their task. It should not be torn apart by dissension.
- Finally, effectiveness is judged by whether the team feels satisfied with its efforts. If the team members are pleased with their efforts, if the experience has been a good one, if time spent away from their normal work has been worth the effort, the team has likely been effective.

What then are the Factors that Contribute towards an Effective Team?

There are three areas of group behaviour that must be addressed for teams to be effective. The team must work hard. The effort that the team puts in to get the job done is dependent on whether the nature of the task motivates the members of the team and whether the goals are challenging. The team must have the right mix of skills to bring to the table. These skills include technical, problem solving and interpersonal skills. The team must be able to develop appropriate approaches to problem solving. This depends on developing a plan of attack and using appropriate techniques for analysis.

The Task itself should be Motivating

The following factors contribute to hard work, skill development and effective problem solving strategies:

- The task itself should be seen as being worthwhile.

It needs to be a whole piece of work with a clear and visible outcome so that people can feel a sense of ownership.

- The outcome of the task should be perceived as being important to other people's lives. It should affect others in the organization or impact on the external customer.
- The job should provide the team with an opportunity for self-regulation. They should decide how the work is to be done. Meaningful feedback should be provided on the how well the team is performing.

The Team Needs Challenging Goals, which are Clearly Defined.

- When challenging goals are set the team will mobilize its efforts to find innovative ways to achieve feats that may have been considered impossible. Providing a challenging job is the most important motivator to sustain group effort.
- Goals provide a sense of direction to the team so that when conflict occurs it is possible to channel the conflict more constructively by returning to the goals for direction.
- The team needs to buy in to the goals. They must have the opportunity to buy in and commit to achieving the goals. Goals need to be challenging, but not impossible to achieve. They also need to be measurable so that progress towards achieving them can be monitored and results confirmed.

Rewards are Important.

- The rewards need to suit the personal characteristics of the people on the team.
- Whatever form the reward takes, it is important that group effort be recognized. One should avoid the destructive effect of trying to single out individuals from the group, when there has been a group effort.
- Rewards merely reinforce these conditions for fostering group effort.

The Team should have the Right Mix of Skills.

- The right mix of skills should be brought to the task at hand. It is also a question of carefully reviewing the job to determine what relevant skills is required and selecting staff so that the team has the right balance. Providing relevant training then makes up any shortfall in skills.
- Technical skills are required. For teams who are trying to improve a process that cuts across department boundaries, each function should be represented. One should achieve a balance of skills. This means avoiding having a preponderance of skills and experience in one specialized area. Sheer numbers may weigh the solution towards the dominant group.
- In the case of permanent work teams it is likely that team members will not have all the task relevant skills at the onset. When the group is new, it is likely that members will bring narrow skills learned in their old roles. They will need to develop broader skills for the new job. To ensure that this is done, training and coaching should be provided.
- The members of the team need to have problem solving and decision-making skills as well as technical skills. When a business is making its first venture into team based work, it is likely that people will not have a good grasp of the techniques related to problem analysis and solution.
- These relevant skills must be acquired, so it will be necessary to provide training. Over a period of time staff will become experienced in problem solving techniques and the organization will develop a repertoire of skills among the staff so this training will not always be necessary.
- Interpersonal skills are also important. This is not as obvious as it may sound. Most people do not listen well. Listening is much more than being quiet when

some else is talking. Active listening is required. Many people do not speak to the point but ramble on or go off at a tangent. Most people do not take criticism well and tend to be defensive about their own opinions.

Agree on a Code of Conduct.

- At the beginning of the team project it is important to develop a code of conduct for meetings. The team needs to agree on a set of rules to ensure that their efforts are purposeful and that all members contribute to the work.
- The most critical rules pertain to attendance, open discussion, using an analytical approach, not pulling rank over other members, planning the work and sharing work assignments. This will ensure that the work is done well and done on time.

The Team Must Develop Effective Problem Solving Strategies.

- For the team to be able to develop an appropriate strategy, it must have a clear definition of the problem, know what resources it has available and the limits, and understand the expectations. It must then develop a problem-solving plan, based on the approach suggested in the part on continuous improvement.
- When this does not happen, people are passive. Their skills and knowledge are not utilized and they waste their time.

Special Teams have Special Issues

From the perspective of organisational improvement we are interested in three types of teams. One is the problem solving team, another is the work team and then there is the senior management team. Problem solving teams are set up with a clearly defined task to investigate a problem and recommend a solution. Sometimes the same team will go on to implement the solution.

When their task is completed the team is disbanded and members go back to their normal organisational duties:

- There are two important issues facing these teams. One is getting started and the other is handing over the recommendations for implementation. The key to getting started is to ensure that the team is committed to achieving an agreed set of goals. Goals serve to focus the team's effort.
- Implementation is important. It will not just happen; it must be planned. The implementers must be brought into the solution stage so that they develop a sense of ownership towards the solution and buy into it. The best way to do this is to have the problem solving team do the implementation.
- Another approach is to phase the implementers into the team so that the membership changes prior to the implementation. Whatever approach is used one should remember that the idea is to implement a solution and not to produce a report.
- Work teams are different in that they are a fixed part of the organization. They have an ongoing function, which is to control a set of activities that make up a discrete operation in the overall business process. They need to focus on the critical factors in their process and to control these factors to ensure a quality product.

3

Organizing the Human Resource Management Department

The functions, functional change, and human potential of lower-level and middle-level managers (LMM) have recently received increased attention in conceptual and empirical analysis. There are various reasons for the special attention devoted to these organization members, who have traditionally been neglected by micro-economic research.

Thus, changed economic, technological, and socio-political factors have induced firms to formulate new strategic aims and to secure their implementation through functional policies. LMM play a dual role in these processes of strategy formulation and, especially, implementation. They are both "change masters" and the recipients of change. They are the targets of top management's human-resource management (HRM) measures, and at the same time actors, initiators, and sponsors of HRM measures applied to their own subordinates. Caught in the middle, they have the difficult task of mediating a firm's policy decisions downward through the hierarchy.

As the purveyors of ideas and information from new strategies, they run the risk of setting into motion aggravating processes of change with regard to their own traditional functions and their accustomed work situation. As the persons affected by change, they are often an important source of resistance to change in the phase of strategy implementations. Thus, uncooperative LMM are often blamed when strategies, once formulated, are—so goes the almost universal complaint—not implemented, or are found to be incapable of implementation. Consequently, the buildup, cultivation, and development of the human potential of LMM, and especially the development of the qualifications needed for change, are of decisive importance for successful implementation of strategic goals. The human potential of LMM is in this respect a strategic success factor. Various theses on the content and the extent of the functional change of LMM have been described in the literature. Some authors expect—especially in connection with the increasing networking of information technology in and among organizations—not only a functional change, but a loss of function for LMM.

Managerial capacity becomes partly superfluous on these levels, or at least undergoes a quantitative thinning out. Nonetheless, those managers who remain are regarded as an important human resource whose relative importance for the growth of a firm is increasing. In most cases, however, it is expected that freed manager capacities will be utilized for expanded and/or new jobs, and not eliminated. This presumption is supported by our own empirical studies.

The two approaches, however, have two points in common that are of relevance for the present study: (1) in both approaches, LMM are regarded as valuable human potential by firms, a potential that is indispensable in order for a firm to be able to cope successfully with future problems; (2) a functional change is accordingly expected for these managers, and that change will place new demands on the activity they perform in their jobs. Against this background, the acquisition of new qualifications by LMM for successfully coping with the new challenges becomes critically important. An analysis of the change of function and the consequent qualification needs for LMM was the object of an international empirical research project.

CHANGES IN THE REQUIREMENTS PLACED ON LMM

PROJECT DESIGN

The results presented are part of an international comparative study in six European countries: the United

Kingdom; Denmark; Holland; France; Italy; and Germany. The project was titled: Study on changing functions of lower and middle management. It was financed by the European Foundation for the Improvement of Living and Working Conditions, located in Dublin.

This foundation is an autonomous EC institution established by the Council of Ministers in 1975 to furnish the EC Commission with scientifically based proposals for improving living and working conditions in the EC member nations.

The set of assumptions guiding research (agreed upon by the international research team) was structured as follows: changed background conditions for economic action require new firm strategies; the implementation is dependent on a set of measures and changes regarding organizational structure and personnel policy.

This process of development of organization and personnel entails changes in the functions and requirements of LMM, which in turns puts pressure on these managers to acquire new qualifications (new qualification needs). The acquisition and practical application of new qualifications are to be secured through appropriate personnel development (PE) and organization development (OE) measures.

Among the essential external factors are economic (competition), technological (microelectronic revolution), and socio-political factors (transformations in values, for example).

The purposes of the research project were:

- To describe the changed demands and functions of LMM and to identify the possible causes of this change.
- To describe personnel and organizational options that are realised or planned for these levels of management in firms.

The acquisition and application of functionally necessary new qualifications by LMM, and how this process is conducted within the firm is regarded in this context as a crucial precondition for ensuring flexibility and efficiency in firms. The following is a report on the German part of the study.

DEMARCATION PROBLEMS

Since there is no generally valid demarcation between "lower-level," "middle-level" and "top-level" management, the conceptual limitations were established as guidelines for our study. The basis for demarcation between the upper- and middle-level management is the legal definition of a managerial employee. Since management functions are in some cases clearly exercised in the staff domain, all staff workers with responsibility for personnel management are classified as middle-level management. Lower-level management is restricted to employees with only one hierarchical level under them.

The results of the interviews, however, revealed that in practice the demarcation of management levels is sometimes made along these lines, sometimes along others, and sometimes is not made at all. Thus, in many firms the first and second levels of the hierarchy are regarded as top management when they work very closely together; in smaller firms, on the other hand, top management usually comprises only the executive level. A distinction between middle-level and lower-level management is generally not made. A comparison of the interview results thus proved to be extremely problematic because of these different defining criteria. It was therefore necessary to diverge from the original standard guidelines and conform to the practices specific to each firm.

CHANGE IN STRATEGIC GOALS, AND IN OBJECTIVES BEARING ON ORGANIZATIONAL STRUCTURE AND PERSONNEL POLICY

Selection of Cases and Method of Study

During the first phase of the empirical investigation, eleven case studies were made. The most important precondition for including a firm in the sample was that information either on its management problems or on how it approached such problems had to be available as far as it was relevant to the questions posed in the study. The pertinent specialized literature, specialized periodicals, and the economic press were used as sources for this. Cases discovered in a literature search and regarded as interesting were selected so that the sample on the whole satisfied the following criteria:

- To include a range of firm sizes.
- To have a sample that was a representative cross-section of over several economic branches.
- If possible, to include several firms within one branch, in order to permit comparison.
- To include at least one multinational firm.

Eleven firms were chosen for the study on the basis of these selection criteria: three from the service sector; four from the electrical industry; three from the automobile industry; and one from the chemical industry. Semi structured interviews with personnel managers were carried out in each firm (a total of fourteen); these managers were drawn from the top or the second highest management level. Since the LMM problem situations have not yet really been defined and formulated by research, and hence there are no standardized research instruments available, we chose an explorative method to reconnoiter the problem (comparative case studies).

Table. Case Study Overview

Branch	Employees	Activity field
Services		
Case A	40,000	Transport firm
Case B	41,000	Media firm
Case C	3,000	Credit institute
		Electrical Industry
Case D	30,000	Computer manufacture
Case E	20,000	Computer manufacturer
Case F	350	Software provider of system solutions
Case G	2,700	Electrical industry Electrical appliances Automobile Industry
Case H	38,000	Automobile manufacture
Case I	50,000	Automobile manufacturer
Case J	130,000	Automobile manufacturer

The most essential aspects of changes, both external and internal to firms, that result in new functional and qualificational requirements for LMM are shown. Increased competition is most often mentioned among the changed background conditions of a firm's business operations. Two aspects should be distinguished: first, markets are becoming increasingly internationalized, and this is associated with intensified competition; second, on the other hand, there is a constraint to compete because of growing saturation on particular markets.

These two aspects are not mutually exclusive. Further, rapid technical progress and the associated rapid obsolescence of products (especially in the data-processing industry) are stressed. Competition-related pressure to innovate grows as the time between technical innovation shrinks. As for socially relevant factors, it is noteworthy that the growing ecological consciousness among the population (e.g., within and toward the automobile industry, the chemical industry, etc.) was mentioned several times as a relevant background condition for business operations.

The transformation of values that has long been discussed in the literature, and is particularly important for shaping the managerial and supervisory structures and processes within an organization, is now ascribed relatively minor importance by the managers surveyed. Change in economic, technical, and social factors entail new strategic goals for firms, with a view toward establishing as close a connection as possible between external change and organizational activities, and, over the long term, toward ensuring company survival.

Among these goals are:

- Growth of the firm, also internationally (especially in the automobile industry, data-processing firms, media firms, paint manufacturers);
- A growing orientation toward the market and toward customers (especially in the service branches);
- Securing technical advantage over competitors
- Improvement in organizational and individual flexibility.

Changes in organizational structure and personnel policy that alter the internal structures and processes of control, operations management, and personnel management, are mentioned particularly as top priority for implementing strategic options.

The organizational level: There is a discernible tendency toward decentralization in many firms. Decentralization is intended to facilitate the delegation of responsibility, which is desired by all the firms studied. Delegation of responsibility is supposed to relieve the burden on top management, and to enlarge the tasks and responsibilities of lower- and middle-level managers.

The motivation and job satisfaction of those concerned should thereby be enhanced. Further, delegation of responsibility should increase a firm's flexibility, since it should allow decisions to be made more quickly and competently. The delegation of tasks and responsibilities also increases proximity to the customer, especially in the service sector. Most of the firms studied are striving for a flatter, less drastic hierarchy, with a view toward adapting organization to the changed situation. The view is heard in some cases that the elimination of one hierarchic level could combat incrustation in bureaucratic structures.

The personnel level: Firms are trying continually to adapt the management capabilities of their managers to the changed demands. Personnel-oriented management is a central principle of management in almost all firms. For managers, this means being required to give more attention to the expectations of those they manage.

In all cases we found that firms are ascribing increasing importance to organizational culture and corporate identify. The end pursued with these two concepts is to bind employees and relevant groups outside the firm more tightly to their organizations. Managers' identification with the firm must especially be strengthened.

Another essential focal point is improving information policy for all employees. The presumption is that the better informed the employee, the more he or she will be inclined to identify with the goals of the firm. The informed employee is an essential building block of the desired corporate identify. In one firm, an open-door philosophy, including top managers as well, is practiced.

There was also a discernible tendency in the firms studied for managers' attitudes toward work and/or toward other areas of life (family, mobility, etc.) to be an increasingly important hiring criterion in personnel recruiting. Adequate specialized qualification is now regarded only as a basic precondition for hiring new employees.

To sum up, we can say that from the standpoint of the managers surveyed, the increasing dynamics of technical economic development and the associated heightened competition on markets are the most salient background conditions of business operations; the strategic objectives and the requisite molding of a firm's internal structure must be oriented to these conditions in the future. The results related to these central points in the German study are considerably similar to the assessments of British, French, Dutch, Danish, and Italian managers who were asked the same question.

This development may be interpreted as an increasing loss of practical market certainties. Coping with the related socioeconomic risks and uncertainties becomes a central challenge to organizations and their members, with a view toward ensuring the organizations' further development and their ability to survive.

The changed background conditions heighten the requirements placed on the control functions of persons and organizations. This development is discernible in the search for new organizational forms and new hiring and behaviour models for an organization's members, which altogether tend towards and increasing individual flexibility, with an eye toward increasing the ability to act and react, with regard to the market and society (i.e., a firm's problem-solving potential).

The principles of mass production, organized bureaucratically to achieve efficiency, are losing more and more of their problem-solving powers, given the new, changed background conditions of economic action. The new quality of the demands on the control functions of firms is also evident in the fact that the ensuing problems of practical economic development, the externalization of which was long regarded as the expression of the capital logic of an individual business, are now themselves becoming an economically conditioned (because they are dependent on the ups and downs of the market) object of a firm's management (e.g., in ecologically sensitive branches such as the automobile and chemical industries). It is to be expected that new qualification needs for LMM will arise with the changed external problem situation and the internal firm structures caught up in a process of change. In addition to specialized skills, which all the respondents regarded as a precondition for assuming management positions, attention is focused especially on social and communicative skills. The personnel managers of all eleven firms surveyed and the middle-level managers themselves see particular deficiencies in these skill domains. The connection between external change, strategic objectives, structural change, and the qualificational needs of LMM will now be illustrated on the basis of four selected examples.

QUALIFICATION NEED, CHOICE OF CASES AND METHOD OF STUDY

Four of the eleven cases in the first research phase were chosen as further intensive case studies to explore certain aspects of the need and acquisition of qualifications. Group discussions and semi-structured interviews were carried out with a total of forty-nine LMM.

The following questions were taken up in each group discussion:

- What new or changed qualifications other than those you now have do you think you will need in the upcoming years?
- What difficulties do you see in the acquisition and application of the new qualifications?

Our questions concerning the group were as open as possible to spur the participants to intensive collaboration. We were able to structure the group discussions roughly in the same way in all three firms. However, the different compositions of the groups must be taken into account in comparing the results: The managers of the paint manufacturing company were especially sensitized to the importance of social skills, compared with the other respondents, because of prior business experience (network management). The strong heterogeneity of the groups showed up in a positive way, thus contributing to obtaining a differentiated response to the questions.

All the members of the credit institution have the same function (branch managers) and belong to the same hierarchical level. Compared to the firm structure, this random sample is nonetheless a relatively representative segment of the lower-level and middle-level management of the firm. The questions were answered relatively summarily. The composition of the group from the computer manufacturer displayed no relevant distinctive features. The participants belong to different functional spheres and different hierarchical levels. There was also nothing exceptional as regards the group's cooperation.

Two other questions were asked in the semi structured interview over and above the themes touched upon in the group discussion. These questions had to do with how the needed qualifications were identified, their acquisition within the firm, and organizational support in acquiring and using these qualifications. "Major" problems, however, that went beyond the individual situation, often punctuated the group discussion, whereas in the interviews the individual, everyday situation of the respondents was stressed. Questions concerning the difficulties in acquiring and using new qualifications elicited responses asserting a lack of learning skills, especially in the interviews.

This may be due to the fact that this point was in particular need of explanation, and to the social control at work during a group discussion. The complaint of "eternal yesterday," which often cropped up in the interviews, is much more difficult to put fort within a group of colleagues.

On the other hand, there is a considerable convergence of methods, especially in regard to qualificational needs and difficulties in acquiring and using them, inasmuch as these needs and difficulties went beyond the particular firm and were common to a certain extent to all. As suggested, therefore forego presenting these points separately to help keep things in perspective. The results of the studies show that the interviewed managers expected a multi-leveled qualificational need because of changes both internal and external to the organization, and not in the last instance in regard to the internal EC market in 1992.

In addition to peculiarities specific to particular firms, qualificational needs that go beyond the particular firm are discernible for LMM:

- Development of social skills.
- Development of strategic knowledge, strengthening market-oriented and customer-oriented thinking.
- Acquisition and broadening of knowledge of languages.
- Development of systematic, holistically oriented thinking.
- Development of individual adaptability and flexibility.

In terms of the first requirement, development of social skills, one outstanding result of the study is that the requirements concerning social skills are ranked in all firms as having the greatest importance for the future. The acquisition of comprehensive social skills thus exceeds all other domains in importance.

The term "social skills" refers broadly to the ability to communicate human closeness and emotional warmth in dealing with colleagues, and so to stress the human side of the job. Employee-oriented management and the ability to communicate, with one's superiors as well, are also regarded as important. The managers of the different firms repeatedly stressed the necessity and importance of teamwork. Within one of these organizations, however, the question comes up to whether social skills are learnable, and if so, to what extent.

The view is expressed that an individual must possess a willingness to assume social responsibility, and that this is a basic precondition that cannot be learned. In the transport firm, the assumption of responsibility and the willingness to "go into other people's problems" are classified, for example, in this domain. Ability to encourage employees, and to counsel them, as well as to mediate in cases of conflict, is regarded as important in the sphere of interaction between superiors and employees. Development of strategic knowledge, strengthening of market-oriented and customer-oriented thinking—an enhanced market orientation is regarded as important by all the surveyed manager groups. It is necessary in order to be able to recognize and make better use of available opportunities.

To achieve a better market orientation, the credit institution, for example, is planning certain complementary structural changes: the branches will henceforth be run as profit centres. The transport firm has already completed a reorganization (decentralization). The respondents working for the paint manufacturer, the credit institution, and the transport firm all stressed that strategic capabilities and skills, as well as strategic thinking, will have a larger role to play among management tasks. The acquisition of these skills will therefore be a focal point in the near future. The respondents of all firms pointed to the necessity of thinking more in international dimensions.

Thus, for example, international standards, as well as divergent trends on markets, must be taken more into account in product development. Because of the changed social background conditions (e.g., the influence of citizens' action groups, a greater environmental consciousness, and legislative restrictions on firms), organizations today interact much more intensively with various strategically relevant interest groups. The managers of the computer manufacturer especially stressed that intensive consideration of the field of force between a firm and its environment is becoming increasingly important for individual managers as well. Since it must be assumed that the demands made of a firm, and hence of its employees, by different social groups will continue to grow, the respondents regarded the ability to deal with these demands as an important skill requirement in the future.

The third requirement—the acquisition and broadening of knowledge of languages—is included because deficient knowledge of foreign languages is mentioned as an important problem in all firms. This does not seem so egregious where Europe 1992 is concerned, but it does show that there is a an elementary need for better language skill qualifications, given the essential changes that may be expected to take place at that time.

Regarding the fourth requirement—the development of systematic, holistically oriented thinking—thinking in terms of contexts and relations is regarded as a new important requirement, especially in the paint manufacturing and computer manufacturing firms. The complexity of tasks is increasing so abruptly that an intelligent approach is only possible if the overall relational context is taken into account. This also requires of managers an ability to think in networks, that is, to include other domains and departments of the firm in the planning and execution of tasks.

In terms of the fifth requirement—the development of individual adaptability and flexibility—on the whole, the respondents of all firms noted that the requirements with regard to individual mobility and flexibility will increase for a variety of organizational contexts. A continuous adaptability to altered situations, a fundamental willingness to learn, and geographic mobility, are some of these requirements.

The assessment shows that technical and specialized know-how are not regarded as top-priority qualification needs. It must be presumed that the relative importance of these qualifications for LMM will decline. Nonetheless, these qualifications are still regarded as important and are considered by the surveyed managers (and personnel directors) to be part of an indispensable basic knowledge.

The meeting of this qualificational need will also be a precondition for the success of European market integration. These integrational trends can be expected to further accelerate technical economic development, and heighten the demands placed on the control functions of organizations and their employees as the protective functions of national markets and the barriers to market entry are gradually dismantled. Social and strategic skills, knowledge of languages, and flexibility must then be seen as necessary individual and organizational prerequisites for dealing competently with openings and networkings in markets as well as in society.

These results are also confirmed by a study done by the personnel consulting firm of Korn and Ferry. These international consultants have analysed the national strengths and weaknesses of managers. Compared to an "ideal Euromanager profile," German managers are weak with regard to team orientation, thinking in international contexts, and motivational and communicative skills. Personal characteristics such as mobility, tolerance, humour, creativity, and understanding of other cultures are also too weak. German managers also have an inadequate knowledge of languages. In light of these findings, the broad agreement with the diagnosis of the managers we surveyed is noteworthy.

CONSEQUENCES FOR HUMAN-RESOURCE MANAGEMENT

The empirical findings make it clear that developing a systematic and coordinated concept for the development and cultivation of the human potential of LMM is a top-priority task, if the changed economic background conditions are to be addressed with maximum effectiveness and if strategic objectives are to be realised.

Remarkably, our studies, as well as Anglo-American studies, show that the LMM themselves—who are directly concerned—consider the need for such a concept more urgent than do top-level managers. This presumably explains why, as is often lamented, it is so difficult for new human resource management concepts to gain headway among top management. The results of our study should therefore serve as an orientation for the top management of firms. The concept of human-resource management, currently the focus of considerable attention in academic discourse, can therefore provide useful guidelines for a firm's personnel policy and for relevant decision making.

HUMAN-RESOURCE MANAGEMENT

Human-resource management is an American concept of resource-oriented personnel management that has recently entered into the German dialog. The view of personnel as potential, as human capacity, and not merely as a cost factor—that is, as a potential that must be systematically planned, maintained, and developed—is central to HRM. But it has been an integral component of German personnel management theory for a long time as well.

Over and above the rhetoric about recognition (the individual is in the centre point of the firm), the HRM concept displays some structural characteristics that are novel for German personnel management theory, at least regarding the clarity of its formulations, and that hence can be useful for the purposes of the present study.

The special characteristics of the HRM concept are:

- Measures of personnel recruitment and development, that hitherto have been separate, are systematically interlinked.
- HRM is locked into a firm's strategic and structural decisions.
- Human resources is seen from the perspective of general management, not from the perspective of some functional sphere (e.g., personnel department).
- Assembly-line management is incorporated into HR responsibility.

The first characteristic alludes to the need for better coordination between the domains of traditional personnel and organizational work (this is the consistency equals efficiency hypothesis). An avowal by top management of the benefit of more participation requires relevant measures of personnel selection, further education, remuneration, and job structuring. Further opportunities for participation for middle-level managers should not be countermanded, for example, by an objective loss of function. A reciprocal linkage and temporal parallelism of decisions concerning corporate strategy, organizational structure, and human-resource measures is necessary to ensure that the successful implementation of strategies does not founder on the deficient human-resource potential of the organization. This perspective has also recently been assimilated by German personnel-management theory.

One task of strategic human resource management is, in the view of the authors, to derive, from in-firm strategies and business units strategies, personnel policy guidelines and measures to serve the strategic goals. The strategic character of these human resource measures is reflected, for example, in the fact that they are geared not to short-term requirements (adaptational measures), but rather to the growth of success potentials and the creation of the personnel prerequisites for this. The linkage between personnel policy (HRM) measures and changes in organizational structure also reflects the interconnection of measures for organizational and personnel development, repeatedly called for in the literature, that represent the preconditions for successful change.

To ensure that HRM has a strategic orientation, this function must be integrated into the sphere of responsibilities of top management. This should counteract the additive, uncoordinated planning and realization of personnel policy that is ubiquitously observed at the firm level (e.g., policy confined to particular departments or functions). Operational HRM measures, however, are (again) the task of every line manager.

In addition to the structural characteristics of the HRM model, which go beyond the traditional approaches of personnel management, four central policy areas may be identified with regard to content.

- Employee influence (participation philosophy);
- Human-resource flow (personnel recruitment, use, and dismissal);
- Reward systems (incentive, remuneration, and participation systems); and
- Work systems (job structuring).

These policy areas are influenced by the interests of participants in the organization (stakeholders), shareholders, management, employees, trade unions, the government and the community, as well as by situational factors, such as employment structure, business strategy, management philosophy, labour-market conditions, trade-union requirements, technology, laws, and societal values. Human-resource management decisions have both immediate organizational outcomes (commitment, competence, congruence, cost-effectiveness) as well as certain long-term consequences (individual well-being, organizational effectiveness, societal well-being). Beer, *et al.*, stress especially the differential efficiency of the integrating coordination and consistency of the four political policy fields among themselves and with the business strategy. It is clear from the standpoint of strategic HRM that HRM measures must be applied complementarily to ensure the buildup and development of human potential.

INTEGRATION OF HRM MEASURES AS A TOP-PRIORITY STRUCTURAL TASK

From the standpoint of the managers interviewed in our study, the deficient integration of discrete measures of personnel policy into a tenable general concept is a weak point that makes the requisite acquisition and use of new qualifications more difficult.

The following difficulties, which are beyond the particular firm, or beyond our particular case studies, reflect this:

- Lack of support from top management;
- Lack of career planning; and
- Lack of incentives.

The first problem, the lack of support from top management, is a point of criticism heard consistently from the respondents, who refer both to the distribution of authority and responsibility at the lower level as well as to the poor example offered by top managers in their thinking and action. Top management must recognize that they function as models and make sure that the values, norms, and principles that are regarded as organizationally correct are also made visible. It is easier for such norms to become a force guiding the action of all of an organization's members; this is also one of the central assumptions of the concept of organizational culture and a guideline for culture-conscious management.

Lip service alone is not enough. Some examples of top-management activities that are conductive to the development of a model function, coupled, of course, with the development of the requisite skills, are:

- Giving LMM margin for maneuver in the use of new qualifications; creating free spaces for experimentation.
- Not permitting (e.g., by systematic rationalization utilizing new information and communication techniques) the centralization of information and decision-making structures to undermine how important the organization considers it that LMM acquire qualifications to improve their management abilities.

The second problem, systematic career planning, gives direction to individual action, in respect to acquiring the requisite qualifications, and supplants incidental, improvised job taking. If career planning is to have any prospects of success, certain preconditions must be met: planning must be couched in the broader framework of planning quantitative and qualitative needs for personnel to firm up the credibility of career planning and to avoid exaggerated promises and frustrations. Career promises by superiors or by the personnel department are perceived by some of the managers surveyed as a "motivation trick" if it is obvious that there are far fewer upward mobility positions available than there are persons who have been promised such a promotion. For this reason, the managers concerned must also be told that planning of careers does not exclude divergences from the plan.

Career planning must not be equated with career guarantees. Whereas systematic career planning has the function of providing long-term direction in the acquisition of qualifications (indirectly effective HRM measures), measures affecting the organization of labour create a direct incentive for the acquisition and practical application of new qualifications. For example, replacement arrangements for the time a manager attends further education are such a measure. Also, managers may be offered assistance to improve their individual time management and their individual work techniques, permitting a more efficient individual organization of their work. This can ease the burden of routine and creates free time that could then be used to acquire and or to apply new qualifications. Relief from routines is ranked as a desirable structuring objective by LMM of all four firms. The results of the survey show clearly that the managers concerned see the personnel policy of the firms studied as highly fragmented. Inconsistencies between particular personnel policy measures reduce or counteract the efficacy of these measures in their target groups' own estimation.

Measures focusing on participation and development should thus be internally consistent with strategic and organizational measures. Where shaping the work situation of LMM is concerned, this means a methodical endeavor to expand their room for action. The case studies also clearly show that the requirement that strategic, structural, and personnel measures be interlinked is justified from the standpoint of efficiency, but is rarely realised in firm practice (as yet). The reason for this may be that the responsibility for HRM measures still rests to a large degree exclusively with the personnel departments, and is still too little regarded as a top-management task. The consistent criticism of the lack of support from top management, which detracts from the effectiveness of relevant personnel policy measures, is an unequivocal argument for increased involvement by top management in HRM responsibility.

PROSPECTS

The findings of the present case studies and the conceptual considerations presented could contribute to a common understanding, both internally, among an organization's members, as well as between researchers and practitioners concerning basic personnel policy problems, and encourage the devising of ways to develop personnel policy practice.

The next step of firm practice, however, cannot be derived deductively from the hypotheses produced by industrial management research. Scientific results can, however, contribute to the systematization of organizational problem situations, and provide guidelines for company decision makers. But the promotion of human resources is not solely the task of a company's management, or indeed of companies in general. If human resources are seen as a competitive advantage of countries poorly supplied with raw materials over countries rich in raw materials, the development of these resources becomes a task of the society as a whole and one of growing importance as well.

Generally speaking, current developments in society and the economy, and in the organization of labour, can from the standpoint of LMM be interpreted as a thrust toward individualization, entailing new risks for those concerned. And among these risks are the loss (due to technical economic factors) of traditional certainties with regard to professional practical knowledge (qualification) and the consequent creation of insecurity and uncertainties. Also, new qualifications are becoming obsolete increasingly rapidly. At the same time, a new kind of dependency arises: the situation of the individual is becoming more and more dependent on the labour market and hence on education and further education. Traditional certainties are losing their protective and binding force as labour market economies are implemented and the supporting edifices created by welfare and labour legislation are dismantled.

Thus, individuals are becoming increasingly institutionally dependent. The challenges to the social partners (also in the European community) lie in the creation and development of overall background conditions in the labour market, in welfare and labour laws, as well as in education policy to improve LMMs' labour-market mobility and to prevent social dumping. Given this background, the requisite meeting of the qualificational needs of LMM must be joined with the creation of supportive marginal and background conditions at the institutional and social levels.

4

Human Resource Management in India

HUMAN RESOURCE MANAGEMENT PRACTICES IN INDIA

Over many centuries India has absorbed managerial ideas and practices from around the world. Early records of trade, from 4500 B.C. to 300 B.C., not only indicate international economic and political links, but also the ideas of social and public administration.

The world's first management book, titled *'Arlhashastra'*, written three millennium before Christ, codified many aspects of human resource practices in Ancient India. This treatise presented notions of the financial administration of the state, guiding principles for trade and commerce, as well as the management of people.

These ideas were to be embedded in organisational thinking for centuries. Increasing trade, that included engagement with the Romans, led to widespread and systematic governance methods by 250 A.D.

During the next 300 years, the first Indian empire, the Gupta Dynasty, encouraged the establishment of rules and regulations for managerial systems, and later from about 1000 A.D. Islam influenced many areas of trade and commerce. A further powerful effect on the managerial history of India was to be provided by the British system of corporate organisation for 200 years. Clearly, the socio cultural roots of Indian heritage are diverse and have been drawn from multiple sources including ideas brought from other parts of the old world. Interestingly, these ideas were essentially secular even when they originated from religious bases. In the contemporary context, the Indian management mindscape continues to be influenced by the residual traces of ancient wisdom as it faces the complexities of global realities.

One stream of holistic wisdom, identified as the Vedantic philosophy, pervades managerial behaviour at all levels of work organisations. This philosophical tradition has its roots in sacred texts from 2000 B.C. and it holds that human nature has a capacity for self transformation and attaining spiritual high ground while facing realities of day to day challenges. Such cultural based tradition and heritage can have a substantial impact on current managerial mindsets in terms of family bonding and mutuality of obligations.

The caste system, which was recorded in the writings of the Greek Ambassador Megasthenes in the third century B.C., is another significant feature of Indian social heritage that for centuries had impacted organisational architecture and managerial practices, and has now become the focus of critical attention in the social, political and legal agenda of the nation.

One of the most significant areas of values and cultural practices has been the caste system. Traditionally, the caste system maintained social or organisational balance. Brahmins (priests and teachers) were at the apex, Kshatriya (rulers and warriors), Vaishya (merchants and managers) and Shwdra (artisans and workers) occupied the lower levels. Those outside the caste hierarchy were called 'untouchables'.

Even decades ago, a typical public enterprise department could be dominated by people belonging to a particular caste. Feelings associated with caste affairs influenced managers in areas like recruitment, promotion and work allocation. Indian institutions codified a list of lower castes and tribal communities called 'scheduled castes and scheduled tribes'.

A strict quota system called, 'reservation' in achieving affirmative equity of castes, has been the eye of political storm in India in recent years. The central government has decreed 15 per cent of recruitment is to be reserved for scheduled castes, and a further seven and half per cent for scheduled tribes. In addition, a further 27 per cent has been decreed for other backward castes. However, the liberalisation of markets and global linkages has created transformation of attitudes towards human resource (HR) policies and practices. Faced with the challenge of responding to the rationale of Western ideas of organisation in the changing social and economic scenario of Indian organisation, practitioners are increasingly taking a broader and reflective perspective of human resource management (HRM) in India.

This manuscript has three main parts. In the first part is provided an overview of important historical events and activity that has influenced contemporary managerial tenets, the second part of the manuscript describes the emerging contemporary Indian HRM practices and indicates some interesting challenges. The concluding part, the third part of the manuscript, succinctly integrates the two preceding parts.

VALUE OF CONTEXT OF HRM IN INDIA

The managerial ideologies in Indian dates back at least four centuries. Arthashastra written by the celebrated Indian scholar-practitioner Chanakya had three key areas of exploration,

- Public policy,
- Administration and utilisation of people,
- Taxation and accounting principles.

Parallel to such pragmatic formulations, a deep rooted value system, drawn from the early Aryan thinking, called vedanta, deeply influenced the societal and institutional values in India. Overall, Indian collective culture had an interesting individualistic core while the civilizational values of duty to family, group and society was always very important while vedantic ideas nurtured an inner private sphere of individualism. There has been considerable interest in the notion that managerial values are a function of the behaviours of managers. England, Dhingra and Agarwal were early scholars who contended that managerial values were critical forces that shape organisational architecture. The relevance of managerial values in shaping modern organisational life is reflected in scholarly literature linking them to corporate culture, organisational commitment and job satisfaction, as well as institutional governance. Thus, understanding the source of these values and in particular societal work values (which link the macro-micro relationships and in turn organisational practices) had become a popular line of enquiry, and a great deal of evidence has been presented to support the importance of national culture in shaping managerial values. One of the most widely read formulations of this literature is the seminal work of Hofstede who popularised the notion of clustering culture in generic dimensions such as power distribution, structuring, social orientation, and time horizons. In turn, these dimensions could be employed to explain relevant work attitudes, job incumbent behaviours and the working arrangements within organisational structures. Two of these dimensions were individualism and collectivism.

The traditional social ethos from the ancient roots, which was developed over centuries, underwent profound transformation during the British rule. Consequently, in the contemporary context multiple layers of values (core traditional values, individual managerial values, and situational values) have emerged. Though the societal values largely remain very much anchored in the ancient traditions they are increasingly reflecting corporate priorities and values of global linkages.

But in the arena of globalisation where priorities of consumerism, technological education, mass media, foreign investment and trade union culture predominate, newer tensions are becoming evident. For instance, contemporary Indian multi national companies and global firms in India have started shifting their emphasis to human resources with their knowledge and experience as the central area of attention in extending new performance boundaries. Considerable research evidence attests to this trend with particular relevance to greenfield organisations with little or no historical baggages in their organisational culture. Within Indian traditions the choice of individualistic or collectivistic behaviour depends on a number of culturally defined variables. The dynamics of these variables are underpinned through three key elements guiding Indian managerial mindscapes. These three constructs are Desh (the location), Kaal (the timing), and Patra (the specific personalities involved). Sinha and Kunungo claim that the interaction of these three variables determines the guidelines for decisional cues.

This managing or nurturing of the outer layer of collectivism in an inner private sphere of individualism is expressed which demonstrates the behavioural anchors in Indian organisational life. Sharma (1996), this culture based framework, which has three types of gunas (attraction), is being increasingly used in employee assessment and organisational team building strategies. The contention is that each guna is a separate contribution to the core of human personalities. The Sattava (or truth orientation) is the sentiment of exalted values in people, organisations or society. Alternatively, the Tamasik guna depicts a negative orientation which can be expressed behaviourally as ignorance, greed or corruption. Those individuals with a Rajasik guna are inherently driven by a desire to make a worthwhile contribution to their surroundings. Collectively, these spiritual orientations, which manifest as Sattava, Tamas or Rajas gunas, articulate as positive or negative HRM functions such as leadership, motivation or other institutional behavioural activity. The culture of Sradha (upward loyalty) and Sneha (mentoring with affection) outline the behavioural anchors derived from the ` roots. The acceptance of 'Sradha' by youngers and the display of 'Sneha' by the seniors have been the root of sustainability of all types of Indian oragnisations. This has a striking similarity to the concepts of *'oyabun'* and *'kobun'* in the Japanese cultural context.

CONTEMPORARY INDIA

In a recent survey of Indian CEO's, it was suggested that Indian managerial leaders were less dependent on their personal charisma, but they emphasised logical and step by step implementation processes. Indian leaders focused on empowerment and accountability in cases of critical turnaround challenges, innovative challenges, innovative technology, product planning and marketing or when other similar challenges were encountered. These social scientists contend. Leaders in other countries often tell about why they chose a peculiar person for a certain role per task, detailing the personal characteristics that made that person right for that situation. They may also consider, in detail, how an assignment would help someone grow and develop their abilities. In general, Indian leaders simply did not discuss how they matched particular people to certain roles or tasks, nor did they usually consider in detail how the personal characteristics of individuals might shape or inform the best way to influence that person.

INDIAN HRM IN TRANSITION

One of the noteworthy features of the Indian workplace is demographic uniqueness. It is estimated that both China and India will have a population of 1.45 billion people by 2030, however, India will have a larger workforce than China. Indeed, it is likely India will have 986 million people of working age in 2030, which well probably be about 300 million more than in 2007.

And by 2050, it is expected India will have 230 million more workers than China and about 500 million more than the United States of America (U.S.). It may be noted that half of India's current population of 1.1 billion people are under of 25 years of age. While this fact is a demographic dividend for the economy, it is also a danger sign for the country's ability to create new jobs at an unprecedented rate. As has been pointed out by Meredith.

When India's young demographic bubble begins to reach working age, India will need far more jobs than currently exist to keep living standards from declining. India today doesn't have enough good jobs for its existing workers, much less for millions of new ones. If it cannot better educate its children and create jobs for then once they reach working age, India faces a population time bomb: The nation will grow poorer and not richer, with hundred of millions of people stuck in poverty. With the retirement age being 55 to 58 years of age in most public sector organisations, Indian workplaces are dominated by youth. Increasing the retirement age in critical areas like universities, schools, hospitals, research institutions and public service is a topic of considerable current debate and agenda of political parties.

The divergent view, that each society has an unique set of national nuances, which guide particular managerial beliefs and actions, is being challenged in Indian society. An emerging dominant perspective is the influence of globalisation on technological advancements, business management, education and communication infrastructures is leading to a converging effect on managerial mindsets and business behaviours.

And when India embraced liberalisation and economic reform in the early 1990s, dramatic changes were set in motion in terms of corporate mindsets and HRM practices as a result of global imperatives and accompanying changes in societal priorities. Indeed, the onset of a burgeoning competitive service sector compelled a demographic shift in worker educational status and heightened the demand for job relevant skills as well as regional diversity. Expectedly, there has been a marked shift towards valuing human resources (HR) in Indian organisations as they become increasingly strategy driven as opposed to the culture of the status quo. Competitive advantage in industries like software services, pharmaceuticals, and biotechnology (where India is seeking to assert global dominance), the significance of HRs is being emphasised.

These relativities were demonstrated in a recent study of three global Indian companies with (235 managers) when evidence was presented that positively linked the HRM practices with organisational performance. In spite of this trend of convergence, a deep sense of locality exists creating more robust 'cross vergence' in the conceptual as well as practical domain. The intellectual sphere, which emphasises the mindset transaction in work organisations, has been significantly impacted by the forces of globalisation. Indeed,

Chatterjee and Pearson (2000) argued, with supporting empirical evidence from 421 senior level Indian managers, that many of the traditional Indian values (respect for seniority, status and group affiliation) have been complemented by newer areas of attention that are more usually linked to globalisation, such as work quality, customer service and innovation.

The most important work related attribute of the study was the opportunity to learn new things at work. Such cross verging trends need to be understood more widely as practitioners face a new reality of human resource development of post industrial economic organisations. The other three spheres, namely the emotional, the socio cultural and the managerial domains are undergoing, similar profound changes. For instance, the socio cultural sphere confronts the dialects of the national macro level reform agenda as well as the challenge of innovating by addressing the hygiene and motivational features of the work place. Consequently, this sphere, which is underpinned by the anchors of Sradha and Sneha, has the opportunity to leverage work setting creativity in dimensions of autonomy, empowerment, multiskilling and various types of job design.

And the emotional sphere, which focuses on creativity and innovation to encapsulate the notions of workplace commitment and collaboration as well as favourable teamwork, brings desirable behavioural elements of transparency and integrity into organisational procedures and practices. The managerial sphere provides the mechanisms for shifting mindsets, for in Indian organisations HRM is viewed to be closely aligned with managerial technical competency. Thus, understanding of the relativity of HRM to strategic intended organisational performance is less well articulated in Indian firms. The current emphasis of reconfiguring cadres, downsizing, delayering and similar arrangements will become less relevant as holistic perspectives gain ground

5

Human Resource and Audit

HR AUDIT

Both public sector and not-for-profit organizations continue to wrestle with the challenges of defining and managing organizational effectiveness. Human resource management teams are drawn increasingly into new strategic and operational initiatives proceeding under a variety of labels, e.g., downsizing, reinvention and business process improvement.

Over the past ten years, a significant number of HR executives joined their organizations' strategic planning teams. Twisting between the realities of fewer resources and expanded accountability, HRM strategic planning often flounders. This is due to the lack of simple, yet compelling management tools for demonstrating how HRM services contribute to the accomplishment of broader organizational objectives.

The author offers a proven model, the HRM Effectiveness Audit, as a guide for establishing a measurement-based, value-added service improvement system. Through partnering and training, the author has helped implement HRM reviews in a variety of organizations, including the U.S. Patent and Trademark Office, Virginia Department of Social Services, and South Carolina Budget and Control Board — Office of Human Resources.

As we move into the 21st century, public sector and not-for-profit organizations continue to wrestle with the challenges of defining and managing their effectiveness. On the federal level, initiatives have been largely driven by Congressional oversight arising from the Government Performance and Results Act of 1993 (GPRA). GPRA requires federal agencies to demonstrate contributions to organizational results through performance measurements and strategic planning.

In 1998, the Office of Personnel Management published the HRM Accountability System Development Guide to provide guidelines to human resource management (HRM) teams. On the state level, executive and legislative mandates to down size and reduce operating costs continue to force HRM teams to re-examine their internal business methods.

Not-for-profits also face strong pressures. For example, to qualify for Medicare payments, health care systems are subject to regular reviews by the Joint Commission on Accreditation of Health Care Organizations (JCAHCO). HRM teams in these organizations must demonstrate their contribution to enhancing the quality of organization-wide services. Yet, with all these initiatives, HRM teams continue to struggle with the challenge of how best to maneuver in the new arena of higher accountability and expectations. In some organizations, the power of the customer has been harnessed. HRM teams take "a partnership approach" with the agencies they serve.

There is a cry for new tools to equip the HRM adequately to participate as a "strategic business partner." This substance offers a practical procedural model for auditing, measuring and improving HRM services. The generic model springs from Ray Borbidge's The HRM Effectiveness Audit written during Borbidge's association with the author.

Over time, this model has been shaped and refined as the result of numerous audits conducted in a variety of public and private sector organizations.

The audit unfolds through four phases:

1. *Phase* I: Ranking Importance of the HRM Service Portfolio
2. *Phase* II: HRM Team Self-Evaluation
3. *Phase* III: Measuring Current Service Levels
4. *Phase* IV: Developing Action Plans

Core Principle: High Involvement of Internal Customers

The audit pivots around the core principle of high participation of internal customers. Many business improvement efforts fail by neglecting to involve customers in the definition of what "effectiveness" means for delivery of a product or service.

In particular, the automotive industry improved its competitive position by more actively engaging customers in product design. Consequently, the industry now effectively challenges international competitors who previously cut deeply into their market share.

In recent years, governmental agencies and not-for-profits also have enlisted their customers to improve organizational effectiveness. The Internal Revenue Service is a prime example. HRM teams within these organizations ask their customers to be partners in improving internal business processes.

The various HRM functions (employment, employee relations, training, etc.) are treated as interrelated processes with three specific elements: inputs, outputs, and customers. This systems model keeps people focused on customer satisfaction.

To illustrate, inputs for the employment function can be defined in terms of the knowledge and skills of the employment staff, capital resources, and budgetary capabilities. Newly hired employees are the outputs. And, the primary customers are those who request the service and ultimately receive the output. In this case, the primary customers are the hiring managers.

Throughout the audit, internal customers are heavily involved in driving the process. In Phase I, internal customers rank the relative importance of the HRM service portfolio. In Phase III, they participate in focus groups to define effectiveness metrics for each HRM service area. And finally, in Phase III they also provide regular feedback on service levels when they complete their satisfaction surveys. The audit team receives benefits from high customer participation leading to a well-executed review that radiates credibility.

Pre-Audit Issues: Naming, Sampling, demographics, Base-lining

The naming issue: The word "audit" suggests a comprehensive review of practices, procedures and results. Audits are associated frequently with financial reviews and may create a sense of apprehension. Each organization undertaking an audit must decide the appropriate name to fit its culture. Alternative names invoking less emotional impact include: "review," "assessment" or "service improvement system." For simplicity, here, as suggested, use the "audit" label throughout. The sampling issue: Teams initiating the audit process ask the question: How widely throughout the organization should we collect data?

The answer depends on organizational size. The prime consideration is: How many managers are there in the mid-level and one level higher? If the task of engaging the entire target population is logistically not feasible, then a sampling plan should be considered. Here's a real case example of how a sampling plan can work. In an audit with a 10,000-employee health care organization, there were approximately 600 mid-level managers across five business units and three management levels (supervisor, manager, director).

The audit team decided to use a stratified random sampling plan to select 120 participants. The 600 managers were placed into a five-by-three matrix. Then, every fifth manager was selected from an alphabetical list of names within each cell of the matrix. This plan ensured representative participation across the organization. Groups were scheduled for 75-minute meetings over a two-day period.

The demographic issue: Audit teams must also determine what demographic characteristics are most important. Surveys normally start with a profile of demographic data. Typical characteristics might include: business unit, functional group, management level, and location. The team must anticipate the various ways for "cutting and slicing" the data to identify unique needs of various subgroups. The base line issue: The first time an audit is performed, a few extra steps are necessary. Specifically, the team must investigate what is most important to measure. Through focus groups, managers articulate their criteria for measuring HRM effectiveness. From these measurements, the audit team creates a valid customer satisfaction survey. In a first-year audit, such focus groups provide the data necessary for completing Phase I and the first part of Phase III of the audit. With these caveats about sampling, demographics, and base lining, let's walk through the four phases of the audit process.

Phase I: Ranking Importance of HRM Service Portfolio

The purpose of Phase I of the audit is to establish the relative importance of the various HRM services in relation to the accomplishment of organizational objectives. As internal customers, mid-level line and staff managers rank a list of HRM services according to the importance of each service toward meeting their business objectives over the coming year.

Each HRM management team decides the appropriate comprehensive list that reflects the scope of HRM services. The eleven service categories span the range of work done by most HRM departments. The first category on the list, HR Department Organization, draws special attention. Although not a direct service per se, HRM department organization does affect how all employees interface with the personnel function.

For example, do managers have a single point of contact, or is the department decentralized by specialization? Note that the way the department is organized can dramatically affect how internal customers view the effectiveness of HRM services.

Typical HRM Service Portfolio:

- HR Department Organization
- HR Planning/Organizational Development
- Recruitment and Selection
- Compensation Administration
- Employee Benefits Administration
- Employee Relations and Communications
- Personnel Policies and Workplace Rules
- EEO/AA and Other Regulatory Compliance

- Training and Development
- Labour Relations
- Safety, Health and Wellness

The work product from Phase I is a spreadsheet that leads to a rank order of importance for all HRM services. To create the spreadsheet, eleven functions are listed down the sheet. Names of participating managers are listed across the top columns. Each column of data represents the rankings of the eleven services. A mean score is calculated for each of the eleven. Finally, the aggregate rank order of importance for the entire portfolio emerges. At this point, an important decision must be made: How deeply down the rank of important HRM services does the audit team wish to explore?

With first-year audits, the author recommends selection of the top four or five ranked HRM services. Through this decision, the audit team limits the scope of its assessment to the most critical. A more narrowly defined focus emerges. Now, the stage is set for Phases II and III.

Phase II: HRM Team Self-Evaluation

The purpose of the self-evaluation phase is to stimulate discussion and challenge the status quo. This phase can be completed anytime before the analysis of survey results in Phase III. Each specialized group completes a "best practices" questionnaire. The best source for this is How to Conduct a Human Resources Effectiveness Audit with questionnaires for all of the eleven service areas. Each of the questionnaires contains 25-40 items. Groups completing the questionnaire compare current practices with a set of standards based on reputable sources, including the Baldridge Quality Award criteria.

Each HRM group completes their part of the questionnaire. Through the last two items in each part, the HRM functional subgroup develops two consensus ratings: one that reflects the group's own perspective about how well their service is delivered, and one that speculates on how the customers of the service will later rate it in the customer satisfaction survey. The consensus ratings are scaled on a five-

or seven-point continuum with the midpoint representing a rating of "adequate." Of the two ratings for each category, the speculative responses carry the most weight. When compared to the "overall" satisfaction survey mean for a particular HRM service, the speculative ratings show how closely attuned the HRM subgroup is to the needs of its customers. An illustration will illumine this point later. Concurrently, with the implementation of Phase II, the audit team can begin Phase III.

Phase III: Measuring Current Service Levels

The purpose of Phase III of the audit is to develop performance metrics for the various HRM services and to measure current satisfaction levels. In the first year of an Audit, the baselining portion of Phase III is part of the focus group activities. Focus groups move from rating the HRM portfolio to defining what effectiveness means for the top four or five services. An open dialogue ensues from the facilitating question, "In your quiet moments, you evaluate the recruitment and selection (e.g.) services provided to you. What are the criteria you use to evaluate how well these services are provided?"

For recruitment and selection, customers may cite a variety of factors: elapsed time from posting position to delivery of the candidate certification list, the quality of candidates, or recruiter response time for communications with hiring managers. There are many possibilities. The demographic portion has been omitted. Notice that respondents are asked to comment on all items rated below "adequate." Such comments provide a wealth of feedback for process improvement work.

When the data is entered into a spreadsheet, not only are the seven-point ratings recorded, but also the comments are categorized. Thus, one quickly gets an overview of the range of comments, rich fuel for subsequent improvement efforts. In the second year audit and beyond, focus groups verify the validity of the survey before it is circulated again. Does it continue to address the major performance issues for that HRM service? If so, then the survey is distributed to collect another set of data points. With a new set of data points, the audit team gauges its progress toward closing performance gaps. Imagine the power of a report that can make statements like this: "The recruitment and selection team reduced the average time to fill vacancies by 24 per cent and boosted its customer satisfaction rating from 3.5 to 5.0 within one year."

PHASE IV: DEVELOPING ACTION PLANS

The purpose of Phase IV of the audit is to develop an HRM business plan based on the priorities emerging from the audit. In this example, the audit focused only on the top four most important HRM services: recruitment and selection, employee relations, compensation, and training and development. The grid has been sorted in ascending order according to the arithmetical mean of the "overall" satisfaction rating.

For example, if the recruitment and selection data in the Phase III column came from survey, then the "3.2" shown in the grid represents the calculated average of all responses to rating indicates that the majority of respondents are dissatisfied with the service level. Note: Even a mean slightly above "adequate" should generate some concern, because it suggests that a significant number of managers are dissatisfied.

The audit team also pays special attention to comparisons of the second and third columns, which indicate how attuned the HRM team is to the needs and expectations of their internal customers. In the example, the recruitment and selection category offers a striking comparison. The recruitment team expected an above-adequate "5" rating. Instead, the internal customers rated this service at "3.2," which is significantly adequate. The question remains, "Why did the recruitment team not know about the pervasive dissatisfaction?" The gap between expectations and reality suggests a need for improved feedback mechanisms.

The grid leads the way for exploration. When the audit team wants to dig deeper, it can isolate the specific issues within the survey, i.e., the underlying source of broader dissatisfaction. The audit team drills down to uncover the sources of overall performance problems. They examine the pattern of responses to the underlying questions within each part. Then, they drill deeper by reviewing the comment categories associated with unsatisfactory ratings.

The beauty of the audit blossoms from the story told by internal customers. Rather than being armed with only anecdotes, the audit team has the ammunition from a powerful round of data collection. On this foundation, the HRM team crafts a persuasive plan of attack for improving its services. Encouragements and Pitfalls every audit team confronts controversial issues such as: group apprehension, backsliding, and report positioning.

Group Apprehensions

At first, HRM teams may reluctantly embrace the audit procedure. Concerns about negative feedback and job security are typical. HRM team leaders should lay the foundation for positive collaboration by explaining the positive benefits of the audit.

Here are two likely benefits that show how the entire HRM team benefits. First, the audit identifies "low-hanging fruit," i.e., easily implemented, low-cost improvements that can dramatically enhance satisfaction ratings. Second, by engaging internal customers throughout the process, many people throughout the organization see the HRM department as responsive, attentive, and business-focused. These points begin to paint the upside picture in favour of the audit.

Backsliding

Maximum value of the audit comes from periodic repetition. With the second and third data points, trends begin to emerge. Performance gaps begin to close. Some widen. New issues arise. Priorities are refocused. The second-year hump is the biggest obstacle.

If the audit is forgotten or deliberately avoided in the second year, a golden opportunity passes. And there is a penalty, too. All the goodwill generated by the first-year audit is squandered. Internal customers become jaded thinking that the first-year exercise was mere lip service.

Report Positioning

Float a draft of the final report to upper management before organization-wide release. This assures that the proposed HRM action plans conform to broader strategic directions. Feedback alters tactics and priorities for service improvements. To illustrate, assume mid-level managers do not rate "regulatory compliance" as a high priority for meeting their business goals. However, if regulatory agencies are threatening their own audit reviews, top management may insist that this area become a top priority.

Regularly administered, the HRM Effectiveness Audit places the HRM team firmly at the table with other strategic business partners. The resulting business plan demonstrates how the HRM team will meet the business needs of its internal customers. The entire process effectively engages customers in a dialogue defining a measurement system for tracking progress in HRM service improvement. If public sector HRM teams expect to clearly show that they deserve the label of a strategic business partner, they will need to adopt methodologies similar to those described herein.

6

Human Resource Planning

CONCEPT OF HRP

- *Definition* 1: Need, Availability, Supply=Demand
  - "HRP includes estimation of how many qualified people are necessary to carry out the assigned activities, how many people will be available, and what, if anything, must be done to ensure personnel supply equals personnel demand at the appropriate point in the future."
- *Definition* 2: Right numbers, Capability, Organization Objectives
  - "HRP is a Process, by which an organization ensures that it has the right number and kind of people at the right place, at the right time, capable of effectively and efficiently completing those tasks that will help the organization achieve its overall objectives."
- *Definition* 3: Translation of objectives into HR numbers
  - "HRP is a process of translating organizational objectives and plans into the number of workers needed to meet those objectives."

Meaning / Purpose of HRP

- In simple words HRP is understood as the process of forecasting an organization's future demand for and supply of the right type of people in the right numbers.

- It is only after HRP is done, that the company can initiate and plan the recruitment and selection process.
- HRP is a sub-system in the total organizational planning.
- HRP facilitates the realization of the company's objectives by providing right type and right number of personnel.
- HRP is important because without a clear-cut manpower planning, estimation of a organization's human resource need is reduced to mere guesswork.

Need and Importance of HRP

Forecast future personnel needs: To avoid the situations of surplus or deficiency of manpower in future, it is important to plan your manpower in advance. For this purpose a proper forecasting of futures business needs helps you to ascertain our future manpower needs. From this angle, HRP plays an important role to predict the right size of manpower in the organization.

Cope with change: HRP enables an enterprise to cope with changes in competitive forces, markets, technology, products and government regulations. Such changes generate changes in job content, skills demands and number of human resources required.

Creating highly talented personnel: Since jobs are becoming highly intellectual and incumbents getting vastly professionalized, HRP helps prevent shortages of labour caused by attritions. Further technology changes would further upgrade or degrade jobs and create manpower shortages. In these situations only accurate human resource planning can help to meet the resource requirements. Further HRP is also an answer to the problems of succession planning.

Protection of weaker parts: A well-conceived personnel planning would also help to protect the interests of the SC/ST, physically handicapped, children of socially oppressed and backward classes who enjoy a certain percentage of employments notwithstanding the constitutional provisions of equal opportunity for all. *International strategies*: International expansion strategies largely depend upon effective HRP. With growing trends towards global operations, the need for HRP further becomes more important as the need to integrate HRP more closely into the organization keeps growing.

This is also because the process of meeting staffing needs from foreign countries grows in a complex manner. Foundation of personnel functions: HRP provides essential information for designing and implementing personnel functions such as recruitment, selection, personnel development, training and development etc. *Increasing investments in HR*: Another importance is the investment that an organization makes in human capital. It is important that employees are used effectively throughout their careers. Because human assets can increase the organization value tremendously as opposed to physical assets

Resistance to change & move: The growing resistance towards change and move, self evaluation, loyalty and dedication making it more difficult to assume that organization can move its employees everywhere. Here HRP becomes very important and needs the resources to be planned carefully.

Other benefits: Following are the other benefits of HRP.

- Upper management has a better view of HR dimensions of business
- Management can anticipate imbalances before they become unmanageable and expensive.
- More time is provided to locate talent
- Better opportunities exists to include women and minorities in future growth plans
- Better planning of assignments to develop managers
- Major and successful demands on local labour markets can be made.

HRP System

HRP System as such includes following elements or sets for planning:

- Overall Organization Objectives

- Business Environment
- Forecasting Manpower Needs
- Assessing Manpower Supply
- Matching Manpower Demand-Supply factors
- Based on these elements we can draw "HRP System Architecture" as under.

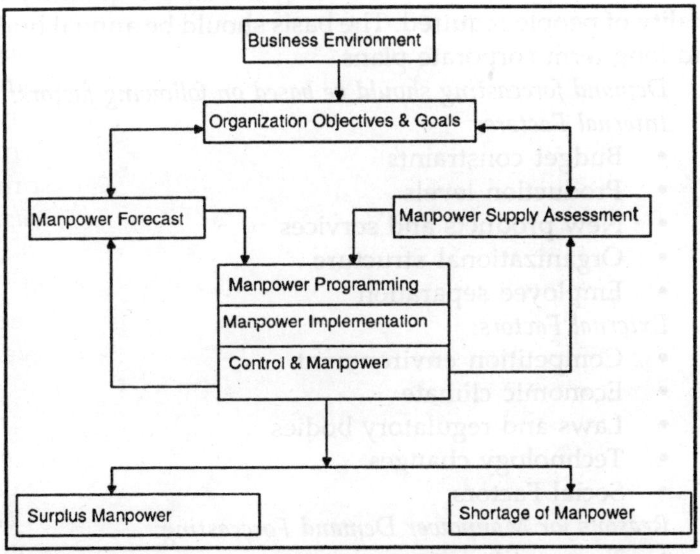

HRP PROCESS

Organizational Objectives and Policies

The objectives of HR plan must be derived from organizational objectives like specific requirements of numbers and characteristics of employees etc. HRP needs to sub-serve the overall objectives by ensuring availability and utilization of human resources.

Specific policies need to be formulated to address the following decisions:

- Internal Hiring or External Hiring?
- Training & Development plans
- Union Constraints
- Job enrichment issues

- Rightsizing organization
- Automation needs
- Continuous availability of adaptive and flexible workforce

Manpower Demand Forecasting

It is the process of estimating the future quantity and quality of people required. The basis should be annual budget and long term corporate plans

Demand forecasting should be based on following factors:

Internal Factors:

- Budget constraints
- Production levels
- New products and services
- Organizational structure
- Employee separation

External Factors:

- Competition environment
- Economic climate
- Laws and regulatory bodies
- Technology changes
- Social Factors

Reasons for Manpower Demand Forecasting:

- To quantify jobs
- To determine the Staff-mix
- To assess staffing levels and avoid unnecessary costs
- Prevent shortages of people
- Monitor compliances of legal requirements with regards to reservations

MANPOWER FORECASTING TECHNIQUES

In this techniques managers across all the levels decide the forecast on their own judgment. This can be bottom-up or top-down approach and judgments can be reviewed across departments, divisions and top management can conclude on final numbers of manpower required.

- *Ration-Trend Analysis*: This technique involves studying past ratios, and forecasting future ratios making some allowance for changes in the organization or its methods.

- *Work Study Techniques*: It is possible when work measurement to calculate the length of operations and the amount of manpower required. The starting point can be production budget, followed by standard hours, output per hour; man-hours required, etc., could be computed.
- *Delphi Techniques*: This technique solicits estimates from a group of experts, and HRP experts normally act as intermediaries, summarizes various responses and report the findings back to experts.
- *Flow Models*: This technique involves the flow of following components. Determine the time required, Establish categories, Count annual movements, Estimate probable transitions. Here demand is a function of replacing those who make a transition.

MANPOWER SUPPLY FORECASTING

This process measures the number of people likely to be available from within and outside the organization after making allowance for absenteeism, internal movements and promotions, wastages, changes in hours and other conditions of work.

Reasons for Manpower Supply Forecasting:

- Clarify Staff-mixes exist in the future
- Assess existing staff levels
- Prevent shortages
- Monitor expected future compliance of legal requirements of job reservations

Supply Analysis covers:

EXISTING HUMAN RESOURCES

HR Audits facilitate analysis of existing employees with skills and abilities. The existing employees can be categorized as skills inventories (non-managers) and managerial inventories (managers)

Skill inventory would include the following:

- Personal data

- Skills
- Special Qualifications
- Salary
- Job History
- Company data
- Capabilities
- Special preferences

Management inventories would include the following:

- Work History
- Strengths
- Weaknesses
- Promotion Potential
- Career Goals
- Personal Data
- Number and Types of Subordinates
- Total Budget Managed
- Previous Management Duties

Internal supply techniques help to assess the following:

- Inflows and outflows (transfers, promotions, separations, resignations, retirements etc.)
- Turnover rate
- Conditions of work (working hours, overtime, etc.)
- Absenteeism (leaves, absences)
- Productivity level
- Job movements (Job rotations or cross functional utilizations)

External Supply:

External sources are required for following reasons:

- New blood,
- New experiences
- Replenish lost personnel
- Organizational growth
- Diversification

External sources can be colleges and universities, consultants, competitors and unsolicited applications.

HR PLAN IMPLEMENTATION

A series of action programmes are initiated as a part of HR plan implementation as under.

RECRUITMENT AND SELECTION

Employees are hired against the job vacancies. Based on the manpower demand and supply forecasts made, hiring of employees is initiated based on supply forecasts. For this internal and external sources of manpower are utilized. A formal selection board is established to interview and select the best of the candidates for the required vacancies. Finally the selected employees also need to be placed on proper jobs. Here some companies recruit employees for specific jobs while others recruit fresh trainees in large number and train them for future manpower needs.

- *Training and Development*: The training and development programme is charted out to cover the number of trainees, existing staff etc. The programmess also cover the identification of resource personnel for conducting development programme, frequency of training and development programmes and budget allocation.
- *Retraining and Redeployment*: New skills are to be imparted to existing staff when technology changes or product line discontinued. Employees need to be redeployed to other departments where they could be gainfully employed.
- *Retention Plan*: Retention plans cover actions, which would reduce avoidable separations of employees. Using compensation plans, performance appraisals, avoiding conflicts, providing green pastures, etc., can do this.

DOWNSIZING PLANS

Where there is surplus workforce trimming of labour force will be necessary. For these identifying and managing redundancies is very essential.

MANAGERIAL SUCCESSION PLANNING

Methods of managerial succession plans may vary. Most successful programmes seem to include top managements involvement and commitment, high-level review of succession plans, formal performance assessment and potential assessment and written development plans for individuals.

A typical succession planning involves following activities:

- Analysis of demand for managers and professionals
- Audit of existing executives
- Projection of future likely supply from internal and external sources
- Individual career path planning
- Career counseling
- Accelerated promotions
- Performance related training and development
- Strategic recruitment

CONTROL AND EVALUATION OF HRP

HR Plan must also clarify responsibilities for control and establish reporting procedures, which will enable achievements to be monitored against the plan. The HR Plan should include budgets, targets and standards. These plans may simply be reports on the numbers employed, recruited against targets etc.

SUCCESSION PLANNING

Meaning of Succession Planning

Succession planning is the process or activities connected with the succession of persons to fill key positions in the organization hierarchy as vacancies arise. The focus of attention is towards 'which' person the succession planning is needed. The focus is not more on career development but it is more towards what kind of person is required to fill the future vacancy. Succession planning focuses on identification of vacancies and locating the probable successor. For example in succession planning the key concern can be who will be next CEO or what will happen if the Marketing Manager retires in coming March.

Importance of Succession Planning

- Succession planning helps when there is a sudden

need arises due to reason or retirement of a key employee.
- Individual employee comes to know in advance the level to which he can rise if he has the ability and aptitude for it.
- Individual employee or successor feels happy when he feels that organization is taking care of his talents and aspirations.
- Succession planning helps create loyalty towards the organization and improved motivation and morale of individual employees.
- Organization gains stable workforce and low employee turnover.
- Ultimately organization becomes successful in accomplishing its goals effectively.

CAREER PLANNING

Career planning is the process or activities offered by the organization to individuals to identify strengths, weaknesses, specific goals and jobs they would like to occupy. Career as a concept means a lifelong sequences of professional, educational and developmental experiences that projects an individual through the world of work. It is a sequence of positions occupied by a person during his life. Career may also be defined as amalgamation of changes in values, attitudes and motivation that occurs as a person grows older. In career planning, organization is concerned with strategic questions of career development. Further the organization is concerned about if it should employ more graduates, more engineers, more scientists or more accountants etc. Career planning provides picture of succession plan for employees as per organizational needs. It focuses on the basis of performance, experience, could be placed where, when and how.

Career planning is a process of integrating the employees' needs and aspirations with organizational requirements.

Objectives of Career Planning:
- Build commitment in the individual
- Develop long-range perspective

- Reduce personal turnover expenses
- Lessen employee obsolescence
- Ensure organizational effectiveness
- Allow individual to achieve personal and work related goals.

Importance of Career Planning

Career planning is important because it helps the individual to explore, choose and strive to derive satisfaction with his own career objectives.

JOB ANALYSIS

Definition 1: Process of Collecting Information

- "Job Analysis is a process of studying and collecting information relating to operations and responsibilities of a specific job. The immediate products of this analysis are 'Job Description' and 'Job Specifications'."

Definition 2: Systematic Exploration of Activities

- "Job Analysis is a systematic exploration of activities within a job. It is a basic technical procedure that is used to define duties and responsibilities and accountabilities of the job."

Definition 3: Identifying Job Requirements

- "Job is a collection of tasks that can be performed by a single employee to contribute to the production of some product or service, provided by the organization. Each job has certain ability requirements (as well as certain rewards) associated with it. Job Analysis is a process used to identify these requirements."

MEANING OF JOB ANALYSIS

Job Analysis is a process of collecting information about a job. The process of job analysis results into two sets of data:

- Job Description
- Job Specification

As a result Job analysis involves the following steps in a logical order.

Steps of Job Analysis:

- Collecting and recording job information
- Checking the job information for accuracy
- Writing job description based on information collected to determine the skills, knowledge, abilities and activities required
- Updating and upgrading this information

PURPOSE OF JOB ANALYSIS

- *Human Resource Planning (HRP)*: The numbers and types of personnel are determined by the jobs, which need to be staffed. Job related information in the form of Job Analysis serves this purpose or use.
- *Recruitment & Selection*: Recruitment precedes job analysis. It helps HR to locate places to obtain employees. It also helps in better continuity and planning in staffing in the organization. Also selecting a good candidate also requires detailed job information. Because the objective of hiring is to match the right candidate for right job
- *Training & Development*: Training and development programmes can be designed depending upon job requirement and analysis. Selection of trainees is also facilitated by job analysis.
- *Job Evaluation*: Job evaluation means determination of relative worth of each job for the purpose of establishing wage and salary credentials. This is possible with the help of job description and specifications; i.e. Job Analysis.
- *Remuneration*: Job analysis also helps in determining wage and salary for all jobs.
- *Performance Appraisal*: Performance appraisal, assessments, rewards, promotions, is facilitated by job analysis by way of fixing standards of job performance.
- *Personnel Information*: Job analysis is vital for building personnel information systems and processes for improving administrative efficiency and providing decision support.
- *Safety & Health*: Job Analysis helps to uncover

hazardous conditions and unhealthy environmental factors so that corrective measures can be taken to minimize and avoid possibility of human injury.

PROCESS OF JOB ANALYSIS

Process 1: Strategic Choices
Process 2: Collecting Information
Process 3: Processing Information
Process 4: Job Description
Process 5: Job Specification

STRATEGIC CHOICES

Extent of involvement of employees: Extent of employee involvement is a debatable point. Too much involvement may result in bias in favour of a job in terms of inflating duties and responsibilities. Too less involvement leads to suspicion about the motives behind the job. Besides it may also lead to inaccurate information. Hence extent of involvement depends on the needs of the organization and employee.

Level of details of job analysis: The nature of jobs being analysed determines the level of details in job analysis. If the purpose were for training programmes or assessing the worth of job, levels of details required would be great. If the purpose is just clarification the details required would be less.

Timing and frequency of Job Analysis: When do you do Job Analysis?

- Initial stage, for new organization
- New Job is created
- Changes in Job, Technology and Processes
- Deficiencies and Disparities in Job
- New compensation plan is introduced
- Updating and upgrading is required.

Past-oriented and future-oriented Job Analysis: For rapidly changing organization more future oriented approach would be desired.

For traditional organizations past oriented analysis would be required. However more future oriented analysis may be derived based on past data.

Sources of Job Data: For job analysis number of human and non-human sources is available besides jobholder himself. Following can be sources of data available for job analysis.

Non-Human Sources	Human Sources
Existing job descriptions and specifications	Job Analysis
Equipment maintenance records	Job Incumbents
Equipment design blueprints	Supervisors
Architectural blueprints of work area	Job Experts
Films of employee working	
Training manuals and materials	
Magazines, newspapers, literatures	

COLLECTING INFORMATION

Information collection is done on the basis of following 3 parameters.

Types of Data for Job Analysis:

- Work Activities
- Interface with other jobs and equipments
- Machines, Tools, Equipments and Work Aids (List, Materials, Products, Services)
- Job Context (Physical, Social, Organizational, Work schedule)
- Personal Requirement (Skills, Education, Training, Experience)

Methods of Data Collection:

- Observation
- Interview
- Questionnaires
- Checklists
- Technical Conference
- Diary Methods

Who to Collect Data?

- Trained Job Analysts
- Supervisors
- Job Incumbents

PROCESSING INFORMATION

Once the job information is collected it needs to be processed, so that it would be useful in various personnel functions. Specifically job related data would be useful to prepare job description and specifications, which form the next two processes of job analysis.

Methods of Data Collection

- *Observation:* Job Analyst carefully observes the jobholder and records the information in terms of what, how the job is done and how much time is taken. It is a simple and accurate method, but is also time consuming and inapplicable to jobs involving mental activities and unobservable job cycles. The analysts must be fully trained observers.
- *Interview:* In this analyst interviews the jobholders, his supervisors to elicit information. It can be Structured or Unstructured Interview. Again this is also a time consuming method in case of large organizations. Plus there is also a problem of bias.
- *Questionnaires:* A standard questionnaire is given to jobholder about his job, which can be filled and given back to supervisors or job analysts. The questionnaire may contain job title, jobholder's name, managers name, reporting staff, description of job, list of main duties and responsibilities etc. It is useful in large number of staffs and less time consuming. However the accuracy of information leaves much to be desired.
- *Checklists:* It is more similar to questionnaire but the response sheet contains fewer subjective judgments and tends to be either yes or no variety. Preparation of checklist is a challenging job itself.
- *Technical Conference:* Here a conference of supervisors is used. However, this method lacks accuracy.
- *Diary Methods:* In this method jobholder is required to note down their activities day by day in their diary. If done faithfully this technique is accurate and eliminates errors caused by memory lapses etc.

Quantitative Methods of Job Data Collection

Position Analysis Questionnaire (PAQ)

PAQ is a highly specialized instrument for analysing any job in terms of employee activities. The PAQ contains 194 job elements on which job is created depending on the degree to which an element is present.

These elements are grouped together into 6 categories:

1. U – Usability / Use of Job
2. I – Importance of Job
3. T – Time
4. P – Possibility of Occurrence of Job
5. A – Applicability of Job
6. S – Specialty Tasks of Job

The primary advantage of PAQ is that it can be used to analyse almost every job. This analysis provides a comparison of a specific job with other job classifications, particularly for selection and remuneration purposes. However PAQ needs to be completed by trained job analysts only rather than incumbents.

Management Position Description Questionnaire (MPDQ)

Highly structured questionnaire, containing 208 elements relating to managerial responsibilities, demand, restrictions and other position characteristics These 208 elements are grouped under 13 categories. PAQ and MPDQ yield standardized information about the worker and the job.

Functional Job Analysis

It is a worker oriented job analytical approach, which attempts to describe the whole person on the job.

Barriers of job analysis:

- Support from Top Management
- Single means and source, reliance on single method rather than combination
- No Training or Motivation to Jobholders
- Activities and Data may be Distorted

JOB DESCRIPTION

"Job Description implies objective listing of the job title, tasks, and responsibilities involved in a job."

Job description is a word picture in writing of the duties, responsibilities and organizational relationships that constitutes a given job or position. It defines continuing work assignment and a scope of responsibility that are sufficiently different from those of the other jobs to warrant a specific title. Job description is a broad statement of purpose, scope, duties and responsibilities of a particular job.

Contents of Job Description:

- Job Identification
- Job Summary
- Job Duties and Responsibilities
- Supervision specification
- Machines, tools and materials
- Work conditions
- Work hazards
- Definition of unusual terms

Format of Job Description:

- Job Title
- Region/Location
- Department
- Reporting to (Operational and Managerial)
- Objective
- Principal duties and responsibilities

Features of Good Job Description:

- Up to date
- Proper Job Title
- Comprehensive Job Summary
- Clear duties and responsibilities
- Easily understandable
- State job requirements
- Specify reporting relationships
- Showcase degrees of difficulties
- Indicates opportunities for career development
- Offer bird's-eye-view of primary responsibilities

JOB SPECIFICATIONS

"Job Specification involves listing of employee qualifications, skills and abilities required to meet the job description. These specifications are needed to do job satisfactorily." In other words it is a statement of minimum and acceptable human qualities necessary to perform job properly. Job specifications seeks to indicate what kind of persons may be expected to most closely approximate the role requirements and thus it is basically concerned with matters of selection, screening and placement and is intended to serve as a guide in hiring.

Contents of Job Specifications:

- Physical Characteristics
- Psychological characteristics
- Personal characteristics
- Responsibilities
- Demographic features

Further the job specifications can be divided into three broad categories:

- Essential Attributes
- Desirable Attributes
- *Contra-Indicators*: Indicators hampering the success of job

JOB EVALUATION

Job Evaluation involves determination of relative worth of each job for the purpose of establishing wage and salary differentials. Relative worth is determined mainly on the basis of job description and job specification only. Job Evaluation helps to determine wages and salary grades for all jobs. Employees need to be compensated depending on the grades of jobs which they occupy.

Remuneration also involves fringe benefits, bonus and other benefits. Clearly remuneration must be based on the relative worth of each job. Ignoring this basic principle results in inequitable compensation. A perception of inequity is a sure way of de-motivating an employee. Job evaluation is a process of analyzing and assessing the various jobs systematically to ascertain their relative worth in an organization. Jobs are evaluated on the basis of content, placed in order of importance. This establishes Job Hierarchies, which is a purpose of fixation of satisfactory wage differentials among various jobs.

SCOPE OF JOB EVALUATION

The job evaluation is done for the purpose of wage and salary differentials, demand for and supply of labour, ability to pay, industrial parity, collective bargaining and the like.

Process of Job Evaluation:

- Defining objectives of job evaluation
  - Identify jobs to be evaluated (Benchmark jobs or all jobs)
  - Who should evaluate job?
  - What training do the evaluators need?
  - How much time involved?
  - What are the criteria for evaluation?
  - Methods of evaluation to be used
- Wage Survey
- Employee Classification
- Establishing wage and salary differentials.

METHODS OF JOB EVALUATION

Analytical Methods:

- *Point Ranking Methods*: Different factors are selected for different jobs with accompanying differences in degrees and points. Factor Comparison Method: The important factors are selected which can be assumed to be common to all jobs. Each of these factors are then ranked with other jobs. The worth of the job is then taken by adding together all the point values.

Non-Analytical Methods:

- *Ranking Method*: Jobs are ranked on the basis of its title or contents. Job is not broken down into factors etc.
- *Job Grading Method*: It is based on the job as a whole and the differentiation is made on the basis of job

classes and grades. In this method it is important to form a grade description to cover discernible differences in skills, responsibilities and other characteristics.

Pitfalls of Job Evaluation:

- Encourages employees on how to advance in position when there may be limited opportunities for enhancement as a result of downsizing.
- It promotes internal focus instead of customer orientation
- Not suitable for forward looking organizations, which has trimmed multiple job titles into two or three broad jobs.

JOB DESIGN

Definition: Integration of work, rewards and qualification:

- "Job Design integrates work content (tasks, functions, relationships), the rewards and qualifications required including skills, knowledge and abilities for each job in a way that meets the needs of employees and the organization."

Steps in Job Design:

- Specification of Individual Tasks
- Specification of Methods of Tasks Performance
- Combination of Tasks into Specific Jobs to be assigned to individuals

Factors Affecting Job Design

Organizational Factors

- Characteristics of Tasks (Planning, Execution and Controlling of Task)
- Work Flow (Process Sequences)
- Ergonomics (Time & Motion Study)
- Work Practices (Set of ways of performing tasks)

Environmental Factors:

- Employee Abilities and Availability
- Social and Cultural Expectations

Behavioural Elements:

- Feedback
- Autonomy
- Use of Abilities
- Variety

TECHNIQUES OF JOB DESIGN

Work Simplification: Job is simplified or specialized. The job is broken down into small parts and each part is assigned to an individual. To be more specific, work simplification is mechanical pacing of work, repetitive work processes, working only on one part of a product, predetermining tools and techniques, restricting interaction amongst employees, few skills requirement. Work simplification is used when jobs are not specialized.

Job Rotation: When incumbents become bore of routine jobs, job rotation is an answer to it. Here jobs remain unchanged, but the incumbents shift from one job to another. On the positive side, it increases the intrinsic reward potential of a job because of different skills and abilities needed to perform it. Workers become more competent in several jobs, know variety of jobs and improve the self-image, personal growth. Further the worker becomes more valuable to the organization. Periodic job changes can improve interdepartmental cooperation. On the negative side, it may not be much enthusiastic or efficiency may not be more. Besides jobs may not improve the relationships between task, while activities and objectives remain unchanged. Further training costs also rise and it can also de-motivate intelligent and ambitious trainees who seek specific responsibilities in their chosen specialties.

Job Enlargement: It means expanding the number of tasks, or duties assigned to a given job. Job enlargement is naturally opposite to work simplification. Adding more tasks or duties to a job does not mean that new skills and abilities are needed. There is only horizontal expansion. It is with same skills taking additional responsibilities like extending working hours etc. Job enlargement may involve breaking up of the existing work system and redesigning a new work system. For this employees also need to be trained to adjust to the new system. Job enlargement is said to contribute to employee motivation but the claim is not validated in practice.

Benefits of Job Enlargement:

- Task Variety
- Meaningful Work Modules
- Full Ability Utilization
- Worker Paced Control
- Meaningful Performance Feedback

Disadvantages of Job Enlargement:

- High Training Costs
- Redesigning existing work system required
- Productivity may not increase necessarily
- Workload increases
- Unions demand pay–hike
- Jobs may still remain boring and routine

Job Enrichment: Job enrichment is improvisation of both tasks efficiency and human satisfaction by building into people's jobs, quite specifically, greater scope for personal achievement and recognition, more challenging and responsible work and more opportunity for individual advancement and growth.

An enriched job will have more responsibility, more autonomy (vertical enrichment), more variety of tasks (horizontal enrichment) and more growth opportunities. The employee does more planning and controlling with less supervision but more self-evaluation. In other words, transferring some of the supervisor's tasks to the employee and making his job enriched.

Benefits of Job enrichment:

- It benefits employee and organization in terms of increased motivation, performance, satisfaction, job involvement and reduced absenteeism.
- Additional features in job meet certain psychological needs of jobholders due to skill variety, identity, significance of job etc.
- It also adds to employee self-esteem and self-control.

- Job enrichment gives status to jobholder and acts as a strong satisfier in one's life.
- Job enrichment stimulates improvements in other areas of organization.
- Empowerment is a by-product of job enrichment. It means passing on more authority and responsibility.

Demerits of Job Enrichment:

- Lazy employees may not be able to take additional responsibilities and power. It won't fetch the desired results for an employee who is not attentive towards his job.
- Unions resistance, increased cost of design and implementation and limited research on long term effect of job enrichment are some of the other demerits.
- Job enrichment itself might not be a great motivator since it is job-intrinsic factor. As per the two-factor motivation theory, job enrichment is not enough. It should be preceded by hygienic factors etc.
- Job enrichment assumes that workers want more responsibilities and those workers who are motivated by less responsibility, job enrichment surely de-motivates them
- Workers participation may affect the enrichment process itself.
- Change is difficult to implement and is always resisted as job enrichment brings in a changes the responsibility.

Autonomous of Self-Directed Teams

Empowerment results in self-directed work teams. A self –directed team is an intact group of employees responsible for whole work segment, they work together, handle day-to-day problems, plan and control, and are highly effective teams.

High Performance Work Design

Improving performance in an environment where positive and demanding goals are set leads to high performance work design. It starts from the principle of autonomous groups working and developing an approach, which enables group to work effectively together in situations where the rate of innovation is very high. Operational flexibility is important and there is the need for employees to gain and apply new skills quickly with minimum supervision. However due to bureaucracy high performance work design does not work.

DESIGNING JOBS – MOTIVATING JOBS

The concept of motivating jobs relates to Job design. Job design affects employee productivity, motivation and satisfaction. Job design is a conscious effort to organize tasks, duties and responsibilities into a unit of work to achieve certain objectives. How a job design creates a motivating job can be seen with the help of certain components of job design, namely, job rotation, job enlargement, job enrichment, work simplification etc.

Work simplification simplifies the job by breaking down the job into small parts. Simplified jobs are easy to perform hence employees find it easy to do. Training requirements are reduced and it benefits the organizations in terms of cost. Job rotation means movement of employees of job to job across the organization. It improves the intrinsic reward potential of a job because of different skills and abilities are needed to perform a job. Workers become more competent in several jobs rather than only one.

It also improves workers self image, provides personal growth and makes workers more valuable to the organization. Periodic job change can improve interdepartmental cooperation. Employees become more understanding to each other's problems. Consequently it provides a high level of motivation to employees because jobs itself become motivators. Hence job rotation helps the job become more motivating.

Job enlargement involves expanding number of tasks or duties assigned to a given job. Job enrichment involves improving task efficiency and human satisfaction. Job enrichment provides greater scope for personal achievement and recognition, more challenging and responsible work and more opportunity for individual advancement and growth. An enriched job gives vertical enrichment in the form of more responsibility and autonomy and a horizontal enrichment in the form of variety of tasks and more growth opportunities. The employee does more planning and controlling with less supervision but more self-evaluation. All these factors lead to increased level of motivation and hence make the jobs more motivated.

Considering examples, we can say that designing jobs is actually using the relevant and right techniques of job design, like rotation, enrichment, simplifications and make the jobs more motivating to perform. So we can say that Designing Jobs is actually creating Motivated Jobs.

JOB SATISFACTION

Job satisfaction is the result of various attitudes possessed by an employee towards his job, related factors and life in general. The attitudes related to job may be wages, supervision, steadiness, working conditions, advancement opportunities, recognitions, fair evaluation of work, social relations on job, prompt settlement of grievances etc. In short job satisfaction is a general attitude, which is the result of many specific attitudes in three areas namely, job factors, individual characteristics and group relationships outside the job.

COMPONENTS OF JOB SATISFACTION

- *Personal factors*: Sex, Dependents, Age, Timings, Intelligence, Education and Personality.
- *Job inherent factors*: Type of work, Skills, Occupational status, Geography, Size of plant
- *Management controlled factors*: Security, Payment, Fringe benefits, Advancement opportunities and Working conditions, Coworkers, Responsibilities, Supervision

Job Satisfaction & Behaviour relationship is described through following examples.

- Satisfaction & Turnover

- Satisfaction & Absenteeism
- Satisfaction & Accidents
- Satisfaction & Job Performance

WORK SAMPLING

Definition: Measuring and quantifying activities "a measurement technique for the quantitative analysis of non-repetitive or irregularly occurring activity."

Meaning of Work Sampling Work sampling is based on the theory that the percentage of the number of observations on a particular activity is a reliable measure of the percentage of the total actual time spent on that activity. Work sampling operates by an observer taking a series of random observations on a particular "thing" of interest (machine, operating room, dock, etc.) to observe its "state" (working, idle, sleeping, empty, etc.).

When enough samples are taken, an analysis of the observations yields a statistically valid indication of the states for each thing analysed. Assume, for example, that you wish to determine the proportion of time a factory operator is working or idle.

Also assume that 200 random observations were made of the operator and during 24 of these he or she was observed to be idle. Therefore, you find that the individual is working 176/200 = 88% of the time.

Advantages of Work Sampling: It is relatively inexpensive to use and extremely helpful in providing a deeper understanding of all types of operations. When properly used, it can help pinpoint those areas, which should be analysed in, further detail and can serve as a measure of the progress being made in improving operations

Questions of work sampling study:

- What is our equipment/asset utilization?
- When we are not adding value to the product, how are we spending our time?
- How are our interdependent systems performing?
- Where should we focus our continuous improvement activities?

Distinction between Work sampling and "Time Studies":

- Work sampling is lower cost because it uses random samples instead of continuous observations.
- Many operators or machines can be studied by a single observer
- Work sampling can span several days or weeks, thus minimizing the effects of day to day load or equipment variations
- Work Sampling tends to minimize operator behaviour modification during observation.
- Work Sampling, in general, does not require a trained time-study analyst to take the observations. Also, stopwatches or other timing devices are not required. Many studies make use of off-shift technicians or operators to take the observations. Work sampling Methodology

An analyst Randomly observes an activity (equipment, operating room, production line) and notes the particular states of the activity at each observation. The ratio of the number of observations of a given state of the activity to the total number of observations taken will approximate the percentage of time that the activity is in that given state. Note that random observations are very critical for a work sampling study. A brief example might be that 77 of 100 observations showed a machine to be running. We might then conclude, within certain statistical limits, that the equipment is operational 77% of the time.

RECRUITMENT AND SELECTION RECRUITMENT

Definition of Recruitment: Finding and Attracting Applications. "Recruitment is the Process of finding and attracting capable applicants for employment. The Process begins when new recruits are sought and ends when their applications are submitted. The result is a pool of application from which new employees are selected."

MEANING OF RECRUITMENT

Recruitment is understood as the process of searching for and obtaining applicants for jobs, from among them the right people can be selected. Though theoretically recruitment process is said to end with the receipt of applications, in practice the activity extends to the screening of applications so as to eliminate those who are not qualified for the job.

PURPOSE AND IMPORTANCE OF RECRUITMENT

- Determine the present and future requirements in conjunction with personnel planning and job analysis activities
- Increase the pool of job candidates at minimum cost
- Help increase success rate of selection process by reducing number of under-qualified or over-qualified applications.
- Reduce the probability that job applicants once selected would leave shortly
- Meet legal and social obligations
- Identify and prepare potential job applicants
- Evaluate effectiveness of various recruitment techniques and sources for job applicants.

FACTORS GOVERNING RECRUITMENT

External Factors:

- Demand and Supply (Specific Skills)
- Unemployment Rate (Area-wise)
- Labour Market Conditions
- Political and Legal Environment (Reservations, Labour laws)
- Image

Internal Factors:

- Recruitment Policy (Internal Hiring or External Hiring?)
- Human Resource Planning (Planning of resources required)
- Size of the Organization (Bigger the size lesser the recruitment problems)
- Cost
- Growth and Expansion Plans

RECRUITMENT PROCESS

Recruitment Planning:

- Number of contacts
- Types of contacts

Recruitment Strategy Development:

- Make or Buy Employees
- Technological Sophistication
- Where to look
- How to look

Internal Recruitment:

- Present employees
- Employee referrals
- Transfers & Promotions
- Former Employees
- Previous Applicants
- Evaluation of Internal Recruitment

External Recruitment:

- Professionals or Trade Associations
- Advertisements
- Employment Exchanges
- Campus Recruitment
- Walk-ins Interviews
- Consultants
- Contractors
- Displaced Persons
- Radio & Television
- Acquisitions & Mergers
- Competitors
- Evaluation of External Recruitment

Searching:

- Source activation
- Selling
- Screening of Applications

Evaluation and Cost Control:

- Salary Cost
- Management & Professional Time spent
- Advertisement Cost

- Producing Supporting literature
- Recruitment Overheads and Expenses
- Cost of Overtime and Outsourcing
- Consultant's fees

Evaluation of Recruitment Process:

- Return rate of applications sent out
- Suitable Candidates for selection
- Retention and Performance of selected candidates
- Recruitment Cost
- Time lapsed data
- Image projection

Internal Recruitment:

Advantages

- Advantages Less Costly
- Candidates already oriented towards organization
- Organizations have better knowledge about internal candidates
- Employee morale and motivation is enhanced

Disadvantages

- Old concept of doing things
- It abets raiding
- Candidates current work may be affected
- Politics play greater roles
- Morale problem for those not promoted.

External Recruitment:

Advantages

- Benefits of new skills and talents
- Benefits of new experiences
- Compliance with reservation policy becomes easy
- Scope for resentment, jealousies, and heartburn are avoided.

Disadvantages

- Better morale and motivation associated with internal recruiting is denied
- It is costly method
- Chances of creeping in false positive and false negative errors
- Adjustment of new employees takes longer time.

SELECTION

MEANING OF SELECTION

Selection is the process of picking up individuals (out of the pool of job applicants) with requisite qualifications and competence to fill jobs in the organization. A formal definition of Selection is as under.

Definition of Selection: Process of differentiating

"Selection is the process of differentiating between applicants in order to identify and hire those with a greater likelihood of success in a job."

Difference Between Recruitment and Selection

Recruitment:

- Recruitment refers to the process of identifying and encouraging prospective employees to apply for jobs.
- Recruitment is said to be positive in its approach as it seeks to attract as many candidates as possible.

Selection:

- Selection is concerned with picking up the right candidates from a pool of applicants.
- Selection on the other hand is negative in its application in as much as it seeks to eliminate as many unqualified applicants as possible in order to identify the right candidates.

PROCESS / STEPS IN SELECTION

- *Preliminary Interview*: The purpose of preliminary interviews is basically to eliminate unqualified applications based on information supplied in application forms. The basic objective is to reject misfits. On the other hands preliminary interviews is often called a courtesy interview and is a good public relations exercise.
- *Selection Tests*: Jobseekers who past the preliminary interviews are called for tests. There are various types of tests conducted depending upon the jobs and the company. These tests can be Aptitude Tests, Personality Tests, and Ability Tests and are conducted to judge how

well an individual can perform tasks related to the job. Besides this there are some other tests also like Interest Tests (activity preferences), Graphology Test (Handwriting), Medical Tests, Psychometric Tests etc.

- *Employment Interview*: The next step in selection is employment interview. Here interview is a formal and in-depth conversation between applicant's acceptability. It is considered to be an excellent selection device. Interviews can be One-to-One, Panel Interview, or Sequential Interviews. Besides there can be Structured and Unstructured interviews, Behavioural Interviews, Stress Interviews.
- *Reference & Background Checks*: Reference checks and background checks are conducted to verify the information provided by the candidates. Reference checks can be through formal letters, telephone conversations. However it is merely a formality and selections decisions are seldom affected by it.
- *Selection Decision*: After obtaining all the information, the most critical step is the selection decision is to be made. The final decision has to be made out of applicants who have passed preliminary interviews, tests, final interviews and reference checks. The views of line managers are considered generally because it is the line manager who is responsible for the performance of the new employee.
- *Physical Examination*: After the selection decision is made, the candidate is required to undergo a physical fitness test. A job offer is often contingent upon the candidate passing the physical examination.
- *Job Offer*: The next step in selection process is job offer to those applicants who have crossed all the previous hurdles. It is made by way of letter of appointment.
- *Contract of Employment*: After the job offer is made and candidates accept the offer, certain documents need to be executed by the employer and the candidate. Here is a need to prepare a formal contract of employment, containing written contractual terms of employment etc.

ESSENTIALS OF A GOOD SELECTION PRACTICE

- Detailed job descriptions and job specifications prepared in advance and endorsed by personnel and line management
- Trained the selectors
- Determine aids to be used for selection process
- Check competence of recruitment consultants before retention
- Involve line managers at all stages
- Attempt to validate the procedure
- Help the appointed candidate to succeed by training and management development

BARRIERS TO EFFECTIVE SELECTION

- *Perception*: We all perceive the world differently. Our limited perceptual ability is obviously a stumbling block to the objective and rational selection of people.
- *Fairness*: Barriers of fairness includes discrimination against religion, region, race or gender etc.
- *Validity*: A test that has been validated can differentiate between the employees who can perform well and those who will not. However it does not predict the job success accurately.
- *Reliability*: A reliable test may fail to predict job performance with precision.
- *Pressure*: Pressure brought on selectors by politicians, bureaucrats, relatives, friends and peers to select particular candidate are also barriers to selection.

7

Training and Development

TRAINING AND DEVELOPMENT

Definition of Training & Development: Improve performance "Training & Development is any attempt to improve current or future employee performance by increasing an employee's ability to perform through learning, usually by changing the employee's attitude or increasing his or her skills and knowledge. The need for Training and Development is determined by the employee's performance deficiency, computed as follows. Training & Development Need = Standard Performance - Actual Performance.

Distinction Between Training and Education

Training	Education
Application oriented	Theoretical Orientation
Job experience	Classroom learning
Specific Task in mind	Covers general concepts
Narrow Perspective	Has Broad Perspective
Training is Job Specific	Education is no bar

Training: Training refers to the process of imparting specific skills. An employee undergoing training is presumed to have had some formal education. No training programme is complete without an element of education. Hence we can say that Training is offered to operatives.

Education: It is a theoretical learning in classrooms. The purpose of education is to teach theoretical concepts and develop a sense of reasoning and judgment. That any training and development programme must contain an element of education is well understood by HR Specialists. Any such programme has university professors as resource persons to enlighten participants about theoretical knowledge of the topics proposed to discuss. In fact organizations depute or encourage employees to do courses on part time basis. CEOs are known to attend refresher courses conducted by business schools. The education is more important for managers and executives rather than low cadre workers. Anyways education is common to all employees, their grades notwithstanding.

Development: Development means those learning opportunities designed to help employees to grow. Development is not primarily skills oriented. Instead it provides the general knowledge and attitudes, which will be helpful to employers in higher positions.

Efforts towards development often depend on personal drive and ambition. Development activities such as those supplied by management development programmes are generally voluntary in nature. Development provides knowledge about business environment, management principles and techniques, human relations, specific industry analysis and the like is useful for better management of a company.

OBJECTIVES OF (MDP) MANAGEMENT DEVELOPMENT PROGRAMMES

Advantages of Development:

- Making them
  - Self-starters
  - Committed
  - Motivated
  - Result oriented
  - Sensitive to environment
  - Understand use of power
- Creating self awareness
- Develop inspiring leadership styles
- Instill zest for excellence
- Teach them about effective communication
- To subordinate their functional loyalties to the interests of the organization

Difference between Training and Development

Training	Development
Training is skills focused learning abilities	Development is creating
Training is presumed to have a formal education	Development is not education dependent
Training needs depend upon lack or deficiency in skills	Development depends on personal drive and ambition
Trainings are generally need based	Development is voluntary
Training is a narrower concept focused on job related skills	Development is a broader concept focused on personality development
Training may not include development	Development includes training wherever necessary
Training is aimed at improving job related efficiency and performance	Development aims at overall personal effectiveness including job efficiencies

What are the Training Inputs?

- Skills
- Education
- Development
- Ethics
- Problem Solving Skills
- Decision Making
- Attitudinal Changes

Importance of Training and Development

- Helps remove performance deficiencies in employees
- Greater stability, flexibility and capacity for growth in an organization
- Accidents, scraps and damages to machinery can be avoided
- Serves as effective source of recruitment
- It is an investment in HR with a promise of better returns in future

- Reduces dissatisfaction, absenteeism, complaints and turnover of employees

Need of Training

Individual level:

- Diagnosis of present problems and future challenges
- Improve individual performance or fix up performance deficiency
- Improve skills or knowledge or any other problem
- To anticipate future skill-needs and prepare employee to handle more challenging tasks
- To prepare for possible job transfers

Group level:

- To face any change in organization strategy at group levels
- When new products and services are launched
- To avoid scraps and accident rates

IDENTIFICATION OF TRAINING NEEDS (METHODS)

Individual Training Needs Identification:

- Performance Appraisals
- Interviews
- Questionnaires
- Attitude Surveys
- Training Progress Feedback
- Work Sampling
- Rating Scales

Group Level Training Needs Identification:

- Organizational Goals and Objectives
- Personnel / Skills Inventories
- Organizational Climate Indices
- Efficiency Indices
- Exit Interviews
- MBO / Work Planning Systems
- Quality Circles
- Customer Satisfaction Survey
- Analysis of Current and Anticipated Changes

Benefits of Training Needs Identification:

- Trainers can be informed about the broader needs in advance
- Trainers Perception Gaps can be reduced between employees and their supervisors trainers can design course inputs closer to the specific needs of the participants
- Diagnosis of causes of performance deficiencies can be done

METHODS OF TRAINING

On the Job Trainings: These methods are generally applied on the workplace while employees is actually working. Following are the on-the-job methods.

ADVANTAGES OF ON-THE-JOB TRAINING

- It is directly in the context of job
- It is often informal
- It is most effective because it is learning by experience
- It is least expensive
- Trainees are highly motivated
- It is free from artificial classroom situations

Disadvantages of on-the-Job Training

- Trainer may not be experienced enough to train
- It is not systematically organized
- Poorly conducted programmes may create safety hazards

On the Job Training Methods

- *Job Rotation*: In this method, usually employees are put on different jobs turn by turn where they learn all sorts of jobs of various departments. The objective is to give a comprehensive awareness about the jobs of different departments. Advantage - employee gets to know how his own and other departments also function. Interdepartmental coordination can be improved, instills team spirit. Disadvantage - It may become too much for an employee to learn. It is not focused on employees own job responsibilities. Employees basic talents may remain under utilized.

- *Job Coaching*: An experienced employee can give a verbal presentation to explain the nitty-gritty's of the job.
- *Job Instruction*: It may consist an instruction or directions to perform a particular task or a function. It may be in the form of orders or steps to perform a task.
- *Apprenticeships*: Generally fresh graduates are put under the experienced employee to learn the functions of job.
- *Internships and Assistantships*: An intern or an assistants are recruited to perform a specific time-bound jobs or projects during their education. It may consist a part of their educational courses.

Off the Job Trainings

These are used away from work places while employees are not working like classroom trainings, seminars etc. Following are the off-the-job methods;

Advantages of Off-the-Job Training

- Trainers are usually experienced enough to train
- It is systematically organized
- Efficiently created programmes may add lot of value

Disadvantages of Off-the-Job Training

- It is not directly in the context of job
- It is often formal
- It is not based on experience
- It is least expensive
- Trainees may not be highly motivated
- It is more artificial in nature

Off the Job Training Methods

- *Classroom Lectures*: It is a verbal lecture presentation by an instructor to a large audience. Advantage - It can be used for large groups. Cost per trainee is low. Disadvantages - Low popularity. It is not learning by practice. It is One-way communication. No authentic feedback mechanism. Likely to boredom.

- *Audio-Visual*: It can be done using Films, Televisions, Video, and Presentations etc. Advantages - Wide range of realistic examples, quality control possible. Disadvantages - One-way communication, No feedback mechanism. No flexibility for different audience.
- *Simulation*: creating a real life situation for decision-making and understanding the actual job conditions give it. Following are some of the simulation methods of trainings
  - *Case Studies*: It is a written description of an actual situation and trainer is supposed to analyse and give his ceases in writing. The cases are generally based on actual organizational situations. It is an ideal method to promote decision-making abilities within the constraints of limited data. Role Plays: Here trainees assume the part of the specific personalities in a case study and enact it in front of the audience. It is more emotional orientation and improves interpersonal relationships. Attitudinal change is another result. These are generally used in MDP.
  - *Sensitivity Trainings*: This is more from the point of view of behavioural assessment, under different circumstances how an individual will behave himself and towards others. There is no preplanned agenda and it is instant. Advantages - increased ability to empathize, listening skills, openness, tolerance, and conflict resolution skills. Disadvantage - Participants may resort to their old habits after the training.
- *Programmed Instructions*: Provided in the form of blocks either in book or a teaching machine using questions and Feedbacks without the intervention of

trainer. Advantages - Self paced, trainees can progress at their own speed, strong motivation for repeat learning, material is structured and self-contained. Disadvantages - Scope for learning is less; cost of books, manuals or machinery is expensive.

- *Computer Aided Instructions*: It is extension of PI method, by using computers. Advantages - Provides accountabilities, modifiable to technological innovations, flexible to time. Disadvantages - High cost.
- Laboratory Training

Barriers to Effective Training:

- Lack of Management commitment
- Inadequate Training budget
- Education degrees lack skills
- Large scale poaching of trained staff
- Non-coordination from workers due to downsizing trends
- Employers and B Schools operating distantly
- Unions influence

How To Make Training Effective?

- Management Commitment
- Training & Business Strategies Integration
- Comprehensive and Systematic Approach
- Continuous and Ongoing approach
- Promoting Learning as Fundamental Value
- Creations of effective training evaluation system

INDUCTION AND ORIENTATION

Definition 1: Planned Introduction

"It is a Planned Introduction of employees to their jobs, their co-workers and the organization per se."

Orientation conveys 4 types of information:

- Daily Work Routine
- Organization Profile
- Importance of Jobs to the organization
- Detailed Orientation Presentations Purpose of Orientation

- To make new employees feel at home in new environment
- To remove their anxiety about new workplace
- To remove their inadequacies about new peers
- To remove worries about their job performance
- To provide them job information, environment

Types of Orientation Programmes:

- Formal or Informal
- Individual or Group
- Serial or Disjunctive

Prerequisites of Effective Orientation Programme:

- Prepare for receiving new employee
- Determine information new employee wants to know
- Determine how to present information
- Completion of Paperwork

Problems of Orientations:

- Busy or Untrained supervisor
- Too much information
- Overloaded with paperwork
- Given menial tasks and discourage interests
- Demanding tasks where failure chances are high
- Employee thrown into action soon
- Wrong perceptions of employees

Difference between Induction and Orientation

Induction referred to formal training programmes that an employee had to complete before they could start work.

Orientation was the informal information giving that made the recruit aware of the comfort issues - where the facilities are, what time lunch is and so forth. How long should the induction process take?

It starts when the job ad is written, continues through the selection process and is not complete until the new team member is comfortable as a full contributor to the organization's goals.

The first hour on day one is a critical component - signing on, issuing keys and passwords, explaining no go zones, emergency procedures, meeting the people that you will interact with all have to be done immediately. Until they are done the newcomer is on the payroll, but is not employed. After that it is a matter of just in time training - expanding the content as new duties are undertaken.

We only Employ new People one at a time - how can we Induct them?

There are some issues, which cannot wait - they vary according to your situation. Perhaps a buddy system on the job may be the best way to deal with these. Other subjects may be incorporated with refresher training for current staff, or handled as participant in an outside programme. Perhaps some can wait until there are groups of people who have started in the last few months.

This may take some creative thinking, but the answer is quite simple - until the new people are integrated then they are less useful. The math is often amazingly simple - not taking the time to train consumes more time than the training would.

What Levels of Staff need Induction?

Everybody. The CEO needs to know different things to the temporary concierge, but everyone needs a planned programme of induction and orientation.

Placement

Placement is allocation of people to jobs. It is assignment or reassignment of an employee to a new or different job.

Multi Skilling

Multi Skilling is The Integrated Skills Programme that has been developed to build on the existing skills of the current work force to reduce redundancies and avoid downsizing situations. The objective of this programme is to gain total integration of skills.

The programme is based around 'on-the-job' & 'off-the-job' competence. That is the ability to do the job on the shop floor (training to gain work experience) and 'off-the-job' (training in the classroom) to gain underpinning knowledge.

The programme requires the individual to demonstrate competence in a number of different skills and this competence is measured and assessed on the job. Multi-skilling of course works best with more advanced skilled workers because their individual skills levels are developed enough where they can fluidly transition from one skill to the next without degradation of a skills performance. If you are multi-skilling and a great percentage of your workers are having problems executing one of the skills effectively it is probably a good signal you need to go back to basics with that skill and pull it out of the multi-skilling sequences.

Another advantage of multi-skilling is the positive effect of what is called "contextual learning". Contextual learning involves discovery and improvement from two skills, which don't, on the surface, appear to have a direct relationship. The disadvantages of multi-skilling include the obvious danger of moving on to quickly toward advanced skills and combinations without sufficiently drilling basic skills. While there is a great desire to learn quickly we think this is one of the reason we are seeing better skilled from some of the best workers. The consequence is that we become "partially skilled". The greater the number of partial skills we develop, the less chance we ever have of reaching our full potential.

CHANGE MANAGEMENT

CHANGE DEFINED

"Change is the window through which the future enters your life." It's all around you, in many types and shapes. You can bring it about yourself or it can come in ways

Why Change Management?

You can bring the change about yourself or it can come in ways that give you little choice about its what, when, and how. Fighting against change can slow it down or divert it, but it won't stop it however. If you wish to succeed in this rapidly changing new world "you must learn to look on change as a friend - one who presents you with an opportunity for growth and improvement."

The rate of change in today's world is constantly increasing. Everything that exists is getting old, wearing out and should be replaced. "Revolutionary technologies, consolidation, well-funded new competition, unpredictable customers, and a quickening in the pace of change hurled unfamiliar conditions at management." True success and long-term prosperity in the new world depends on your ability to adapt to different and constantly changing conditions. The strategic selection of the best strategic positioning in the playing field, or the Business Space, your firm must take is complicated by the fact that the characteristics of the Business Space change over time. Today, the world is a different place than it was yesterday. "At certain points, the difference becomes material. Successful firms recognize change. Very successful ones anticipate it." Evolutionary (Planned) Change versus Revolutionary Action

How you change a business unit to adapt to shifting economy and markets is a matter of management style. Evolutionary change, that involves setting direction, allocating responsibilities, and establishing reasonable timelines for achieving objectives, is relatively painless. However, it is rarely fast enough or comprehensive enough to move ahead of the curve in an evolving world where stakes are high, and the response time is short. When faced with market-driven urgency, abrupt and sometimes disruptive change, such as dramatic downsizing or re-engineering, may be required to keep the company competitive. In situations when timing is critical to success, and companies must get more efficient and productive rapidly, revolutionary change is demanded.

When choosing between evolutionary change and revolutionary action, a leader must pursue a balanced and pragmatic approach. Swinging too far to revolutionary extreme may create "an organizational culture that is so impatient, and so focused on change, that it fails to give new initiatives and new personnel time to take root, stabilize, and grow. What's more, it creates a high-tension environment that intimidates rather than nurtures people, leaving them with little or no emotional investment in the company.

RESISTANCE TO CHANGE

Most people don't like change because they don't like being changed. "If you want to make enemies, try to change something", advised Woodrow Wilson. When seeking to change an organization, it's strategy or processes, leaders run into Newton's law that a body at rest tends to stay at rest. Advocates for change are greeted with suspicion, anger, resistance, and even sabotage. "Not invented here" syndrome also keeps many sound ideas from gaining the objective assessment they deserve.

Today's World Realities

The magnitude of today's environmental, competitive, and global market change is unprecedented.

It's a very interesting and exciting world, but it's also volatile and chaotic:

- Volatility describes the economy's rate of change: extremely fast, with explosive upsurges and sudden downturns.
- Chaos describes the direction of the economy's changes: we're not sure exactly where we're headed, but we are swinging between the various alternatives at a very high speed.

To cope with an unpredictable world you must build an enormous amount of flexibility into your organization. While you cannot predict the future, you can get a handle on trends, which is a way to take advantage of change and convert risks into opportunities.

Creating Change for Improvement and Competitive Advantage

Change creates opportunities, but only for those who recognize and seize it. "Seeing is the first step, seizing the second, and continuously innovating is the third." Innovation redefines growth opportunities. As current products are becoming obsolete faster than ever, in order to survive and prosper, organizations continually need to improve, innovate and modify their products and services. The Silicon Valley slogan "Eat lunch and you are lunch" is more than a reflection of increasingly intense work ethic. Riding the wave of change is becoming the most important part of the business. While the economy is shifting and innovation is rampant, "doing it the same way" is a recipe for corporate extinction.

Successful change efforts are those where the choices both are internally consistent and fit key external and situational variables. "You have to find subtle ways to introduce change, new concepts, and give feedback to people so that they can accept and grow with it."

Anticipating Change

There is big difference between anticipating and guessing. Anticipation means expecting, being aware of something in advance, to regard it as possible. The ability to anticipate is one of the key ingredients of efficient speed and change management. "Being able to anticipate that which is likely to occur in the next few months and the next few years is enough to give you an edge over 99% of the population who simply go along with whatever happens."

How can you see the future? Actually, anticipation is natural - everyone does it every day. Unfortunately, most people limit exercising their anticipatory skills to daily routine matters. All you really need to start applying these skills for your business is a small head start.

Starting with Yourself

The best place to start change is with yourself. If whatever you do doesn't work, you must be flexible - you must change your action plan if the current one does not produce the required results. If you want other people to change, you must be prepared to make the first step yourself. If you cannot change your environment, you should change your attitude. To achieve effective personal change, consider practicing the NLP Technology of Achievement that was specially developed to discover how people can excel, and most particularly when managing change - how to create the 'difference that makes the difference'... More leading change the old ways of management no longer work and will never work again. Successful change requires leadership. When change fails to occur as planned, the cause if often to be found at a deeper level, rooted in the inappropriate behaviour, beliefs, attitudes, and assumptions of would-be leaders. Leadership is all about the process of change: how to stay ahead of it, master it, benefit from the opportunities it brings. The best leaders strike first by taking the offensive against economic cycles, market trends, and competitors.

They discover the most effective ways for achieving significant change - "a change that identifies the realities of the business environment and reorders them so that a new force is able to leverage, rather than resist, those realities in order to achieve a competitive advantage."

The following system will help you to unleash the power of your organization and reshape it into a more competitive enterprise:

- Develop a vision. To create a seamless bridge from the vision to action, start with your top management team - they should understand and embrace your vision.
- Align all your people against the endgame. Invite their opinion regarding critical issues such as the direction you should be headed, the changes you have to make, and the resources you have to acquire.
- Using the employee feedback, develop a strategic plan. Stay laser-focused on the methods that will drive your business unit towards its stated objectives.
- Build a diverse leadership group representing all the key constituencies of your organization. They will share responsibility for plan management.
- Share detail information about the company and the change progress - people have to understand where you are and where you are going in order to contribute effectively to your mission.

MANAGING ORGANIZATIONAL CHANGE

Success in business doesn't come from feeling comfortable. In today's technology-driven world, business life cycles have accelerated exponentially. The challenge is to keep a step ahead of changing market conditions, new technologies and human resources issues. The wheel of business evolution is a framework and set of tools, which enables you to manage the complex process of organizational change and transformation more effectively. The sequence of the eight segments - business environment, business ecosystem, business design, leadership style, organizational values, management process, knowledge management systems, and performance measures - reflects the learning cycle that occurs when outside-in or bottom-up learning takes place.

BEHAVIOURAL CHANGE

The challenge and the shape of an organization's behavioural change programme depend on the corporate culture and the targeted behaviours that need to be changed. Your change programme needs to be explicitly built around these challenges. "Very often, these programmes involve the creation of incentives which elegantly reinforce the desired behaviour (and therein reinforce the change loop in the learning dynamic)." ...Motivating Employees to Embrace Change

You have a choice of instruments to motivate your people to embrace change. Performance-incentive levers are especially useful in driving those who lack direction or initiative. You may also encourage employee feedback on where and how the company can take corrective action and reward employees for their contribution. In any case, "once you open the gates and encourage employees to serve as agents of change, you must demonstrate that their input will have a real-world impact on the way your company does business."

On the other side, you have to be rather aggressive when dealing with people who view change as a threat and create roadblocks that stall progress. Anyone who thinks that it's harmless to make exceptions for a few people and shift resources to accommodate poor performers is missing an important point. "It's not a few people who are at stake, it's the corporate culture", Miles Greer, of Savannah Electric. "By permitting those who resist or retaliate against change to remain in the company, you broadcast a message that suggests supporting the company's mission statement is optional. Even worse, you permit the least-committed employees to taint and influence the attitude and performance of their peers."

MOVING WITH SPEED

In the new economy where everything is moving faster and it's only going to get faster, the new mantra is, "Do it more with less and do it faster." To be able to move with speed, companies need to establish a change-friendly environment and develop four major competencies: fast thinking, fast decision making, fast acting, and sustaining speed.

Making quick decisions through establishing guiding Principles. Fast companies that have demonstrated the ability to sustain surge and velocity all have established sets of guiding principles to help them make quick decisions. Abandoning theoretical and politically correct 'values' and bureaucratic procedures in favour of a practical, down-to-earth list of guiding principles will help your company make the decision-making process much faster. Only one question will need to be asked of any proposed course of action: Does it fit our guiding principles?

8

Work Life, Job Satisfaction and Morale

Of the thousands of public sector agencies at the federal, state and local levels of government in the United States, a very small percentage are in economic, political or legal situations that allow them to be a community, state or regional leader in terms of employee pay. Organizations that have adopted a pay or compensation philosophy as a market pay "leader" have generally come, not surprisingly, from the private sector.

It is generally difficult for public sector organizations to adopt "market leader" pay philosophies since such a philosophy would generally translate to a greater tax burden for citizens, who can be expected to harbor reservations, at the very least, about the "appropriateness" of a "market leader" pay strategy. In fact as the 1976 ICMA text on personnel administration notes, "It is doubtful that taxpayers would tolerate public employees' salaries exceeding those of their counterparts in industry."

Many or perhaps most public sector organizations are committed to a commonly accepted concept in public compensation theory, that is, to pay public sector employees at "prevailing wages." The concept of "prevailing wages" is generally defined as wages that match the external market for similar positions at approximately the 50th percentile, meaning approximately fifty per cent of similar jobs in the community have lower pay ranges and fifty per cent have higher pay ranges. This pay policy is also commonly referred to as a "neither lead nor lag" policy. Community pay leaders, on the other hand, go well beyond the prevailing wage concept and typically set employee pay ranges in the 70th through 90th percentile.

Are there advantages that accrue to an organization that adopts a community pay leader position? Edward E. Lawler III, there may indeed be certain payoffs from pursuing a policy of being a top-notch payer. Lawler notes that, "Such organizations as IBM and Hewlett-Packard have for a long time recognized that if they pay well, they will have very little turnover and be able to pick from among a large number of job applicants." Would public sector organizations realise any benefits if they were able to be community pay leaders? The following paragraphs describe the results for one public sector pay leader.

A PAY LEADER FROM THE PUBLIC SECTOR

Few public agencies are in a position to be a community, state or regional pay leader, but there are exceptions. One such exception is the municipal water utility in Denver, Colorado. This non-union organization, with approximately one thousand employees, is an independent agency of the City and County of Denver with its own policy-setting Board of Commissioners and its own civil service system.

The agency serves water to over 900,000 people, more than a quarter of the state's population, through 250,000 water taps. Its operations are funded through water rates and other fees. Essentially the agency is financially structured as an enterprise fund that does not rely on property taxes. For several years this agency has been a community pay leader and has positioned itself at approximately the 75th percentile of market pay rates.

The pay leader position has brought expected and unexpected results for the agency. As expected and as private firms have found, being a pay leader has resulted in a very low employee turnover rate and has contributed to a large pool of applicants vying for job openings. The most important unexpected result has been the low level of job satisfaction expressed by the agency's employees. In January of 1992 the Mountain States Employers Council, Inc. conducted an Employee Opinion Survey of all agency employees. The response rate for the Survey was 86 per cent. The Mountain States Employers Council had previously conducted many similar Employee Opinion Surveys in the Denver metropolitan area, therefore, the Survey used at the agency contained 34 standard questions with norms developed by previous participants.

Mountain States Employers Council divided the standard questions into several categories comparing the agency scores for these categories to the community norms that had been developed. Two points of interest emerged from an examination of the responses. First, in the category of pay-related questions and the category of benefit-related questions the agency's employees were significantly more positive about pay and benefits than the community norms. Second, in the category of questions related to employee job satisfaction the agency's employees were significantly less satisfied than the community norm.

The agency employee scores that deviated most significantly from the norms in a positive direction involved three questions pertaining to satisfaction with pay increases, satisfaction with the benefit package, and satisfaction with communication about how pay is determined.

The most negative scores in terms of community norms concerned the job satisfaction issues of: opportunities for advancement; promotion policies; supervisory support of quality work; and consistency in the application of disciplinary procedures.

Analysing the survey findings using the perspective of the community norms developed by the Mountain States Employers Council, the following points are clear.

On the positive side:

- Agency employees were generally very satisfied with their base pay and pay increases.
- Agency employees were generally very satisfied with the agency's benefit package.

- Agency employees were generally very satisfied with the equipment they use to perform their jobs.
- Employees felt that they had good job security.
- Employees were satisfied that the agency was concerned about employee safety.
- Employees felt that the amount of work they were asked to do was fair and reasonable.
- Employees felt personally responsible for "top quality" in performing their jobs.

On the negative side:

- Agency employees generally did not feel that promotions were given to the most qualified people.
- Agency employees generally felt very dissatisfied with their chances for advancement. On a related question employees believed that there were not enough opportunities for advancement for qualified people.
- Many agency employees strongly believed that "who you know" was important for getting ahead.
- Many agency employees believed that there were "communication problems" between different parts or departments of the agency.
- Comments from a significant number of employees expressed dissatisfaction with the agency's Affirmative Action policies.
- Employees were also dissatisfied with Human Resources and felt the HR department was not responsive to their needs.

Perhaps the best indicator in the Survey of overall employee job dissatisfaction involved the question "Would you accept a job at another company, doing the same job as you do here, with the same pay and benefits?" Compared to the community norm, a significant percentage of agency employees indicated they would accept another job elsewhere for similar pay and benefits.

The problem is, of course, when you work for a community pay and benefits leader and have excellent job security, the opportunity for finding a similar job elsewhere in the community (the Denver metropolitan area) with equivalent pay and benefits is very limited.

THE RAMIFICATIONS OF BEING A PUBLIC SECTOR PAY LEADER

The single most important consequence attributable, at least in large part, to the pay leader position has been a very low turnover of employees. The agency's turnover rate has persistently been in the two to four per cent range during much of the past decade. While on the surface a very low employee turnover rate may appear desirable, it does have its drawbacks.

For example, there are very few advancement opportunities for employees and intense interest focuses on any promotional opportunity that comes along. Additionally there is extreme unhappiness in the general employee population with any programme or civil service policy, rule or procedure seen as adversely affecting an individual's chances for advancement.

In fact a very low turnover rate makes programmes to ensure workforce diversity much more difficult. In an substance on turnover in the federal government, Gregory Lewis notes that although turnover may be costly for the federal government, it does have some benefits such as bringing "fresh blood" into an organization and in offering promotion opportunities for lower level employees. Lewis further notes that "turnover was key to improving the representation of women and minorities."

Exacerbating the problem of job dissatisfaction at the agency is a relatively recent change from a "promote from within" policy to one of more aggressively opening promotional opportunities to both internal and external candidates. Making job satisfaction problems worse, the agency's excellent Tuition Reimbursement Programme and nearby college campuses have motivated many employees to obtain college degrees.

A highly educated workforce may appear to be a good thing, but there now appear to be a substantial number of lower level agency employees with college degrees and very little opportunity for advancement. This combination of factors is predictably one that does not lead to a workforce with high levels of job satisfaction. There are, of course, factors other than lack of job advancement opportunities that may be contributing to employee job dissatisfaction.

INTERNAL EQUITY

Individuals in organizations generally make two distinct types of pay comparisons when deciding whether or not they are being fairly compensated: internal comparisons of pay with other employees within the organization and external market comparisons. Of these two types of pay comparisons Lawler believes that external market comparisons are most important.

He states that "If external comparisons are poor, an individual will usually leave as soon as he or she can find another job." While external equity is important so is the matter of internal equity. If employees perceive a lack of internal equity between jobs within the organization, morale problems will undoubtedly result.

The agency in question was aware of potential problems resulting from a lack of internal equity among the 300 plus job classifications. A point-factor job evaluation system was used to determine the relative worth of each job and to place each job in the job worth hierarchy in the appropriate pay grade. Wallace and Fay note that job evaluation systems cannot, by themselves, be the answer to all problems concerning internal equity.

Agency employees have, however, expressed very little dissatisfaction with the job evaluation system in use or with comparisons of internal equity in general. There is a job audit procedure in place at the agency so that employees or their supervisors are able to request an audit of any job they perceive incorrectly placed in a particular pay grade.

ORGANIZATION CULTURE

The agency does appear to be undergoing a gradual shift in organizational culture away from a conservative, "family-like" culture. The agency's culture has also reflected at least some of the elements of an "entitlement culture" described by Judith Bardwick. In an entitlement culture, according to Bardwick, employees have so much security that they don't have to earn their rewards. Bardwick states that "When people don't have to earn what they get, they soon take for granted what they receive. The real irony is that they're not grateful for what they get. Instead, they want more. It is the terrible cycle of entitlement." Pay policies can certainly contribute to a culture of entitlement. For example, if employee pays above the market rate of pay (in this case step 4 is the market step in a 9 step pay system) is not pay at risk, then it may be seen as an entitlement by employees.

It would seem logical that as the agency attempts to modify its organizational culture the level of employee job satisfaction could decrease. However, since job security at the agency remains intact, the impact of a gradual change in organization culture cannot fully explain the level of employee job dissatisfaction evidenced in the Employee Opinion Survey.

MANAGEMENT PROBLEMS

The Survey results could also be indicative of "poor" management at the agency. A large majority of respondents, however, did rate the agency Manager as doing a "satisfactory" or a "better than satisfactory" job. The agency also has a strong supervisory training programme which should, in theory at least, lead to a well-trained management team. Undoubtedly some agency managers are less than fully competent, but on the whole, the Survey does not indicate an incompetent management team or a poorly managed organization.

In reflecting on the Survey results and recent interviews with an unscientific sample of agency employees, it must be concluded that the position of being a community pay leader was primarily responsible for accomplishing the agency objective of low employee turnover. It must also be concluded that the accomplishment of the low turnover objective contributed significantly to the general level of employee job dissatisfaction the agency has experienced. As the agency's Manager of Employment and Compensation during this period, we can certainly state that a higher-than-average level of employee job dissatisfaction was not the intended consequence of maintaining a position as a community pay leader. Edward Lawler has perhaps summed it up best when he noted that "There is some research that suggests that high pay rates can lead to high motivation.

However, motivation from this source seems to be very short-lived. Most individuals quickly decide that they deserve whatever pay rate they receive and do not try to perform better in order to deserve it." With no evidence of increased productivity at the agency it must be concluded that Lawler's words ring true for this public sector agency.

NEW DIRECTIONS - A PROPOSAL

Few public sector organizations, as noted earlier, appear to be in a position where they can legitimately pursue a strategy of being a community, state or regional pay leader. In any case, the sense is that a pay leader policy does not tend to produce desired results in public sector organizations with elaborate civil service systems. This is a private sector practice that does not translate well to the public sector.

In many organizations, both public and private, the overall aging of the workforce translates to fewer promotional opportunities and more "plateaued" employees. Even for public agencies that have the ability to pay and can afford to be community pay leaders, it would seem that there needs to be a better understanding of nonmonetary career motivators.

Being a pay leader attracts people who are interested in high pay, though they may not necessarily interested in "public service." Perry and Wise note that utilitarian incentives, such as individual pay and benefits, are not likely to be critical determinants of outputs when individuals identify with the mission of the organization, provided that the incentives are maintained at satisfactory or prevailing levels.

They also conclude that "Public service motivation is likely to be positively related to an individual's organizational commitment. Individuals who are highly committed are likely to be highly motivated to remain with their organizations and to perform." A failure to attract employees who have at least some level of public service motivation may result in employees who are dissatisfied with their jobs in a public sector agency. The goal is not, it seems, to create utilitarian incentives that attract the "best and the brightest," but rather to provide a level of incentives to attract the best and the brightest who are motivated, for any number of reasons, to serve in the public sector. One key point is that whatever the cause of public sector employee job dissatisfaction, the use of high levels of utilitarian incentives (pay and benefits) alone cannot overcome it. The result will be highly paid, dissatisfied employees. There is a direction that seems to make more sense for public sector employers then simply "upping the ante" to compete with high flying private enterprises.

As Romzek notes, utilitarian incentives are important to attract and retain high quality public employees, but they are not enough. Of equal importance is the necessity for public agencies to foster a commitment by employees to the values and mission of the organization. In addition to fostering employee commitment to organizational values and mission, public sector managers can impact employee turnover rates through a better understanding of career dynamics.

Thomas Barth argues that the Career Anchor Theory developed by Edgar Schein could provide a conceptual framework for understanding career motivation. Barth notes that "Schein maintains that as employees progress through their careers they are engaged in a process of self-discovery that reveals career anchors of which they were not initially aware.

If this discovery leads to the cease that they are not in the right job or career path, employees have three principal options:

1. The employee leaves;
2. The employee stays and represses the career anchor;
3. The employee and the organization restructure the job or provide other opportunities within the organization to tap the employee's career anchor."

Public managers who seek a motivated workforce with low turnover would be wise to provide enough flexibility in their civil service policies, rules and procedures to encourage the restructuring of jobs, or the use of job rotation, or special duty assignments so that employees have an opportunity to discover their particular career anchors.

Employees who are motivated to serve in the public sector and who have found a career anchor which matches their individual needs are much more likely to express satisfaction with their jobs than public sector employees who are highly paid, but lack an appropriate career anchor and a commitment to the values and mission of their organization.

The importance of communication in organizational functioning is historically well recognized. However, a noticeable need still exists to examine organizational communication measures as they relate to other organizational concepts. Two organizational concepts that are of interest to management practitioners and researchers are job performance and job satisfaction. Their interest emerges from the fact that the quality of job performance and satisfaction may determine the quality of organizational life and effectiveness. Clearly communication plays a major role in one's job satisfaction (usually measured in multidimensional terms). How an employee perceives a supervisor's communication style, credibility, and content as well as the organizations communication system will to some extent influence the amount of satisfaction (morale) he or she receives from the job. Pincus, in a field study of 327 hospital nurses, found a positive relationship between communication and job performance; but the communication-satisfaction link was stronger, particularly in supervisor communication, climate, and personal feedback.

The study confirmed "the vital importance of employee-immediate supervisor communication on employee job satisfaction". Another study in the public sector reported strong positive relationships between job satisfaction and communication satisfaction with the supervisor and his or her receptivity to information. In fact, after a review of the literature since the mid-1970's, King, Lahiff, and Hatfield report "a consistently clear and positive pattern of relationships between an employee's perceptions of communications and his or her job satisfaction". On the other hand, the influence of communication upon an employee's job performance (usually measured by perceived quality and quantity of output) is not nearly as clear.

A review of the research literature suggests a general link between communication and performance; but perhaps because of varying methodologies and definitions, the results are often mixed. A study by Clampitt and Downs involving a service organization and a manufacturer has uncovered new evidence concerning the relationship.

First, their study, using both interviews and the Communication Satisfaction Questionnaire (CSQ), found that all eight communication satisfaction dimensions impacted the employees' productivity. Although such dimensions as "communication with coworkers," "meetings and memos;' and "corporate-wide information," impacted productivity somewhat, employees in both organizations perceived "personal feedback" from their supervisor to have the highest impact.

Second, satisfaction of an employee with a particular dimension of communication did not necessarily mean his or her productivity was affected. It appears that the relationship between performance and communication is more job specific than originally thought. Thus, abundant research linking communication with both job performance and satisfaction exists. What is lacking in the literature, however, is an investigation of the relationship among the three variables, particularly with communication as a moderating influence.

Zedeck indicates that the moderator approach is a systematic way of studying in what manner organizational and individual facets exert their influence and alter the relationship among target variables. Cohen and Cohen add that a moderator variable refers to "a variable V which interacts with another so as to ... enhance predictability of criterion".

Theoretically, higher links of communication should increase the relationship between an employee's job performance and the satisfaction with that job. Thus, this study assumes that organizational communication is one of those organizational variables that may exert a moderating effect on the relationship between job performance and satisfaction. The primary purpose of this study is to determine the moderating effects, if any, of organizational communication upon the employee performance-satisfaction relationship. That is, if employees are exposed to appropriate communication (trust, accuracy, etc.), job performance will in turn be improved leading to increased job satisfaction.

The relationship between performance and satisfaction is highly variable. Literature reviews conducted by Brayfield and Crockett, Herzberg, Mausner, Peterson, and Capwell, Vroom, and others reflect this variability. Schwab and Cummings noted the highly variable and weak to moderate relationship between job performance and job satisfaction; they observed that these conditions may result from the impact of organizational or individual moderator. Consequently, the moderating approach to the study of the association of performance and satisfaction has emerged. However, the idea is not new.

Brayfield and Crockett criticized researchers for paying too little attention to individual and organizational factors in job performance-job satisfaction relationship studies. Researchers have already found that the relationship may be moderated by employees' self-esteem, need for achievement, organizational rewards, managerial level, job fit, and organizational pressure for performance and experienced time pressure.

Jacobs and Solomon and Bhagat have indicated a need for further research to identify other situational variables that may be moderating the relationship between job performance and job satisfaction. The current investigation proposes that organizational communication is one of those situational variables that possibly exerts an effect on the job performance-job satisfaction relationship. Such a proposition emerges from two sources. First, Schwab and Cummings suggest that variables which differentially affect performance and satisfaction become potential moderators of performance-satisfaction relationships. Since organizational communication has been shown to be related to both job performance and job satisfaction, a likely hypothesis is that organizational communication moderates the job performance-job satisfaction relationship.

Secondly, Porter and Lawler hypothesized and found support for the proposition that variations in job performance are primarily responsible for variations in satisfaction. In a review of the literature, Schwab and Cummings also found support for this proposition. Therefore, since organizational communication has been shown to be related to job performance, it again seems appropriate to expect organizational communication to moderate the relationship between job performance and job satisfaction.

The term organizational communication, as used in this research, encompasses 7 of the 15 dimensions of communication identified by Roberts and O'Reilly: trust in superiors, perceived influence of superiors, accuracy of information, desire for interaction, satisfaction with communication, information load (underload and overload), and directionality of communication (upward, downward, and lateral). These dimensions were selected because they have been shown to be related to job performance in several ways.

First, trust in superiors, influence of superiors, accuracy of information, desire for interaction, and satisfaction with communication have shown a direct relationship with job performance. Second, studies conducted by O'Reilly and O'Reilly and Roberts indicate that communication overload tends to have an inverse and underload a direct relationship with job performance. Lastly, although conflicting results have been reported, upward and downward communication appear to be directly related and lateral communication inversely related to performance. The preceding review concerning the relationship of job performance to job satisfaction and the association of organizational communication to performance-satisfaction serves as the basis for the two hypotheses that are tested. The first hypothesis mainly serves to replicate previous studies. The second constitutes the primary purpose for conducting this investigation.

- *H1*: Job performance will be directly and moderately related to job satisfaction.
- *H2*: Organizational communication - trust in superiors, influence of superiors, desire for interaction, accuracy of information, satisfaction with communication, information load, and directionality of communication - will be a moderator of the job performance-job satisfaction relationship.

Six hundred twenty-nine (629) employees from two companies were identified originally to participate in the study. Seventeen (17) of them were excluded because of business trips, sickness, or vacations. Thus 612 employees existed as potential subjects to receive the survey instruments. Companies A and B are within a diameter of no more than 40 miles in a large metropolitan area of the southern part of the United States. Company A with 27 employees is the headquarters of a firm that manufactures and markets a comprehensive line of heavy duty premium quality lubricants. Company B with 602 employees is a division of a multinational firm that deals with the research, design, engineering, and manufacturing of rotary blast hole bits, downhole percussion bits, hammers, raise reaming heads, and cutters.

Three hundred and two individuals (49.35% of the 612 potential subjects) completed and returned usable research instruments, 23 from Company A and 279 from Company B. The sample was comprised of 249 male respondents and 53 females. In terms of age, 20% were less than 30 years old, 54% between 30 and 49, and 26% were more than 49 years old. Finally, 14% of the respondents reported having worked for their employer for less than 5 years, 31% from 5 to 9 years, 22% from 10 to 14 years, and 33% for 15 years or more.

MEASURES

JOB PERFORMANCE

An overall measure of job performance was obtained by combining self-rated performance scores and supervisory rating scores from two 7-point Likert-type scales assessing performance in terms of quality and quantity. The integration of supervisory and self-ratings of performance may constitute a more objective measure of performance. When asked to evaluate the quality of their performance, participants were requested to respond to the following two questions: (a) How would you rate the quality of your own performance in your job? and (b) How do you think your supervisor would rate the quality of your performance? Two identical questions were asked about the quantity of performance.

Supervisors were simply requested to assess the performance of their subordinates in terms of quality and quantity, separately. Both participants and supervisors rated the quality and quantity of performance using the following 7-point scale: excellent = 7; very good = 6; good = 5; average = 4; fair = 3; poor = 2; and very poor = 1.

The aggregate score of the two scales (quality and quantity) from both respondents and supervisors was taken as the measure of performance. The self-rated score of quality for each participant was determined and averaged with that provided by the supervisor. The same procedure was used to calculate the score of relationship was also found between the two measures of quantity obtained in the same fashion (r = .19). After the integration took place, the correlation between the performance dimensions of quality and quantity (r = .62) was significant at p 01.

JOB SATISFACTION

The Job Descriptive Index or JDI was the means for measuring job satisfaction.

The JDI assesses five dimensions of job satisfaction:

1. Satisfaction with work,
2. Satisfaction with pay,
3. Satisfaction with promotions,
4. Satisfaction with supervision,
5. Satisfaction with coworkers. The JDI has been described as one of the most carefully developed scales for measuring job satisfaction. Its continuous validity makes it an index with the greatest acceptance among management researchers.

ORGANIZATIONAL COMMUNICATION

The Roberts and O'Reilly organizational communication questionnaire was used to measure organizational communication as operationalized in this investigation. Roberts and O'Reilly reported that their instrument had desirable psychometric properties. The mode of data collection was a pretested questionnaire. The readability of the instrument was tested via a graduate class in statistics at a local university.

After securing copies of the lists of employees of the participating firms, a numbered copy of the questionnaire was distributed to each member of the sample. Each individual was told that the number on the questionnaire would be used only as a means for matching statistical data and that no one else would see the number except the researchers.

This number was later used to identify each respondent's supervisor. The internal mail system of each of the participating organizations was used to deliver the research instrument and introductory letter. The completed questionnaire was to be mailed to the Department of Management of a nearby university.

A total of 316 employees completed and returned their questionnaires. Of this total, seven had removed their identification numbers. Two others were improperly answered. Consequently, 307 usable questionnaires were left. The task was then to ask supervisors to rate respondents' performance.

With the assistance of the Director of Human Resources of each participating firm, the immediate supervisor of each respondent was identified using the number assigned to each returned questionnaire. Seventy-nine supervisors were identified. Again, the internal mail systems of the participating organizations were used to deliver the performance scale and related materials to the supervisors. The job performance assessments were to be returned to the University.

One supervisor of three individuals did not respond. Also, during the two weeks taken by supervisors to assess participants' performance, one of the original respondents resigned while another was dismissed. These two respondents were therefore dropped from the list of actual respondents. The elimination of these last five participants left a total of 302 participants for whom supervisors provided performance evaluations. This total of respondents represents a 49.35% rate of return.

With a span of control ranging from 2 to 8 subordinates, none of the 78 supervisors who participated in the assessment of respondents' performance accounted for a disproportionate amount of the data collected.

Further, no event, project, or activity was detected that might have influenced participants' performance during the period that lapsed between the time respondents completed the research instrument and the time supervisors conducted the performance assessment.

STATISTICAL ANALYSES

Hypothesis one was tested by noting whether the correlation between job performance and job satisfaction was positive and significant. Hypothesis two, concerning the expected moderating influence of organizational communication on the performance-satisfaction relationship, was assessed by moderated regression analysis.

Since the theoretical argument that performance leads to satisfaction has been adopted in this investigation, satisfaction was treated as the criterion, with performance and organizational communication as predictors.

Following Saunders and Zedeck, the basic regression equations included the interaction or cross-product of the predictors. This addition provided the following three regression equations for evaluation purposes, where Y is satisfaction, X is performance, Z is organizational communication, and a to d are constants.

- $Y = a + bX$
- $Y = a + bX + cZ$
- $Y = a + bX + cZ + dXZ$

Zedeck states that "if Equations 2 and 3 are significantly different from Equation 1, but not from each other, then the variable [the suggested moderator, organizational communication] is an independent predictor and not a moderator variable". Therefore, for this investigation, a moderator exists only in situations in which a predictor-moderator interaction term accounts for a significant amount of criterion variance after both predictor and moderator variables have entered the regression equation. Moderated regression analyses were conducted for all organizational communication dimensions investigated. This effort also provided any predicting effects detected. The mean, standard deviation and median for each variable show high variability in participants' responses. To compare them, all scores were reduced to a seven-point Likert-type scale.

Results for the relationship between performance and satisfaction show a direct and moderate relationship between them. Thus hypothesis 1 is accepted. The highest correlation was between performance and satisfaction with work, and the lowest between performance and satisfaction with coworkers. Assessment of the potential moderating effect of organizational communication on the relationship between job performance and job satisfaction, the central issue of this study, begins with a review of the correlation matrix. In general, the communication dimensions (potential moderators) show varying degrees of covariance with both the independent variable (job performance) and the dependent variable (job satisfaction).

Of the seven communication dimensions investigated, directionality of communication (upward, downward, and lateral) and communication load (underload and overload) would appear to have the greatest potential as moderators. Conversely, trust in superiors, perceived influence of superiors, accuracy of information, desire for interaction, and satisfaction with communication appear to have the least potential. These inferences are made following Zedeck's logic. Besides classifying a suppressor variable as one type of moderator, he indicates that "a suppressor variable is correlated with the predictor and uncorrelated with the criterion, whereas a moderator is uncorrelated with the criterion".

Table. Descriptive Statistics (n = 302)

Variables	Mean	SD	Median
Job Performance	5.30	72	5.37
Job Satisfaction			
With Work	4.46	1.44	4.66
With Supervision	5.24	1.44	5.57
With Pay	3.87	1.70	4.15
With Promotion	2.78	2.07	1.68
With Coworkers	5.11	1.48	5.44
Organizational Communication			
Upward Communication	2.38	1.53	2.25
Downward Communication	1.81	1.68	1.40
Lateral Communication	2.79	1.68	3.30
Trust in Superiors	5.04	1.49	5.33
Perceived Influence	4.68	1.45	4.67
Accuracy	4.99	1.07	5.00
Desire for Interaction	5.02	1.2	5.00
Information Overload	2.34	1.19	2.00
Information Underload	3.22	1.22	3.00
Satisfaction with Communication	4.91	1.26	5.00

Results from the moderated regression analyses, provide very weak support for organizational communication as a moderator of the performance-satisfaction relationship. Only "accuracy of information" and "lateral communication" received some support as moderators.

Table. Summary of Relationships Between Job Performance and Job Satisfaction Dimensions (n = 302)

Job Satisfaction Dimension	Correlation Coefficient
With Work	.24(**)
With Supervision	.15(**)
With Pay	.10(*)
With Promotion	.17(**)
With Coworkers	.09

* p [less than] .05
** p [less than] .01

More specifically, the relationship between performance and satisfaction with work is significantly greater for individuals scoring high in accuracy of communication than for persons scoring low in the same communication dimension. In addition, the relationship between performance and satisfaction with pay is greater for individuals scoring low in lateral communication than for those scoring high.

Despite the significant interactions detected, organizational communication, as defined in this research, received weak statistical support as a moderator. Many of the communication dimensions investigated acted as main predictors in 30 of the 50 (60%) regression equations evaluated.

The organizational communication dimensions with the highest support as predictors were trust in superiors, influence of superiors, accuracy of information, desire for interaction, satisfaction with communication, and communication load.

The aim of this investigation is to explore the moderating influence of organizational communication on the relationship between job performance and job satisfaction. The study also re-examines the association between these last two variables. Results show that job performance has a direct, weak-to-moderate relationship with job satisfaction.

It also replicates the finding by Petty, McGee, and Cavender, who used meta-analysis (a statistical technique which accumulates findings across studies). Thus, previous and current findings suggest, once again, that changes in one of the two variables (performance or satisfaction) may only weakly or moderately influence the other.

Organizational communication received weak support as a moderator of the relationship between performance and satisfaction. Only 2 of the 50 interactions were significant: satisfaction with work was influenced by the interaction of accuracy of information and satisfaction with pay was impacted by the interaction of lateral communication. The correlation between performance and satisfaction with work was greater for individuals scoring high in accuracy of communication than for participants scoring low. It appears that appropriate and accurate information may enhance both performance and satisfaction with work. This finding implies that individuals receiving proper, correct, and clear information may perform adequately, which in turn may give rise to positive feelings about their jobs, or vice versa. Supervisors might be able to promote adequate levels of job performance and job satisfaction among their employees by providing them with appropriate and accurate information.

On the other hand, individuals scoring low in lateral communication reflected a greater correlation between performance and satisfaction with pay than respondents scoring high. This finding suggests that employees subjected to low levels of lateral communication may be less inclined to make nondesirable comparisons of job related features, including pay, which in turn may negatively affect both performance and satisfaction with pay.

Such a suggestion may be especially true in places where salary or wage differences are not perceived as adequate or consistent. Ample opportunity for lateral communication may increase the possibility of perceiving pay as inadequate when compared with the contribution being made. Further investigation of this speculation may prove beneficial to management practitioners.

When considering the very weak support that organizational communication received as a moderator, one question arises. Why was such support so weak? Two factors may help answer this question. First, this investigation used a very rigorous statistical procedure for detecting moderating effects - moderated regression analysis. Second, many of the communication dimensions studied received strong support as independent predictors.

Thirty of the 50 relationships investigated showed that the integrated communication dimensions acted as predictors. Zedeck suggests that moderators are very difficult to find when the change after adding the proposed moderators as a predictor to the regression equation is high to start with. In this study, the change resulting from the addition of a proposed communication moderator to a particular model as a predictor was equal. Because of this phenomenon, six of the seven communication dimensions investigated - trust in superiors, influence of superiors, accuracy of information, desire for interaction, satisfaction with communication, and communication load - received strong support as predictors of job satisfaction.

In addition, job satisfaction was treated as the dependent variable when conducting the moderated regression analysis. Considering that virtually every dimension of communication investigated related to both job performance and job satisfaction in the same manner, it is then plausible to suggest that the main effects of organizational communication are compatible with two of the central theories in the literature concerning the causal relationship between performance and satisfaction:

(a) Job performance - [greater than] job satisfaction,
(b) Job satisfaction - [greater than] job performance.

For example, high levels of accuracy of information may lead to high levels of performance, and successful performance may promote job satisfaction. The sequence may also function in reverse. High levels of accuracy of communication may lead to high levels of job satisfaction, and favourable perception of satisfaction may enhance job performance.

What appears evident from this research is that regardless of the direction of the job performance-job satisfaction relation, organizational communication appears to be an important predictor of both variables. Thus, communication can be an effective tool that practitioners may use to enhance these two dimensions. Downs, Clampitt, and Pfeiffer argue this same point.

Finally, some methodological observations should be made. Admittedly, measuring organizational and individual constructs by aggregating self-reported data from research participants, as was done in this study, is controversial. The basic criticism "is essentially that researchers using survey methods have simply combined disparate perceptions into fallacious averages". In this study, however, the researchers are confident that the investigated measures of job performance, job satisfaction, and organizational communication are meaningful. First, these findings about the relationship between job performance and job satisfaction mirrored those of previous studies, suggesting that the variables analysed were not just fallacious or spurious averages.

Second, a graphical analysis of residuals yielded properties that suggested that the residuals were independent, had zero mean, had a common variance, and followed a normal distribution. Therefore, these reasons provide strong support for the point that the data collected adequately represent the constructs investigated in this study.

That organization communication received strong support as a predictor of job satisfaction and weak support as a moderator of the job performance-job satisfaction relationship is the major cease of this research. Although some relationships did not prove significant as hypothesized, communication did prove to be important in organizational functioning nonetheless.

And such importance undergirds the need for the continued investigation of communication in organizations. These findings, combined with the use of rigorous statistical procedures and the research design of relating communication to significant output variables, make this study unique in its contribution.

But more research into these complex relationships is needed by business communication scientists. Downs, Clampitt, and Pfeiffer note that, "Perhaps the opportunities are rare, and the choices few, when both objectives [performance and satisfaction] can be achieved through a single communication strategy". Business communication researchers might consider alternate strategies and combinations of strategies in future research investigations.

First, this study did not take a skills approach in defining communication and relating it to performance-satisfaction outputs. Perhaps an investigation of writing (letters and reports) and speaking in the context of this research effort might prove interesting. If specific skill levels are examined, they should be approached within the proper research context, design, and process for meaningful results to occur.

Moreover, this study used only organizational communication as defined by Roberts and O'Reilly. Other constructs of communication such as the Communication Satisfaction Questionnaire or the Interpersonal Communication Relationship Inventory could be used to determine the moderating effects of communication. Or, to determine the influence of the supervisor's interpersonal capacity on the performance-satisfaction relationship, the Index of Interpersonal Communication Competence could be used.

The various definitions of communication in the literature call for several research possibilities to analyse the performance-communication-satisfaction trilogy in organizations. The opportunities for additional research are exciting, to be sure. Business communication researchers need to tap these opportunities as they investigate the complex and dynamic process of communication in organizations.

9

Worker Participation

WORKERS' PARTICIPATION IN MANAGEMENT

Broadly, worker's participation in management means associating representatives of workers at every stage of decision-making. Participative management is considered as a process by which the worker's share in decision-making extends beyond the decisions that are implicit in the specific content of the jobs they do. This amounts to the workers having a share in the reaching of final managerial decisions in an enterprise.

Definition 1: Association of Workers in decision-making process. Workers' participation may be taken to cover all terms of association of workers and their representatives with the decision-making process, ranging from exchange of information, consultations, decisions and negotiations to more institutionalized forms such as the presence of the workers' members on management or supervisory boards or even management by workers themselves.

SCOPE OF WORKERS' PARTICIPATION

Scope of workers participation ranges over three managerial decision-making stages.

- *Social Decisions*: Hours of work, welfare measures, work rules, safety, health, sanitation and noise control.
- *Personnel Decisions*: Recruitment and selection, promotions and transfers, grievance settlements, work distribution

- *Economic Decisions*: Methods of manufacturing, automation, layoffs, shutdowns, mergers and acquisitions and other financial aspects.

Methods of Workers' Participation in Management:

- Board Level
- Ownership
- Complete Control
- Staff Councils
- Joint Councils
- Collective Bargaining
- Job Enlargement and Enrichment
- Suggestion Schemes
- Quality Circles
- Empowered Teams
- Total Quality Management
- Financial Participation

Prerequisites of Successful Participation:

- Clearly defined and complementary Objectives
- Free flow of information and communication
- Representatives of workers from workers themselves
- Outside trade union participation should be avoided
- Workers' education and training
- No threat by participation
- Association at all levels of decision-making

Benefits of Participation:

- Gives identity to an employee
- Motivates employee
- Self-esteem, job satisfaction and cooperation improves
- Reduced conflicts and stress
- More commitment to goals
- Less resistance to change
- Less labour problems
- Better quality suggestions expected

UNIONS

Employee associations are popularly known as unions. However these unions are not confined to only strikes and negotiations. Their role is much wider than this. Unions make their presence felt in recruitment and selection, promotions, training, termination or lay off. Many programmes, which contribute to the Quality of Work Life (QWL) and productivity, are undertaken by management in consultation with and with the cooperation of the unions. Unions also participate in deciding wage and salary structure and negotiate revisions once in 3 or 5 years.

Trade unions are voluntary organizations of workers or employers formed to promote their interests through collective action. Trade unions Act 1926 defines a trade union as a combination, whether temporary or permanent formed primarily for the purpose of regulating the relation between

- Workmen and Employers
- Workmen and Workmen
- Employers and Employers

For imposing restrictive conditions on the conduct of any trade or business and includes any federation of two or more trade unions

Why do employees join Trade Unions?

To protect themselves against exploitation by management

- By force
- Dissatisfaction
- Lack of Power
- Union Instrumentality

ROLE OF CONSTRUCTIVE AND POSITIVE UNION

Unions have a crucial role to play in Industrial Relations. Unions have following broad role.

- To redress the bargaining advantage of the individual worker vis-à-vis the individual employer, by substituting joint or collective action for individual action.
- To secure improved terms and conditions of employment for its members and the maximum degree of security to enjoy these terms and conditions.

- To obtain improved status for the worker in his work or her work
- To increase the extent to which unions can exercise democratic control over decisions, which affect their interests by power sharing at the national, corporate and plant levels.

The union power is exerted primarily at two levels. Industry level to establish joint regulation on basic wages and hours with an employer's association. Plant level, where the shop stewards organizations exercise joint control over some aspects of the organization of work and localized terms and conditions of employment. Unions are party to national, local and plant level agreements, which govern their actions to a greater or lesser extent, depending on their power and on local circumstances.

UNFAIR LABOUR PRACTICES

Industrial Disputes Act 1947 specifies the following as unfair labour practices

- To interfere, restrain, coerce workmen in the exercise of their right to organize, form, join or assist a trade union.
- Threatening workmen with discharge or dismissal
- Threatening of lockout or closure
- Granting wage increases to undermine trade union efforts
- To dominate, interfere with or support financially or socially by taking active interest in forming own trade union, and
- Showing partiality or granting favour to one of several trade unions to a non-recognized trade union
- To establish employer sponsored trade unions
- To encourage or discourage memberships in any trade union by discriminating workman by punishing or discharging, changing seniority ratings, refuse promotions, giving unmerited promotions, discharging union office bearers
- To discharge or dismiss workmen by victimizing, not

in good faith, implicating in criminal case, for patently false reasons

- To abolish work of a regular nature
- To transfer workmen
- To show favouritism or partiality
- To replace workers
- To recruit workmen during legal strikes
- To indulge in acts of violence or force
- To refuse collective bargaining
- Proposing and continuing lockouts

ORGANIZATIONAL DOWNSIZING

Downsizing necessarily means reducing work force to an optimal level depending upon the business conditions and organizational needs. It is said that an organization should be rightly staffed, i.e. It should not be overstaffed and or understaffed.

RETRENCHMENT

It means termination of service. It is a termination for reasons other than disciplinary actions, retirement or superannuating, expiry and termination of contract or prolonged illness. Retrenchment compensation and notice for retrenchment are only preconditions for retrenchment and not a right, which a retrenched worker can claim. If notice and compensation are not given, the worker will not be called as retrenched. Compensation is payable for 15 days wages for every completed year of service besides one month's notice or pay in lieu of notice. But employee should have completed at least one year of complete service in order to receive compensation.

Layoffs

Lay of is inability of the employer to provide employment to workers due to circumstances beyond his control such as shortage of power, coal, breakdown of machinery, natural calamity etc. It is not a termination of service. Lay off compensation can be claimed as a statutory right by the worker if he has completed one year of continuous service or has worked for 240 days on the surface or 190 days underground in 12 calendar months. Compensation payable is half of the wages.

Voluntary Retirement Schemes VRS are announced when there is a huge pool of old aged manpower occupying senior positions amounting to surplus. Many organizations are providing liberal incentives to leave before age of superannuating. VRS in other words is a retirement before the age of retirement.

MEANING OF ORGANIZATION

ORGANIZATIONAL STRUCTURE

Structure is the formal decision-making framework by which job tasks are divided, grouped, and coordinated. Formalization is an important aspect of structure. It is the extent to which the units of the organization are explicitly defined and its policies, procedures, and goals are clearly stated. It is the official organizational structure conceived and built by top management. The formal organization can be seen and represented in chart form. An organization chart displays the organizational structure and shows job titles, lines of authority, and relationships between departments.

ORGANISATION CHARTS

The organization charts are the sample and an understandable way showing the formal organization structure-It gives a clear overview of the shape and structure of an organization. It is an order and the design of an organization captured in a visual form.

It is a blue print or a basis for proper conceptualization, further thinking, a discussion board for further modifications without affecting the actual changes. The organization chart well drawn, can give an insight in to the organization, its hierarchical structure line and staff authority, authority and responsibility levels, chain of command, line of delegated authority, decentralization or otherwise in an organization, span of control etc. It also helps and guides the management in evolving changes with the changes in the environment and for faster realization of goals. It is a good guide for the new recruits in their initiation in the organization and in understanding the authority responsibility levels including his own.

Formal Organisation

The intentional structure of roles in a formally organised enterprise is a formal organisation. It should have an attribute of flexibility, room for discretion and the recognition of individual talents and the capacities. In a group functioning the individual effort will have to be chanelize through the group leader and has to be for the organization's good.

Informal Structure

The informal organization is the network, unrelated to the firm's formal authority structure, of social interactions among its employees. It is the personal and social relationships that arise spontaneously as people associate with one another in the work environment. The supervisor must realise that the informal organization affects the formal organization. The informal organization can pressure group members to conform to the expectations of the informal group that conflict with those of the formal organization.

This can result in the generation of false information or rumors and resistance to change desired by management. The supervisor should recognize the existence of information groups, identify the roles member play within these groups, and use knowledge of the groups to work effectively with them. The informal organization can make the formal organization more effective by providing support to management, stability to the environment, and useful communication channels.

Matrix Structure in a matrix organization, teams are formed and team members report to two or more managers. Matrix structures utilize functional and divisional chains of command simultaneously in the same part of the organization, commonly for one-of-a-kind projects. It is used to develop a new product, to ensure the continuing success of a product to which several departments directly contribute, and to solve a difficult problem. By superimposing a project structure upon the functional structure, a matrix organization is formed that allows the organization to take advantage of new opportunities.

This structure assigns specialists from different functional departments to work on one or more projects being led by project managers. The matrix concept facilitates working on concurrent projects by creating a dual chain of command, the project (programme, systems, or product) manager and the functional manager.

Project managers have authority over activities geared toward achieving organizational goals while functional managers have authority over promotion decisions and performance reviews. An example is an aerospace firm with a contract from NASA.

Divisional Structure

In a divisional organization, corporate divisions operate as relatively autonomous businesses under the larger corporate umbrella. In a conglomerate organization, divisions may be unrelated. Divisional structures are made up of self-contained strategic business units that each produces a single product. For example, General Motors' divisions include Chevrolet, Oldsmobile, Pontiac, and Cadillac.

A central headquarters, focusing or results, coordinates and controls the activities, and provides support services between divisions. Functional departments accomplish division goals. A weakness however, is the tendency to duplicate activities among divisions.

Organic structure on the other hand, the organic structure is more flexible, more adaptable to a participative form of management, and less concerned with a clearly defined structure. The organic organization is open to the environment in order to capitalize upon new opportunities. Organic organizations have a flat structure with only one or two levels of management. Flat organizations emphasize a decentralized approach to management that encourage high employee involvement in decisions. The purpose of this structure is to create independent small businesses or enterprises that can rapidly respond to customers' needs or changes in the business environment. The supervisor tends to have a more personal relationship with his or her employees. Functional structure functions or divisions arrange traditional organizations.

In a functional organization, authority is determined by the relationships between group functions and activities. Functional structures group similar or related occupational specialties or processes together under the familiar headings of finance, manufacturing, marketing, accounts receivable, research, surgery, and photo finishing. Economy is achieved through specialization. However, the organization risks losing sight of its overall interests as different departments pursue their own goals.

10

Counseling for Effective Human Resource Development

AN OVERVIEW

"People are our most important resource" has become far more than an obligatory line in an annual report. Organizational career development (OCD) has evolved over the last several decades and has emerged as a competitive strategy for enhancing organizational effectiveness through a well-developed workforce.

Before painting an accurate picture of how OCD has changed over the last few decades, we need to set the context by sketching various "big-picture" transformations that have occurred in the business landscape. First, bottom line margins of success can no longer be guaranteed by technological advances; competitiveness means mastery of interpersonal communication, teamwork, and critical thinking.

New information and communications technologies, along with harsh global economic realities (e.g. downsizing), now require new ways of looking not only at career development but also at the appropriate balance between individual and organizational needs. Finally, career development is increasingly taking place in a context of systems that connect such development with other HR initiatives and practices.

In order to assess the impact of these changes, we decided, in the early 1990s, to embark on a full-fledged reexamination of OCD. Our aim was to determine how far the field has come, attitudinally and practically, since 1978-the year in which the American Management Association sponsored a major survey of OCD practice. That study revealed "widespread support" for career planning but also a "wide gap" between actual and ideal practice. The essential questions prompting our own investigation were these: What is the current state of the practice of career development in larger organizations? How have things changed since 1978? And what new ideas or trends are in the offing-that is, what is the state-of-the-art of OCD?

UPDATING THE 1978 SURVEY

Our study made use of both broad-based surveys and structured telephone interviews. We conducted a random sampling of 1,000 U.S., corporations and 96 federal agencies; in addition, our survey targeted samples of between 500 and 1,000 European, Australian, and Singaporean corporations. (As suggested, discuss the results of each sample, starting with the U.S., one and then comparing it with the foreign ones.)

Because the career development systems of large organizations are typically more visible than those in smaller organizations and thus afford richer data, we concentrated on large entities (over 40 per cent of which were international) in diverse industries. Our survey had a healthy 26 per cent response rate, and we believe that the results (although unstratified) offer a meaningful representation of OCD trends in bigger organizations.

Directed at HR executives, our survey instrument (like that of the 1978 study) included questions on the following issues:

- The prevalence of career development systems (defined as "processes and practices that link individual career goals with the organization's HR needs");
- System "drivers" (factors prompting system design and implementation);
- Corporate attitudes toward OCD;
- Implementation (audiences and structures);
- Perceived effectiveness; and
- Outcomes and assessment.

OCD Practice: Findings From Our Recent Survey

Nearly 70 per cent of our U.S respondents had or were launching career development systems; most of those systems were either less than a year old or over six years old. Organizations without systems cited three main reasons for this lack: insufficient top-management support, inadequate budgetary resources, and lack of organizational capability or interest.

Factors That Encourage Career Devekioment Systems

Why do organizations have or start career development systems? We asked respondents to indicate the top three factors that influenced the development of their career development systems. Surprisingly, the two reasons most often cited by our survey respondents had to do with upward mobility: (1) a desire to promote from within (23 per cent) and (2) a shortage of promotable talent (14 per cent).

A third often-cited factor, organizational commitment to development, actually ranked considerably higher among government respondents. Significantly, the development of an organization's strategic plan was cited nearly as frequently (i.e., by 12 per cent of all respondents) as a shortage of promotable talent. To our surprise, only 8 per cent of all respondents alluded to the desire to motivate employees under conditions of limited growth-and a mere 2 per cent cited a desire to improve worker productivity.

These findings were the first of several signals indicating the durability of a traditional view of career growth as synonymous with upward mobility. In developing their systems, most respondents believed that their main audience was salaried (i.e., exempt) employees.

Almost 75 per cent targeted "fast-track" management candidates or "high-potentials," and over half targeted management trainees. Again, the major emphases seemed to be on enhancing upward mobility and building bench strength (i.e., the ability to replace departing employees quickly and effectively).

Attitudes Toward OCD

With regard to our respondents' attitudes toward OCD, several themes emerged from the survey. Organizations, managers, and employees alike viewed career development as important. Supervisors were seen as playing a vital but problematic developmental role. Career development was viewed as directly relevant to strategic business planning: fully 85 per cent of our survey respondents agreed with the statement that career development programmes must be linked with strategic planning.

Finally, career development was perceived as having many of the positive effects (such as enhanced skills) but few of the negative ones (such as loss of good employees through movement to other employers) sometimes associated with it. Significantly, the "drivers" or prompts for career development did not always mesh logically with attitudes toward it.

Thus, while neither motivational or productivity-related reasons were cited by our survey respondents as major drivers for the design and implementation of their systems, respondents nonetheless stated that career development enhances job performance and should be tied to strategic plans.

It appears that assumptions about the benefits of a career development system are not what drive system design and implementation; once the system is in place, however, it tends to engender positive attitudes and garner managerial support. The actual impetus for system development seems to be quite specific to individual organizations and their cultures and business needs.

OCD System Audiences, Tools, and Techniques

As noted earlier, salaried employees were the main target of most respondents' developmental efforts. Interestingly, more than twice as many governmental respondents than private-sector ones (i.e., 75 per cent) targeted new employees. Although this finding surprised us, it seems likely that within the private sector, as both the projected number of available new entrants and their skills decrease, organizations will have no choice but to attend more closely to the new employee and his or her developmental needs. Traditional career development practices predominated in our survey pool. Nearly 60 per cent of all respondents had development programmes, including training/development and tuition reimbursement (as well as job enrichment and redesign). Over half had job matching programmes, and roughly 45 per cent offered individual career development discussions. Processes for assessing organizational potential and tools for employee self-assessments were available in roughly 30 and 45 per cent, respectively, of all organizations. Internal labour-market information exchanges were present in about one-quarter.

The emphasis on internal promotion and development of bench strength was clearly evidenced by the prevalence of development programmes (broadly defined) and job matching programmes. Yet it remains unclear, in our view, how such programmes can succeed over the long term. Without a heavier use of employee and manager self-assessments and without access to career and organizational information, how can individuals undertake job moves (either upward or lateral) effectively? In the end, our findings on common career development practices seem to beg the basic question of what really constitutes development in today's organizations.

IMPLEMENTATION OF OCD SYSTEMS

About half of all our respondents used a task force or advisory group to design or implement their systems. Staffing was generally lean: less than 25 per cent of all systems had a full-time staff person devoted to career development. Typically, the responsibility for development was viewed as one shared by employees, managers, and the organization-with the employee, however, bearing the largest share (i.e., over half of the responsibility).

Significantly, less than 50 per cent of all respondents were training their line managers to hold career discussions. In our minds this finding raises important questions about how effectively OCD systems can be implemented when neither training nor accountability are consistent features of the manager's role.

PERCEIVED EFFECTIVENESS OF OCD PRACTICES

Among our respondents, the three practices with the highest effectiveness ratings were tuition reimbursement, internal training and development programmes, and external seminars and workshops. These are all traditional training and development activities not necessarily linked to a career development strategy. The same holds true for employee orientation and job posting programmes, which also received high effectiveness ratings.

Tools that we had thought were commonly accepted components of career development systems - including career planning workshops, stand-alone career workbooks, and computer software - received surprisingly low prevalence and effectiveness ratings. (Only 34 per cent of our respondents used career planning workshops; only 15 per cent offered workbooks; and a mere 13 per cent had computer software for career development.) Perceptions of low effectiveness may be attributable to the fact that often these tools are not formally linked to systems or HR initiatives, leaving tool usage as an isolated activity.

Although a notably high percentage of respondents reported that line managers were holding career discussions with their employees, less than 25 per cent described those discussions as effective. This perception of ineffectiveness may well stem from the fact, noted earlier, that fewer than half of the respondents were actually training their managers to hold career discussions.

RESPONDENTS' ASSESSMENTS OF THEIR SYSTEMS

Although government respondents were somewhat more inclined to evaluate their processes, the organizations we surveyed had few formal means of determining whether their career development systems were achieving their aims. The most common evaluation method was informal verbal feedback with nearly two-thirds of respondents relying on that method. From an informal standpoint, we asked respondents to assess their systems through a series of open-ended questions. Less than one-third of the corporate sample rated their systems as effective or very effective-in marked contrast to respondents in the government sample, whose effectiveness ratings were about 20 points higher. In fact, nearly half of the corporate respondents were only lukewarm about their systems.

Despite these results, most respondents expressed the belief that their systems produced positive outcomes and recognized the need for greater accountability, formality, and systemization. Overall, two variables that seemed to influence positive perceptions of effectiveness were the length of time in which a system had been in place and the number of full-time staff devoted to career development.

These findings buttressed our belief that systems take time to develop and need sufficient resources to thrive. We also believe that as line managers become more integral to a career development system's implementation (and are held accountable for their role in the process), they will contribute directly and continuously to its effectiveness and thereby positively influence the perceptions of all the players in the system.

COMPARING THE STATE OF THE PRACTICE FROM 1978 TO 1990

In 1978, over 1,100 members of the AMA (half of whom were from manufacturing) were mailed a questionnaire regarding their career planning and management practices; 225 organizations responded to this questionnaire. The survey instrument was similar to that used in our 1990 survey (for the American sample). To our surprise, the results of the two surveys were strikingly similar despite downsizing, delayering, and other significant changes in the overall business climate. The state of the practice underwent few radical transformations in the 1980s.

Both the 1978 and 1990 survey respondents named the desire to promote from within and a shortage of promotable talent as key drivers of their career development efforts. Thus, "climbing the corporate ladder" persists as a goal in a variety of organizational cultures, despite mounting evidence that this notion is no longer as realistic or relevant as it once was. This finding surprised us in light of the currently pressing need to motivate employees in conditions of limited growth; the two emphases seem at odds. (It may be, however, that attitudes about upward mobility take time to catch up to economic reality.)

Career counseling by line managers increased (from 56 to 83 per cent), as did training for these managers (from 25 to 44 per cent); however, the 1990 survey sample reported continued dissatisfaction with the manager's role. One might speculate that although a growing number of organizations view their managers as crucial to any formalized, integrated, and strategically oriented OCD effort, not all organizations are clear on how to prepare and use their managers in developmental activities.

Computer software for career development, expected by many to become very popular during the 1980s, fared poorly in ratings by the 1990 survey respondents: only 13 per cent reported using such software, and of those users, less than half rated it effective or very effective. Job posting was the only practice that grew significantly from 1978 to 1990 and was seen positively by respondents-probably because of shifts toward openness and ongoing communication in many corporate cultures.

What about attitudes toward OCD? It appears that they, too, have not changed drastically from 1978 to the present. As noted, the latest survey respondents, like their predecessors, stressed the problematic role of the manager in the development process as well as the burdensome nature of the process for supervisors. In our view these findings once again imply a need for more and better training of managers in their multiple roles as coaches, developers, and creators of links to business strategy.

Regardless of perceived problems, the respondents in both surveys stated that they were witnessing an increase in the systemization of career development practices and a burgeoning range and efficiency of tools and techniques. It thus seems that although certain trends exist, the field of OCD has by no means settled into a uniform or predictable future direction. It remains a "work in progress," powerfully influenced by specific circumstances and conditions.

FOREIGN VERSUS DOMESTIC OCD PRACTICES AND ATTITUDES

The European, Australian, and Singaporean samples of our survey were by no means a homogenous group; they differed from one another and, as a whole, from the U.S., sample. The European sample comprised 70 respondents in several different countries, whereas the other two samples comprised 200 respondents from each country (Australia and Singapore).

As in the United States, the desire of foreign companies to develop people from within and to make an organizational commitment to career development were major factors contributing to system design and implementation. Development of the organization's strategic plan was a third top-ranked factor. What basic beliefs were shared by survey respondents in all four samples?

Most respondents reported a belief in some version of the following:

- Senior management values career development and seeks to link it with the organization's strategic plan.
- Career development enhances the use of employee skills and helps people deal with a low-growth environment; however, most supervisors aren't equipped to conduct career discussions.
- Employee participation in career development should be voluntary, not mandatory.

The latter belief was held especially strongly among American respondents, who tended to focus on the role of the individual employee. American respondents also had weaker perceptions of senior managerial "buy-in" to career development and to the strategic link than did their foreign counterparts.

An emphasis on in-house training and development and on external seminars or workshops-coupled with the relative lack of practices that help "solid citizens" as well as high-potential employees-characterized all four samples. Despite the fact that the global business environment may not be one in which "up" is the only or best direction for career growth, organizations are apparently still clinging to the traditional notion of development as upward mobility within a clearly defined corporate hierarchy.

How do domestic and foreign attitudes compare with regard to outcomes? Only 29 per cent of American respondents rated their systems as effective or very effective, as opposed to 52 per cent in Australia, 58 per cent in Europe, and 62 per cent in Singapore. This attitudinal divergence may be reflected in these relevant facts: fewer full-time career development staff are available in most American organizations, fewer career discussions are held between employees and their managers, and the link between strategic planning and career development is weaker.

Across the board, respondents cited several benefits of career development systems-regardless of either their effectiveness ratings or specific prompts for their design. Among the key benefits named were the following:

- Better planning and management of human resources;
- Increased competitive advantage; and
- Enhanced skills, motivation, and employee retention.

When asked what they would do differently, respondents around the world often cited more systemization, accountability, and evaluation as well as more training and involvement of managers. Most also reported a need for greater commitment of resources. Future plans typically included strategies to expand current programmes and increase systemization and linkages. Respondents also reported that managers would be receiving greater support in their crucial role in the developmental process.

This last point bears noting, especially in light of the evident consensus among foreign respondents regarding the value of career discussions between managers and employees. Only in the American sample were such discussions not included as one of the top five developmental practices. This finding points up the doubts of senior American managers about their line managers' ability to hold useful career discussions-which in turn suggests a basic ambivalence about the efficacy of increased training (or on-the-job experience) in coaching employees. A kind of "Catch-22" may be operating here: although senior managers support career development on a philosophical level, they may not always be lending practical support to the supervisors who play such a key role in making development happen.

In the American context, then, it appears that the linkages between effective management, workforce development, and the bottom line are not consistently strong. Within certain organizations, however, appreciation of the strategic significance of career development is clearly part of a broader new understanding of what makes for organizational growth, stability, and profitability over the long run.

BASING NEW SYSTEMS ON NEW UNDERSTANDINGS

How do today's organizations deal with the development-related issues and challenges identified by our survey respondents? By closely examining a number of state-of-the-art career development systems and practices from both a "macro" (strategic) and "micro" (operational) focus, we have gained some useful insights into practitioners' approaches and concerns. We describe one system and one practice that exemplify positive responses to the HR challenges faced by large American organizations.

DESIGNING A CAREER DEVELOPMENT SYSTEM WITH LONG-TERM BENEFITS

In the late 1980s, executives at Amoco Production Company (APC), a subsidiary of Amoco Corporation, decided that career development would no longer be about upward mobility for fast-track employees; rather, it would address development, contribution, and impact. Through a four-phase design and implementation process, APC has created a career development system whose features not only integrates with other HR initiatives but also help APC continuously align the skills and interests of individual employees with corporate business objectives.

The system, called Amoco Career Management (ACM), facilitates strategic staffing-that is, getting the right person in the right place at the right time. APC carefully considered the question of how to obtain "buy-in" to the new system. In the first and second phases of system design, a steering committee was formed and charged with the task of assessing (with the aid of an employee advisory group) the current state of career development within the company, employee needs, the competitive environment, and best practices in the industry. This information was then incorporated into the company's vision of career development as a process linked with business development-a vision generated by senior managers and disseminated throughout the organization.

Next (in the third phase), the steering committee created design teams that worked on self-assessments and training, process and accountability, career discussions and individual development planning, and information. In the final phase, a "roll-out" and marketing plan were designed and implemented. An implementation team also spearheaded customization of the process for field and international locations.

The system's key feature is career discussions between employees and their supervisors, which are supported by individual development plans and the team development strategy. The employees draft individual development plans (IDPs) outlining their specific career goals and action plans and then bring their IDPs to the career discussion.

The supervisors provide the team development strategy which they have developed based on the team's projected direction and business challenges and the needed competencies and skills. The result of the career discussion is a revised IDP that aligns employee competencies with the business goals and strategy. Outcomes may include job enrichment, job change, and self-development. Supporting features of the ACM system include employee education and supervisor training, an all employee meeting, assessment workshops, job posting or canvassing (ASNAP-Amoco Self-Nomination Process), and management feedback and review linked to the career discussion. Other HR initiatives, such as performance management and continuous improvement, are integrated with the ACM system; in addition, efforts are underway to align the system with succession planning, diversity, and promotion and reward systems.

Although earlier HR initiatives at APC were designed on the basis of a paradigm in which career success was defined solely in terms of promotion, the organization's new approach calls for efforts to achieve a long-term competitive advantage, not just individual advancement. This paradigm shift requires perseverance and commitment from all corporate sectors, along with a reassessment of HR practices to ensure integration with basic strategic goals.

USING CAREER INFORMATION AS A DEVELOPMENTAL TOOL

While APC's system evolved through a carefully staged design and implementation process, not all organizations choose to proceed as APC has done. Some organizations design one innovative developmental practice that can then either "spearhead" additional innovations or serve as a vital nexus for a larger systemization effort.

3M Corporation is a case in point. At the end of the 1980s, the company conducted an employee survey that revealed a need for better and more readily available information on job opportunities. Hiring managers needed help in identifying internal candidates, and 3M's increasingly diverse work-force needed to know more about necessary skills and qualifications for different job requirements.

A job information system (JIS) was deemed an appropriate solution. The JIS now in place complements 3M's existing HR review process, in which managers nominate people for jobs on the basis of potential and suitability. The JIS covers only self-nominators, and its data are used more regularly than the annual HR data. All jobs (up through management) are posted on the system; vacancies are listed electronically for 10 working days during which employees can access information on jobs through their computers.

A telephone hotline provides answers to questions about specific positions. Employees can apply to any job for which they feel they are qualified; hiring managers respond to all applicants, even those not interviewed. The JIS was developed by a task force that included HR, staff, and line personnel. It was piloted extensively and publicized through a variety of in-house communication mechanisms.

Significantly, evaluations of this new practice have revealed that nearly half of all job applications have been for non promotions-which indicates that many 3M employees are thinking developmentally, not simply in terms of promotion. Employees say that they understand their career options more clearly and realistically, and managers report many positive successes in locating the right employees for the right jobs. Linkages with other HR initiatives have been and are being forged.

A career resource manual cites job posting as a resource, and a "Career Directions" workshop offers a part on internal job seeking designed to tie in with the JIS. Although system designers recognize that efforts to coordinate various career-related tools must be ongoing, they also state that there is nothing that 3M would do differently if it were starting over: the JIS was so well-piloted and -advertised that it has become a highly effective asset for both the company and its employees.

ADVICE FROM STATE-OF-THE-ART ORGANIZATIONS

Several themes were repeatedly articulated by the HR executives we interviewed at 3M, APC, and other farsighted organizations that were designing, implementing, or evaluating career development systems.

In particular, the following four caveats were often voiced:

- Involve top management right from the start: visible senior champions are indispensable.
- Establish guiding principles for OCD early and base them on knowledge of the organization's culture, strategic objectives, and criteria for success.
- Develop systems from the line up; always involve diverse employees and managers in all phases-from design to evaluation.
- Stay flexible: business units need to make the career development system work for their own situations and needs.

CAREERS IN THE CONTEXT OF WORKPLACE CHANGE

At home and abroad, changes in structure and operation are becoming commonplace as organizations struggle to gain and maintain a competitive advantage. Organizational restructuring has contributed heavily to a new orientation toward OCD. As companies downsize, merge, and reorganize, managers and employees alike are realizing that uncertainty and change are facts of organizational life.

Also being reshaped are workforces themselves. More and more businesses are moving away from large staffs to a model in which a smaller core of workers is aided by numerous part-timers and independent contractors. This shift has in turn prompted a change in the implicit psychological contract between employers and employees.

Employers now offer opportunities for growth rather than lifelong security; on the employees' side, loyalty is more likely to extend to a profession than to an organization. Additionally, many workers are reassessing the balance between work and leisure, and organizations have had to become content with the altered priorities of a "baby-bust" generation of workers for whom work is not necessarily the best path to personal fulfillment.

Demographics, too, are occasioning major shifts in the way organizations address the work-life balance. Time for childrearing and for elder care is a high priority for large numbers of employees in today's workforce-specially for dual-career couples who juggle numerous (and often competing) demands on their time and schedules.

What other factors impinge on OCD practice now and are expected to do so even more strongly in the future? We foresee heightened attention to Total Quality Management (TQM) initiatives; further empowerment of employees so that workteams can be genuinely autonomous; and changes in skill and competency requirements-especially enhanced communications skills, adaptability, and the ability to keep the focus on the customer.

These trends, coupled with the globalization of business and the continuous development of new technologies in nearly every industry, bring new challenges and possibilities to HR practitioners. It seems clear, to name just one example, that employees will need portfolios of transferable skills; hence, cross-training and retraining are sure to gain in importance.

Our survey findings, combined with our experience in the field, have led us to believe strongly in the competitive advantages of integrating development planning and strategic planning. The use of "systems thinking" can do much to revitalize development planning-as can moves toward greater openness and regular communication of missions and goals. Yet although these are healthy features, several other concerns must be addressed if authentically strategic benefits are to accrue from career development.

Perhaps the most pressing of these is the future of the manager's role in developing employees. It is imperative that managers be held accountable for development and be strongly supported in this process. As our survey respondents repeatedly stressed, most managers need coaching to become good coaches themselves.

Also necessary are expanded peer-learning methodologies and other team-based approaches to development. It is evident that self-managed workteams will carry increased bottom-line responsibility. Their developmental needs will have to be carefully assessed if they are to perform effectively. For teams and individuals alike, on-the-job training and learning should be the norm. One-shot training programmes have been shown to be far less effective than ongoing, workplace-based reinforcements of new skills and knowledge. In a similar vein, organizations are going to need to dedicate more resources to identifying and developing transferable competencies (such as adaptability to change) that employees can use in diverse settings to achieve shifting strategic objectives.

No discussion of OCD can be meaningful without reference to the need for evaluations of programmes-for without these, neither effectiveness nor accountability can be ensured. Measurement and continuous improvement should be part of the implementation of career development systems at all stages. Moreover, organizations must be able to step back periodically and conduct "macro" evaluations of the effects of OCD on their business performance as a whole: that is, not just individual programme assessments but "big-picture" evaluations of the effect of programme outcomes on business generally.

Finally, it is crucial that quality initiatives be tied to development. Quality cannot be considered in a vacuum. As organizations dedicate resources to OCD and as each employee takes charge of his or her own development, quality will invariably be enhanced

11

Human Relations

AN OVERVIEW

"If men were angels, no government would be necessary. If angels were to govern men, neither external nor internal controls on government would be necessary," This statement about the human condition from Federalist 51 posits a view of people which most authors of Total Quality Management have chosen to ignore. When reviewing the literature on quality management, one is struck by the absence of any mention of individuals who have problems in the work place, and the reader is left with the cease that "men are angels."

There is an assumption that all employees with the right type of training and the proper coaching will fit into the TQM organization. Johnston, in summarizing various authors on the attitudes toward workers, stated that "under TQM, the workers are viewed as the greatest source of improvements."

Workers who are managed correctly will take responsibility for their work, be committed to the organization, and have ownership of the service or product. "Absenteeism and sick leave abuse are not a problem when workers feel like they are an important part of the business." While this deduction is derived from MacGregor's Theory Y view of employees, work and management, it fails to provide for the prospect that some employees' behaviour may not be modified by coaching and training, and that other measures, such as termination, may have to be utilized to correct the situation.

The literature assumes that the employees involved in a TQM organization manifest a love for their work and are interested in doing their best for the organization. The purpose of this substance is not to engage in a lengthy debate about the merits of Theory Y, but to recognize that in most organizations, the universality of these assumptions has its limits. In many organizations, some people were initially selected who did not fully subscribe to the organization's culture nor to the work ethic. Some persons lacked basic qualities such as trust, which, as one author noted, for an organization to manage without managers, one must assume that "employees are trustworthy adults."

Most organizations, particularly public ones, are not created anew when they start the total quality experience. TQM is being implemented in on-going organizations that contain some individuals who lack some of the basic attributes to perform efficiently and effectively, and the organizations have failed to either correct or remove the problem employee. Without a significant modification in behaviour or a severance from the organization, these individuals imperil an organization's implementation of TQM. To fully develop the plan for discipline and how it would be conducted in a TQM organization, it is necessary to review some of the basic concepts of TQM.

CONCEPTS OF TQM

Total Quality Management, as many authors have noted, is a total philosophy for running an organization. It has as its main objective the meeting of both internal and external customer's expectations through continuously improving all processes and products. It uses basic statistical tools to measure and refine work processes. Since quality is a top-level management responsibility, they must provide the work environment and organizational conditions to allow this to occur.

The refinement, measurement and improvement comes from the workers closest to the daily processes. These workers have the knowledge and experience to make these improvements. However, unlike other processes which solicit employee input such as suggestion systems or quality circles, the quality management system takes the next logical step. Workers are organized into teams and given the power to modify and adapt the process as the team feels necessary. TQM writers argue that for the process to be successful, work groups must be "empowered" to function as a self-directed team.

This theoretical prospective has been translated into practice when one reviews the standards for the Baldridge Award, the Deming Prize (two major awards for total quality organizations), or the ISO 9000 certification. The ISO is the International Organization for Standardization in Geneva, Switzerland. ISO 9000 is a series of five standards for quality management. As an organization moves from the traditional work group to the empowered team, the organization is rated higher.

Three types of teams have been suggested:

1. Semi-autonomous teams - led by supervisor;
2. Semi-managing teams - led by elective leader;
3. Semi-designing teams - have authority to determine their own composition and external relations.

There also needs to be a division in the processes which are under the control of the team. First, there is the issue of the production process. Questions need to be answered as to how much autonomy the team would have in terms of work processes, such as task design, machinery, allocation of tasks among workers, needed training, etc. Second, there is the issue of personnel decisions. Traditional hierarchical organization theory establishes the primary responsibility for basic personnel decisions to the supervisory role.

Since supervisors have the responsibility for ensuring that the work is completed, the supervisor has the intimate knowledge of the work place to determine the degree to which various workers are contributing to or hindering the work process. Consequently, the supervisor is in the best position to recommend disciplinary action, merit increases, and to conduct performance appraisals.

The supervisor, having extensive knowledge of the requirements of the work process, also should have a primary role in choosing the employees who will be able to perform the tasks. The role of the supervisor has been codified in the National Labour Relations Act and similar state and local statutes which govern the collective bargaining process. For example, the Educational Employment Relations Act of the State of California offers a typical definition.

"Supervisory employee" means any employee, regardless of job description, having authority in the interest of the employer to hire, transfer, suspend, lay off, promote, discharge, assign, reward or discipline other employees, or the responsibility to assign work to and direct them, or to adjust their grievances, or effectively recommend such action, if, in connection with the foregoing functions, the exercise of that authority is not of a merely routine or clerical nature, but requires the use of independent judgement.

The logic of empowering work teams to control production leads to the extension that the employees themselves would be just as knowledgeable, or more knowledgeable than supervisors about who would be best for the job, or how individual employees are performing. It should be noted that just because a team has control over work processes, it does not necessarily follow that the team must also have control over personnel issues.

However, for the concept of team self-direction and empowerment to be meaningful, a strong, compelling argument can be made for the team to have control over personnel issues. Some authors have raised the concern that team members would not be objective in their evaluations of employees; either they would treat the person as a friend and not be willing to confront the employee if there were problems, or, possibly, they would want to drive an employee out who did not conform to the group's non-work related norms. However, the same criticism can be made regarding the objectivity of the supervisor.

Comparative research is lacking to indicate whether personnel decisions made by a supervisor are better or worse than those made by a team. As was noted earlier, there is a dearth of any empirical studies regarding the conduct of discipline by a team. Although one can argue that teams can make as objective personnel decisions as supervisors, two conditions need to be present in order for the system to properly function. First, the team must have developed good interactive skills, have worked as a cohesive team, and have mastered controlling work processes.

Team self-direction is a developmental process. In making the transition to a work team, employees need to learn how to function as a group and begin working on production processes with which they have a high degree of familiarity. The success or failure of the team to be able to modify work processes is an indicator as to whether the team is able to be empowered with the personnel decision process.

If a team has been judged mature enough to handle personnel decisions, then the team must receive extensive training in the personnel process as the second condition. (This poses an interesting problem. Who determines if the team is mature enough? Management, the team itself, other teams automatic if certain conditions are present).

Training in the personnel process is another one of the components of training in which quality management mandates. The team has already received task and work improvement training, e.g., statistics, quality control methodology, and training in group processes. Training in personnel procedures requires that the team understand the basic requirements of equal employment law.

Selection requires that the team understands the process both from an organizational and legal perspective. Discipline also requires training. This training component would cover the interpersonal aspects of confrontation, problem definition, and clarification, progressive discipline, employee legal rights, and the concept of just cause, or whatever the organization uses as the basis for discipline.

In summary, personnel decision making is a logical extension of the team empowerment process. For the team to function, it must be experienced and mature in group processes and it must receive training in both the legal aspects of personnel selection as well as the organizational policies which govern personnel.

DISCIPLINE PROCESS MODELS FOR TEAMS

Although there are many variations on organizational structures for disciplinary processing, there would appear to be three major models that can be constructed around the degree of autonomy that the organization will allow. The first model is the team as recommended. The team makes what it feels are appropriate recommendations for discipline to management and then management may accept, modify or reflect the recommendations as necessary. This model safeguards the organization from legal or technical problems that might arise in a disciplinary hearing. If the organization was serious about optimizing empowerment, this model could provide a developmental step in the process of full team self-direction.

The second model is at the opposite end of the spectrum. In this model the team is completely autonomous in making personnel decisions. Team members are completely responsible for selection and disciplinary decisions. This model can only be implemented when the team has developed sufficient maturity and has been trained in personnel procedures. Barkman has suggested that one of the team members might receive advance human resources training and serve as a resource to the team.

The third model falls between the extremes of the first two models. The team proposes the disciplinary plan, but instead of being reviewed by management, the plan is reviewed by members of other work teams who may make modifications accordingly. This model allows for peer review, which should prevent any inappropriate extreme action from occurring.

It is important to note that any of the three models or their variations are considered to be the last, extreme step. For all three models, quality theorists posit that an important preliminary step must occur: there must be informal intervention by team members to work with an employee who is having problems. Every effort has to be made to counsel and assist an employee. If additional training is necessary, it must be provided. The employee must receive every opportunity to improve before any formal mechanism of discipline is implemented. The human resources department could serve as an expert to the team as the team develops its disciplinary plan and could assist the team to avoid any legal problems. Although the would suggest that with maturity and training, a team should be able to be empowered to handle discipline, there are some serious issues and problems that need to be addressed before empowerment in this area can be fully implemented.

ISSUES AND PROBLEMS

The disciplinary process, more than the selection process, is a minefield of procedural dictates. In the public sector the employee's employment has been viewed by the courts as a property right. As a consequence, the courts have developed procedural safeguards to ensure that the employee's due process rights are not violated. The safeguards have been developed based on the experience of the traditional hierarchical organizations and would require some adaptation in a system that utilized empowered teams for discipline.

Another question in the public sector is that the law often reserves the authority for personnel actions to the agency head or manager responsible for the jurisdiction, e.g. the appointing authority; or, it reserves the right to the governing board, e.g. Board of Education. If a team has been empowered, then the personnel authority would have to act as ratifiers and should not change the recommendation. Whether courts would allow the appointing authority or governing board to abrogate their responsibility in this area is questionable unless the basic authorizing statutes were revised.

This problem reinforces the need for management and the governing body to be committed to the tenants of quality management and the consequences of empowerment. At the present time some managers or boards will overrule recommendations for discipline, not because of flaws in the disciplinary procedure, but for political reasons. It is unlikely that the political pressures will disappear just because a jurisdiction has implemented quality management. Last, that union has been a significant force in the development of the quality management process. As the electromation decision of the NLRB points out, work place teams should be carefully constructed to avoid violating the NLRA. State public employment relations boards will probably rule in much the same way if unions challenge a work team experiment. The involvement of employee organizations is a necessary and sufficient condition for the implementation of any quality management programme.

There is a paucity of research of discipline in a team setting. One author noted that research on selection out is scarce, although firings, layoffs, and retirements are a part of organizational life. "Researchers spend virtually no time studying selection out." In a recently published book on human resources and quality management, the author noted that since only the most sophisticated organizations have empowered teams with personnel decision, "there are few stories to tell."

The research agenda in this area covers subjects that concern a variety of disciplines. Legal scholars need to review the impact of the team approach on the property rights issue. Group theorists need to research the issues of group dynamics in the discipline process. What types of conditions must be present for a team to function effectively? Does the potential for excluding a colleague from a work team prevent a team from acting on a problem, i.e. does an avoidance syndrome occur? This process causes significant role modification for managers and supervisors. They move from controllers and directors to coaches and resource personnel. What mechanisms are needed to alleviate the fears and anxieties that such a role shift causes?

If team empowerment in this area increases, then practitioners need to have solid, empirically based research for making design and implementation decisions rather than limited anecdotal evidence. If Total Quality Management is truly more than a fad, and is going to serve as a basis of organizational structuring in the next century, these decisions must be based on good research to avoid costly and damaging decisions. Proponents of quality management have argued that employees need to work in teams and be empowered to make decisions regarding production processes. Logically, the empowered team should also be able to handle the personnel decisions so that the team controls both the process and the persons who carry out the process.

Three separate models for team organization were proposed: recommended; autonomous decider; and a synthesis of the two, using other teams as reviewers. Mature teams and training appear to be necessary conditions for success. The public sector organization is faced with problems in implementing this process, due to procedural safeguards that are present in the disciplinary process, and the surrender of authority by appointing authorities and governing boards. All organizations need to involve employee organizations extensively in the planning and design of empowered teams.

12

Collective Bargaining

INTRODUCTION

The ILO Declaration on Fundamental Principles and Rights at Work adopted in 1998 could not be clearer: "the effective recognition of the right to collective bargaining" and "the elimination of discrimination in respect of employment and occupation" are both so central to the ILO's social justice mandate and Decent Work Agenda that they are two of the four fundamental principles which Members of the ILO have a "good faith obligation ... to respect, to promote and to realise".

Both are among the immutable principles embodied in the ILO Constitution and represent robust standards of egalitarian and democratic inspiration that stress the centrality of enfranchisement within the world of work, reflected in the ILO's Right to Organise and Collective Bargaining Convention, 1949, and the Discrimina-tion (Employment and Occupation) Convention, 1958 . For generations, both these principles have been dynamically interpreted and applied by the ILO's supervisory machinery.

And now, with the adoption of the ILO Declaration, both are urgently reaffirmed by the ILO and its Members "in a situation of growing economic interdependence" as essential components to promote a vision of "sustainable development" that see the economic and the social as mutually reinforcing. Despite the ILO's longstanding commitment to collective bargaining and the elimination of discrimination, initiatives to explore the interface between the two principles have only recently emerged, and have focused overwhelmingly on gender equality. The ILO Declaration resists the impulse to establish a hierarchy between collective bargaining and equality, merely setting these principles apart from the broader range of labour standards. In an increasingly integrated transnational context that challenges traditional labour regulation structures, the time is now ripe to investigate the complex and changing relationship between these two fundamental principles and rights at work.

Despite an overwhelming rate of ratification of Convention No. 98, effective recognition of the right to collective bargaining remains elusive for the vast majority of workers. Globally, only a minority of workers benefit from the free and fair representation of their collective rights, needs and interests. Unequal access to collective bargaining shows how far dominant paradigms of collective bargaining have failed to reflect the plural structures of work, notably in the informal economy and in the developing world. Moreover, emerging post-Fordist paradigms pose difficult challenges to the founding concepts on which twentieth-century industrial relations were constructed.

This starting-point is important beyond its basic reminder that although the ILO's decent work vision applies to all workers, effective recognition of the right to collective bargaining is a "good" that remains merely an aspiration for many. In a limited number of countries, collective bargaining has been the principal means by which terms of employment are set; in other countries at the other end of the spectrum, collective bargaining is accessible only to a small number of workers.

In most countries, moreover, those excluded from the effective exercise of collective bargaining rights include a disproportionate number of workers hailing from groups traditionally discriminated against on grounds including race, sex, religion, and national extraction. Unequal access to collective representation is thus doubly problematic, because it challenges the internal "effectiveness" of collective bargaining and because it reinforces and potentially deepens inequality faced by groups traditionally discriminated against.

As a result, inequality of access to collective representation is a challenge to arguments that privilege traditional collective bargaining mechanisms, particularly if the mechanisms involved favour the most privileged workers to the detriment of the least privileged. The uneasy coexistence between equality at work, broadly understood, and the cardinal emphasis in the ILO Declaration on the need for recognition of the right to collective bargaining to be "effective".

It will be argued that, with due regard to their application to varied social contexts, collective bargaining frameworks are not equality-neutral; rather, the choice of collective bargaining framework can be crucial in determining whether systemic obstacles to equality of access to collective bargaining can be removed. Moreover, in an increasingly complex, integrating world, special care needs to be taken to cultivate new sites for social dialogue, sites that ensure representation for traditionally marginalized or excluded groups.

The is also examines situations in which workers do exercise their fundamental rights to freedom of association and to bargain collectively, in order to consider another level of interface with the fundamental right and principle of equality: the interaction between collective bargaining, the majoritarian mechanism for workplace governance; and the structurally "minority" position of equality-seeking groups in many workforces.

It considers the controversial but real possibility that one fundamental principle could in fact impede the effective recognition of the other. Despite this possibility, the cease is advanced that collective bargaining, whose rationale is deeply rooted in notions of social justice, egalitarianism, democratic participation, and freedom, holds great potential to enhance equality. However, in order to fulfill the equality mandate, collective bargaining must be grounded in a demonstrable commitment on the part of the social partners to promote equality, a commitment evident not only in the provisions of agreements, but also in how "representation" itself is constructed, and how bargaining takes place. Finally, to the extent that the State privileges collective bargaining as the vehicle for private ordering of workplace relationships, it has a cardinal role to play in ensuring that collective bargaining enhances rather than impedes equality concerns. The final part builds on the industrial relations literature on the public-private dichotomy, emphasizing the pluralist nature of labour relations through which state enabling mechanisms permit the social partners to evolve agreements to govern their workplace.

It posits the need for a regulatory environment that reduces barriers to access to collective bargaining, that sets parameters to prohibit discriminatory collective bargains, and that leaves room for collective bargaining's democratic participation mechanisms to achieve equality goals.

UNEQUAL ACCESS TO COLLECTIVE BARGAINING

Unequal access to collective bargaining is a challenge to equality. This broad view of equality draws upon the deeply egalitarian convictions that characterize the quest for social justice within the world of work. It also focuses on the purpose of protection against discrimination, namely to affirm the equal worth and dignity of all human beings. It seeks to ensure that equality, whose fundamental nature is recognized within the ILO's normative universe and beyond, is also a reality in working people's lives.

A purposive approach is required given the mandate in the ILO Constitution and in its normative system to include all workers, thereby affirming their equal worth and dignity. Unequal access to collective bargaining represents a major challenge to equality, one that the Declaration calls on the ILO and its constituency to address.

EXCLUSIONARY IMPLICATIONS OF THE FORDIST PARADIGM

In the design and application of machinery to give effect to the right to collective bargaining, certain categories of worker were forgotten, overlooked or quite simply excluded because they were not part of the dominant paradigm. Such discrimination is systemic, in that it is embedded in social and institutional practices, policies or rules. As the dominant paradigm has shifted, the inequalities have deepened because the vehicles to render collective bargaining effective failed to capture the increasingly plural workplace realities. Moreover, the workers excluded from the actual scope of collective bargaining tend also to be from groups traditionally disadvantaged on the basis of race, gender, disability and other prohibited grounds of discrimination.

Most collective bargaining systems developed and refined over the twentieth century sought primarily to respond to the regulatory challenges of industrial production workplaces. Collective bargaining mechanisms tend to include relative degrees of recognition of (often constitutionally enshrined) freedom of association, including protection against reprisals for trade union membership.

The recognition is often buttressed by mechanisms to ensure that collective bargaining is legally recognized (in voluntarist traditions, by dislodging the common law presumption that they are illegal). Recognition may occur at several levels, and may change with the form of production from enterprise level, industry level, national level, and more recently (and exceptionally) transnational or regional level.

Whether they were premised on decentralized collective bargaining based on democratic participation at the individual workplace or enterprise level, or on more centralized structures emphasizing broader notions of industrial citizenship in social policy, the collective bargaining systems that came to predominate are commonly captured within the framework of the Fordist paradigm. Fordism functioned in an era of mass production in large workplaces, which spurred on an industrial model of employment.

It combined with Taylorist scientific management approaches, leading to industrial de-skilling, since the components of any given production process could be broken down into individual repetitive tasks that most labourers could perform; their execution could be timed and monitored by employers along an assembly line. Since employers and workers were likely to be based in a given factory located within the same country for which production was destined, the workers were essentially also the consumers. Consequently, there was incentive for employers to pay workers good, rising wages, to enable them in turn to buy the products that they produced.

They also needed leisure time so that they could exercise their purchasing power, and consume the goods they bought. These workplace gains were consolidated by Keynesian macroeconomic policies that encouraged governments to spend in the creation of a welfare state.

Liberal economic policies were increasingly embedded in society. It is increasingly acknowledged that even at the height of industrialization, models built on Fordism could not capture the full range of workplace organization. Basic regulatory mechanisms, particularly in the industrial relations system prevalent in the United States and Canada (the Wagner Act tradition), simply excluded certain categories of workers from legislation recognizing freedom of association and the effective right to bargain collectively.

Employment in agricultural and domestic settings was routinely excluded, on the assumption that the work "naturally" fell outside the industrial model, sometimes quite literally because of the absence of an industrial workplace. In some ways, this "natural" exclusion parallels the exclusion in practice of small workplaces, which have traditionally been quite difficult for unions to organize, and in which many historically marginalized groups have tended to work.

More telling today is the inability of many excluded categories to make effective use of their freedom of association and right to bargain collectively when these are granted by legislative mechanisms that merely include these workers, without taking their specific workplace organization into consideration.

Like the broader regulatory and distributive systems encapsulating them, collective bargaining systems of the Fordist era were also national in scope. They took the nation-State and state sovereignty as given, and operated within those confines. Even as accumulation exceeded the consumption capacities of individual States, and trade in goods and foreign direct investment became essential to sustain the mode of production, national borders were carefully guarded to protect workers in industrialized countries from migrant workers prepared to accept working conditions less favourable than those enjoyed by the nationals.

Prevailing occupational segregation of immigrant workers and racial, ethnic and religious minority workers in formal workplaces with low levels of organization or in the informal economy further limited these workers' access to collective bargaining. In contrast, productive relations existing outside a particular nation-State were not considered to fall within the distributional range with which the social partner in a given country should be concerned.

Along with protective legislation, collective bargaining preserved and enriched gains within - but not beyond - a given State. Despite classic justifications based on citizenship rights to share in the fruit of citizens' productive participation and to exclude non-citizens, the national scope of distributive justice increasingly failed to capture the reality of production that crossed national borders, necessarily delinking itself from consumption.

Certainly, many fictions of Fordism have resulted in a number of de facto exclusions from the effective recognition and exercise of collective bargaining rights. One was that women did not have to work because men were the family breadwinners. Though women had worked outside the home long before, throughout, and since the height of Fordism, their work was mostly in precarious conditions and for low wages; they were a reserve labour force to be drawn upon when men were not available.

There was no need to pay women a family wage, as men were the breadwinners. Women were also penalized in that social benefits were often tied to employment, so the male breadwinner also controlled access to social safety nets, including health benefits and retirement pensions. In other cases, particularly workers from disadvantaged groups, workforce participation occurred in the ghettoized occupations perceived to be their proper sphere. In its preoccupation with production, Fordism excluded women's reproductive work, as well as the associated "non-productive," "invaluable" labour of love in the home, assumed to be without value in the labour market. When the wife/mother's labour was replaced, the work was performed by women (and some men) from disadvantaged groups - earlier through slavery or indentured servitude, later through restrictive migration schemes or bonded labour.

Thus, the inadequate value attributed to the work was reinforced. It is a testament to the depth of this dichotomy that domestic work is traditionally excluded from many collective bargaining systems. The exclusions, coupled with the limits placed on women's participation even when they are unionized, compound the exclusionary effects.

Another fiction of Fordism was the presumed homogeneous society. Traditional Fordist accounts failed to acknowledge the labour market segmentation of racial, ethnic and religious minority workers in industrialized societies, as well as that of immigrant workers, who were often relegated to less desirable, comparatively low-status jobs.

Certainly Fordism's egalitarian focus on scientific management - emphasizing transparency in job classifications, requirements and pay levels - supported the contention that collective bargaining was amenable to general principles of non-discrimination. In some contexts, racial minority groups were granted (limited and uneasy) access to the waged labour market and to unionization, although this access was insufficient to prevent racial and related forms of discrimination once employment with access to collective bargaining had been achieved. The workers' minority status in society and in many industries, as well as their segmentation in less desirable occupations and industries, is reflected in (and reflective of) their comparatively limited bargaining power.

In other primarily developing countries, racial, ethnic, religious (and in some cases linguistic) equality is linked to struggles against colonial control over economic and political life. Many trade unions emerged as central social actors in the newly independent States, and played a leading role in promoting broad structural societal change to reverse entrenched racial segregation. However, little attention has been paid to the ways in which racial, ethnic and religious heterogeneity in the country may have influenced access to employment and collective bargaining.

Social partners have found it difficult to identify ways in which collective bargaining can help eradicate systemic racial inequality, probably because of the conceptual difficulties associated with racism, discrimination on the basis of ethnicity and religion, and the relative lack of power of historically disadvantaged groups to influence collective bargaining. There has been a lamentable dearth of material analysing the connections between discrimination and collective bargaining. Although it is valuable to analyse and comment on new forms of discrimination, it is crucial to ensure that old forms, such as racial discrimination, continue to be addressed.

Fordism also assumed away other divergences from the "norm". Thus, job applicants with disabilities were simply not hired; "accommodation" of persons with disabilities, by modifying the workplace or enabling the worker to undertake different tasks or the same tasks differently, came much later. Workers who developed work-related disabilities sometimes simply lost their jobs after prolonged absence from work.

Entitlement to some limited compensation, through long-term disability pay and to some extent accommodation through more flexible approaches to otherwise rigid seniority and job classification systems, was only gradually achieved. Production schedules were organized in shifts; although those shifts recognized dominant norms (e.g. Sundays off in traditionally Christian societies), the religious beliefs of workers outside the dominant social groups were not readily recognized and accommodated.

In their emphasis on transparency through "colour-blind" seniority and merit-based job classification, Fordist hiring, promotion and disciplinary practices were potentially able to foster greater racial and ethnic integration rather than accentuating difference. Yet in fact workers from the dominant social groups benefited disproportionately from these facially neutral rules and for many reasons, including past discrimination, hostile work environments, harassment, job segregation based on traditional roles for women, interruptions for childrearing and recent workplace attachments linked to immigration status.

In particular, systemic discrimination resulting in labour market segregation and in some cases in exclusion from the labour market meant that workers from certain racial or ethnic groups were effectively excluded from access to collective bargaining that recognized their rights and interests. The categories of worker who tended to be excluded, expressly or implicitly, during the Fordist era largely correspond to the categories enumerated in Convention No. Ill as requiring protection from discrimination.

Domestic workers are predominantly women from racial and other minority backgrounds; to exclude (in law or on a de facto basis) domestic work from the reach of collective bargaining has a particularly marked impact on these vulnerable women. Similarly, agricultural workers, notably in industrialized countries, are disproportionately racial minority and foreign workers; therefore their exclusion from collective bargaining legislation in some countries has a disparate impact in terms of race, national and ethnic origin. Workers in the informal economy, atypical, part-time and precarious contractual workers, and workers facing occupational segregation are predominantly women, workers from racial, ethnic and religious minorities, immigrants, workers with disabilities, and young people.

Moreover, even if all the express exclusions from collective bargaining regimes were reversed, this would not solve the problem of unequal access to collective bargaining, because access to trade unions and collective bargaining is much more difficult in certain sectors of the economy. Workers' inadequate bargaining power is an important explanation for the difficulty of unionizing workers in certain sectors. Even if unions manage to secure a foothold within a particular workplace or industry and begin collective bargaining, they often encounter a second layer of difficulty in negotiating favourable working conditions. If the union cannot achieve any significant gains through collective bargaining because of inadequate bargaining power, of course, its support will gradually wither away.

Where the legal and socio-economic realities of certain kinds of work render collective organization difficult and where workers lack sufficient bargaining power despite being organized, collective bargaining reveals its limited ability to ensure equality at work. Indeed, it may even accentuate the gap between workers with effective bargaining power and those without it.

EFFECTIVE RECOGNITION

If traditional collective bargaining regimes exclude certain categories of worker, the question inevitably arises as to whether the right to collective bargaining is effectively recognized. It is our assertion that the term "effective" must be understood in a way that is sensitive to the interface between fundamental principles and rights at work. In other words, collective bargaining mechanisms cannot be considered to be effective if they structurally exclude from access to collective bargaining those disadvantaged workers to whom Convention No. Ill guarantees equality.

To some extent this is also a challenge to traditional arguments that favour certain collective bargaining frameworks over others. To be effective, collective bargaining mechanisms must be fully inclusive, particularly of those workers who have faced historical disadvantage of the kind that Convention No. Ill strives to eliminate. The effective recognition of the right to collective bargaining is embedded in a robust conception of freedom of association that reaffirms the need for democratic governance to infuse working peoples' lived experience.

As a vehicle for achieving and promoting dignity at work, it reflects both the process and the opportunity of freedom, which are integral to the cross-cutting goal of development. Linking freedom of association with effective access to collective bargaining not only recognizes rights and freedoms, but also gives participants the means, or "voice", through which to make their needs known, and in a way that enables the social partners to seek to meet those needs within and beyond the workplace.

The empowering capacity of freedom of association and of the right to bargain collectively is part of a broad conception of freedom, recognizing that "protection" cannot simply be conferred; rather, stakeholders must play an integral role in articulating their own needs. Like other rights, freedom of association and collective bargaining are "not only pivotal in inducing social responses to economic needs, they are also central to the conceptualization of economic needs themselves".

For these reasons, the broad definition of collective bargaining found in ILO Convention No. 98 is entirely consonant with ensuring that workers have a say in the decisions that matter to them; accordingly, the ILO has applied the principle "in an uncompromisingly broad manner, albeit one that recognizes a wide diversity of industrial relations systems".

Indeed, in its concern for promoting social justice, the ILO has championed the companion notion of social dialogue, embracing autonomous participation by tripartite constituencies in a broad range of economic and social policy-making activities, notably at the national, transnational and international levels. This form of tripartism is rooted in "the acceptance of societal pluralism".

The fact that the ILO situates the fundamental freedom of collective bargaining within the broad framework of social dialogue illustrates the ILO's commitment not to a particular regulatory vehicle, but to ensuring that the underlying democratic principle of workers' participation through their freely chosen representatives is safeguarded. For the great diversity of industrial relations systems reflects the great diversity of legal traditions and regulatory frameworks around the world. Whether industrial relations frameworks were received and implemented with success may mirror the relative effectiveness with which broader regulatory frameworks were received, particularly in developing countries and transition countries. Yet there is an added dimension in the labour regulation area.

Regulatory mechanisms for the effective recognition of the right to collective bargaining are largely premised on the existence of a significantly industrialized economy, so transplanting the models to parts of the world where industrialization is just beginning virtually guarantees an uneasy coexistence.

The mechanisms must not only be adjusted to the existing legal, political, and socio-cultural context, but also to the mode of organization of the local labour market. Therefore, a system that ensures effective recognition of the right to collective bargaining in the advanced industrial country where it originated may prove able to ensure only weak recognition of the right of collective bargaining in less industrialized countries.

This problem is of considerable concern in developing countries and in the more fragile transition economies. Because the formal sector is small in these countries, the number of workplaces in which collective bargaining can be applied is limited. Not surprisingly, therefore, collective bargaining tends to be restricted to the public and semi-public sectors of these countries, excluding most workers. Consequently, traditional collective bargaining mechanisms have been ineffective at reaching most workers in many developing countries, thereby compromising equality of treatment.

ECONOMIC RESTRUCTURING AND THE GROWING GAP

Economic restructuring raises challenges for the interface between collective bargaining and equality that can no longer be readily ignored. The difficulties of access to collective bargaining experienced in many parts of the developing world and faced by disadvantaged groups in industrialized countries are increasingly felt by mainstream workers in industrialized and newly industrialized countries. As Manuela Tomei has argued in her description of the "new heterogeneity of informality": Neither "atypical" forms of employment nor the "informal" sector can be viewed as residual categories any more; they are rather integral to the overall development dynamics. Quality of employment varies along a continuum which does not follow the dichotomy formal/informal. Not all jobs in the informal sector are necessarily of poor quality nor do all formal sector jobs qualify as good jobs. Insecurity of tenure, job precarity and irregularity, lack of or limited social protection are increasingly common features of formal activities as well.

Mainstream workers find it increasingly difficult to resist downward pressures on their negotiated gains. Their labour rights attained in part through collective bargaining and social dialogue are increasingly considered to be anti-competitive costs inefficiently allocated through the monopolistic behaviour of unfairly favoured interest groups. There have been limited attempts at labour relations reform, but the basic Fordist premises of collective bargaining systems have not been comprehensively revised. Failure to counteract downward pressures may exacerbate discrimination and discourage attempts to promote equality, particularly in negotiating contexts.

A cardinal example of the changes affecting industrialized and newly industrialized countries is the shift away from a production-based economy to a much-expanded service economy with technology-driven growth. The rapid development and proliferation of new technology have brought about marked changes in the nature and organization of work.

As a result, more workers hold levels of responsibility and control that limit their right to organize under certain domestic labour laws. A system of rigid job classification with fixed, clearly identifiable job requirements has yielded to one where multiskilling, teamwork and "life-long learning" are increasingly expected. In particular, life-long learning implies workers' ongoing training and career changes undertaken not only for their own interest but also to ensure their flexibility and therefore continuing "employability". These changes shake up conventional understanding of the paradigmatic worker, while reducing the ability to rely on fixed, apparently objective criteria to determine "merit". They leave room for more subjective criteria in hiring and promotion practices, while making the ability to fit within a particular dominant cultural norm more explicit. These new requirements may also have adverse effects on equality.

Though territorial borders no longer matter in the ways that they did in the Fordist era, they have been crucial in the development of clusters of particular economic activity and of an intricate web of niche-based service relationships. Consider that primarily young, female offshore telemarketers with impeccable French-language skills based in North African countries with strong telecommunications infrastructures, notably Morocco and Tunisia, can work remotely delivering their virtual services to consumers in France. More supple regulatory frameworks may contribute to the performance of this work on an atypical, contingent basis.

These conditions do not facilitate conventional workplace organization. Even the cornerstone notion of production, initially most amenable to mid-twentieth century views of collective bargaining, has changed so dramatically that Fordist assumptions no longer readily apply. Broadly characterized as the new international division of labour, flexible systems of accumulation have developed through which corporations outsource production to smaller producers and component assemblers around the world.

These fragile micro- and small enterprises linked to a complex web of supply networks are a new and dynamic source of employment along the global production chain that further complicates the informal/formal sector divide in much of the developing world. There are many accounts of exploitative labour practices in those workplaces; the much feared but empirically unverified assumption of a "race to the bottom" has itself fostered a form of regulatory chill that defies more rigorous analysis. Applying enforceable, socially just rules across territorial boundaries to individual workplaces, thereby linking plants around the world with distant multinational enterprises and the consuming public, represents a formidable challenge, especially if it involves ensuring that these new regulatory initiatives do not "run the risk of supplanting rather than buttressing democratic participation in the workplace".

In the increasingly post-Fordist economy, management and ownership structures in the public and para-public sectors have been changed to promote flexibility. Indeed, in the United Kingdom and New Zealand, as noted in Ozaki, "the flexibilization of employment contracts in the public sector preceded the rapid spread in the 1990s of flexible employment in the private sector" even though public-sector reforms were initiated on the basis of "an imagined vision of the private sector". These changes were observed particularly in many developing and least-developed countries that had experienced structural adjustment intended to ensure flexibility in the formal sector, itself quite small.

The changes have tended to reduce workers' capacity to engage in collective bargaining in sectors with traditionally high levels of relatively effective collective bargaining. Some democratic governments in developing and industrialized countries have tried to lead by example by implementing employment equity programmes; however, since the workers from disadvantaged groups who may be hired tend to have the least seniority, they may also be the first to lose their employment when contracting out and other flexible employment practices are introduced.

Of course, privatization and new public-sector management strategies are not invariably problematic as regards non-discrimination in employment, occupation and the right to collective bargaining. Indeed, democratic governments have long drawn heavily on public procurement schemes to enforce employment-equity goals on private contractors bidding for government contracts; theoretically, equity objectives could be attached to more contemporary forms of contracting. Yet the transition from secure unionized work, predominated by workers from dominant social groups to individualized, precarious forms of employment, predominated by disadvantaged groups, is at the crux of the issue. The contracting-out issue illustrates why the impact of unequal access is not system-neutral. Industrial relations systems that restrict the scope or duration of collective bargaining over contracting out may contribute to the loss of collective bargaining rights in the sectors concerned.

Systems that require information-sharing, consultation and negotiation over restructuring may reduce the impact of the resulting changes. Meanwhile, other approaches to privatization may have a direct effect on workers' standard access to collective bargaining machinery. For example, initiatives to privatize a range of equality-enhancing public services, such as affordable childcare, may actually complicate access to the labour market for workers with family responsibilities, and minimize their ability to participate meaningfully in workplace governance through collective bargaining.

Negotiating Equality at Work

It is sometimes suggested that collective bargaining is concerned with industrial and economic issues, whereas human rights and equality are concerned with social issues. Human rights questions should be addressed through legislative reform; and economic questions are the appropriate focus of collective bargaining.

However, the conceptual divide between the economic and the social is narrowing and the connections between the two emphasized. While legislative reform to advance human rights protection is essential, particularly given the limited extent of unionization, legislation should reinforce rather than undermine the role of collective bargaining in the human rights domain.

Moreover, human rights are involved in basic economic issues - wages, restructuring, contracting out, the rise of atypical work, job security, workplace benefits, working conditions - which are at the heart of traditional collective bargaining. All these economic issues have serious implications for equality at work. Similarly, social issues, such as family-related leave, training opportunities, non-discrimination and protection from harassment at work, have significant economic implications.

The potential to advance equality through collective bargaining may be limited because of the restricted scope of collective bargaining. In many industries and workplaces, collective bargaining does not cover employment issues central to equality and non-discrimination, i.e. recruitment, promotion and training. In some countries, collective bargaining focuses on wages and employment benefits rather than on work organization. There have been divisive debates about management rights and the appropriate scope of collective bargaining.

Does the collective bargain simply replace the individual contract of employment or does the collective bargaining process usher in a fundamental shift in all work-related decision-making, and constitute a form of co-determination, a new constitutional framework for the workplace, a new workplace rule of law?

Though collective bargaining may accurately be described as limited in scope and as focusing on wages and benefits, it could potentially address all aspects of life at work, including those at the heart of equality at work. As a means of ensuring worker participation in a range of issues affecting working people's lives and of advancing fairness, respect and well-being, collective bargaining is directly relevant to equality at work.

Tension Between Majority Interests and Minority Rights

Paradoxically, collective bargaining has been both part of the problem and part of the solution to the elimination of inequality and discrimination at work. Collective bargaining usually reflects the priorities and needs of the dominant workers in a particular workplace or industry. In some instances, the problem is one of omission or failure to include on the collective bargaining agenda issues of concern to workers from under-represented groups (e.g. women, racial or religious minorities). This may still be true even when, because of the segregated nature of labour markets, most workers at a particular workplace actually belong to an historically disadvantaged group.

In other cases, direct conflicts emerge between the provisions of collective agreements and the need to accommodate differences and be attentive to human rights. There are examples of trade unions "utilizing the ideology of racism and actively colluding with employers to restrict the job opportunities" of racial and ethnic minority workers. When faced with unemployment and lay-offs, trade unions have sometimes endorsed racist and exclusionary anti-immigration policies.

Similarly, when female workers were viewed as a threat to the employment opportunities of male workers, male-dominated trade unions embraced the family wage and separate-spheres ideologies in order to limit employment opportunities for women. Despite the changes undergone by many workplaces, collective bargaining priorities have not always been adjusted accordingly, resulting in conflicts between traditional trade union demands and the needs of workers who do not correspond to the traditional worker profile.

Debates about the merits of equality rights versus seniority illustrate the potential risks of majoritarianism. Originally, the allocation of workplace benefits and opportunities based on seniority (or length of service) was based on the idea that the approach would advance fairness, protect against favouritism or arbitrary management decisions, and ultimately benefit everyone equally because each employee eventually built up seniority over the years.

The application of seniority rules in the modern economic context, however, does not always advance fair and equal treatment of women and minority groups for one important reason: equal access to employment does not exist, and so women and minority workers often build up considerably less seniority than do majority male workers.

Thus, seniority rules can both accentuate the effects of past exclusion and reinforce the privileges of "insiders" - privileges too often built upon the discriminatory exclusion of "outsiders". However, criticizing the seniority system appears to open the door to greater managerial discretion in the allocation of jobs, benefits and promotion.

It is important therefore to criticize the discriminatory effects of seniority, while developing creative alternatives that respect the positive aspects of seniority systems, for example, by specifying exclusions to the application of seniority provisions in order to accommodate workstation changes and facilitate job opportunities for disabled workers.

The potential conflict between majority interests and minority rights is sometimes seen as a parallel to that between collective and individual rights. Equality rights are perceived in terms of individual rights while collective bargaining is seen as a mechanism for the pursuit of collective or social goals. Collective struggles to end discrimination in the workplace have been hampered by this dichotomy, according to some scholars who consider that civil rights laws have focused on individual rights while labour laws have advanced group rights.

The cogency of this distinction is questionable. As regards discrimination, in particular, it is the group aspect of the unfair treatment that brings it under the rubric of equal rights. Though equal rights are often evoked by individuals, they are closely linked to group rights. Moreover, a growing literature on equality rights emphasizes the systemic and relational aspects of discrimination.

Rather than locating problems of exclusion and discrimination in the individuals or groups who experience inequality, they are understood to result from the social and institutional consequences of not conforming to dominant norms. For equality to be achieved, therefore, institutional change must occur such that the lives of both the minority and the majority are transformed and enriched.

Finally, though trade unions have not always advanced women's or minority group rights in the workplace, they have done so on a number of occasions. Indeed, in some contexts, without trade union advocacy and the collective pursuit of human rights claims (e.g. pay equity or comparable worth), there would be virtually no protection or enforcement of human rights.

INCLUSIVE DEMOCRACY

The key response to the omission of the concerns and needs of historically disadvantaged minority groups from collective bargaining is to ensure these groups' inclusion in the collective bargaining process. For collective bargaining to enhance equality, individuals from such groups must be consulted about their needs and interests and must be represented at the bargaining table.

In this regard, it is helpful to learn from important research on gender equality and collective bargaining, which consistently highlights the need to include women workers in the collective bargaining process. Equitable representation within union decision-making structures and equality-enhancing union policies are repeatedly identified as prerequisites for advancing equality through collective bargaining.

Not only does this validate the experience, knowledge and insights of those who live the realities of exclusion and discrimination, it also enhances collective bargaining's inclusive function enabling the democratic participation of all workers, not simply those who represent the majority in a particular industry or enterprise. When voicing their specific needs and interests, historically disadvantaged groups have not always been encouraged to claim their rights because of trade union fear that this would undermine worker solidarity.

Some have argued that "identity politics" risks undermining unified class-based perspectives. Others have suggested that the integration of trade union representatives in national policy-making has too often been "predicated upon the homogenization of the heterogeneous demands of workers". Nevertheless, there has been growing recognition that the very varied interests and needs within the labour movement deserve to be articulated and addressed. Indeed, some have argued that, far from being undermined, solidarity can be strengthened by recognizing diversity. Effective participation is essential to understand the nature of inequality and to identify creative solutions that can be advanced through the collective bargaining process.

Beyond the need for consultation with individuals and groups with experience of discrimination, research on gender equality and trade unions emphasizes the importance of training individuals from under represented groups to participate in trade union activities and collective bargaining. Here, insights from the gender domain are pertinent to other disadvantaged groups.

Democratic participation in trade union activities and involvement in other workplace-related questions require individuals to know how to operate effectively within the union and at the workplace. Without direct training and education, this may remain beyond the reach of many women workers and minority workers.

Furthermore, if workers from disadvantaged groups are included in negotiating teams and are chosen to participate in collective bargaining, this will help reduce the risk of the needs and concerns of minority groups becoming marginalized during the collective bargaining process. It is particularly useful to have representatives of a minority community who are able to consult effectively with their group.

It is also important to ensure that those elected properly reflect the diversity of the workforce they represent, so that leadership positions are shown to be accessible to all. Questions of representation of diverse interests and groups are complex. How should the various groups be defined? To what extent can individuals from groups historically subject to exclusion and disadvantage at work represent their own group's interests?

For membership of a particular group does not necessarily mean that one holds the same values or ideas as others in that group. How can one guard against problems of tokenism and the legitimation of inequality through an unequal structure of group representation? Moreover, consultation and participation are only effective if there is an audience willing to listen to and take seriously views and voices that are usually silenced or marginalized.

Ensuring that the interests of historically disadvantaged groups are not traded off in the heat of collective bargaining is another challenge. Human rights legislation can play a significant role here, by setting a non-negotiable floor of human rights protection, which both employers and unions must respect. Collective bargaining can then focus on how best to implement human rights guarantees, rather than requiring the parties to bargain about what should be non-negotiable, namely, respect for the rights of equality-seeking groups.

EQUALITY AND THE CONTENT OF COLLECTIVE AGREEMENTS

The pursuit of substantive equality engages employers, unions and workers in a process of institutional and social change, requiring a fundamental rethinking of the world of work to open it up to diversity. Yet, significant change is not always easy to accomplish through collective bargaining because of the latter's nature and given resistance to changing policies or practices that may challenge hard-won gains, even when these no longer create an inclusive atmosphere in the workplace.

Three key aspects of the pursuit of substantive equality through collective bargaining may be identified: a commitment to equality; mechanisms for identifying inequality and discrimination; and creative remedial measures and strategies.

COMMITMENT TO EQUALITY

For equality to be advanced through collective bargaining, trade unions and employers must be committed to the idea. At different times in the past, trade unions have not consistently aligned their interests and commitments with those of women workers and workers from minority groups. Nevertheless, trade unions are now according higher priority to equality questions at the bargaining table.

Gender equality has been a particular focus of trade unions' concern. Although racial inequality has deep historical roots and has caused enormous harm, trade unions have only recently begun to make policy statements denouncing racism and endorsing solidarity across racial, ethnic and religious differences. In recent years, collective bargaining has been relied upon to advance the equal rights of social groups that were not traditionally protected by anti-discrimination laws.

The private ordering dimensions of collective bargaining, whereby the parties themselves negotiate anti-discrimination protection, are particularly important for these groups in the absence of legal and legislative reform. For example, a growing body of research endeavours to document and compare, across nations, the actions taken by organized labour in relation to sexual diversity issues. Innovations in the area of disability rights have also been advanced by trade unions.

With respect to trade union commitment to equality, two observations deserve mention. First, research suggests that when trade unions accord high priority to equality concerns in negotiations, these are much more likely to be met. A recent study concluded that "newer items are unlikely to be achieved unless they are high-priority items.

It would appear that policy does make a difference and that there is real scope for proactive policy stances" second, trade unions' commitment to equality is threatened by an external environment characterized by "increased domestic and international competition and new management strategies" favouring cost-cutting (including closures and mergers), downsizing, outsourcing, use of temporary and part-time workers and privatization.

It has been suggested that much less importance is likely to be accorded to equality during periods of economic recession, restructuring and insecurity. Employers' commitment to equality is also critical. The chances of achieving equality through collective bargaining are greatly enhanced if commitment is secured from both parties.

Moreover, it is important to identify the impact on equality of management strategies adopted in the face of intensified global competition. These often have human rights implications because of their disproportionate impact on vulnerable and socially disadvantaged groups. Although employers sometimes argue that the costs of equality are an obstacle to change, it is increasingly being recognized that the costs of inequality are enormous.

MECHANISMS TO IDENTIFY INEQUALITY AND DISCRIMINATION

When preparing for collective bargaining and setting their bargaining demands and priorities, both unions and employers should include an assessment of existing problems of inequality and discrirnination. It is essential to involve historically excluded and disadvantaged groups in the identification of problems of inequality. When technical knowledge is needed to analyse systems and statistical patterns of exclusion and discrimination (e.g. pay equity), the collective expertise of trade unions and human resource departments can make an important contribution.

There is also a need to set up ongoing mechanisms to identify systemic and policy problems of inequality in industrial relations systems that set a limited timeframe for collective bargaining. In some collective agreements, equity, accommodation or human rights committees are established, with management and worker representatives, to monitor existing equality initiatives, identify new problems and recommend policy and workplace changes.

Monitoring has been identified as a critical component of effective equality policies. It is important to ensure that industrial democracy and collective bargaining reinforce rather than undermine each other. Some research suggests that worker democracy initiatives are in fact more likely to develop in unionized workplaces; earlier research had sometimes linked industrial democracy and quality of work initiatives with efforts to discourage unionization. Legislative initiatives to advance equality in pay equity and employment equity often give an important implementation and monitoring role to trade unions, as the autonomous voice of workers.

CREATIVE REMEDIAL MEASURES AND STRATEGIES

Collective agreements increasingly contain general non-discrimination clauses, which prohibit discrimination in the workplace on the basis of specific grounds. It is also important to include a provision specifically prohibiting harassment in the workplace. These clauses are significant because they affirm a consensus regarding the general normative importance of equality at work.

To the extent that a collective agreement represents the rule of law for the workplace, equality must be included as a founding normative principle. Equality rights clauses may also serve as interpretive aids to other provisions in a collective agreement. In case of ambiguity or possible contradictory provisions in the collective agreement, a non-discrimination clause may reinforce interpretations that are consistent with equality.

Non-discrimination clauses vary as regards the grounds for protection which they invoke. They may mirror existing human rights legislation, incorporate human rights standards by reference, or go beyond statutory protection (which is critically important where the protection provided by the law is inadequate). While equality clauses often invoke separate group-based grounds of discrimination, individual identities tend to transcend singular grounds.

Solidarity may be enhanced through an integrated approach that does not limit equality-enhancing provisions to special treatment for particular groups. Nonetheless, it is important to be attentive to the specificity of individual experience of inequality and to name those inequalities in group-based terms, when necessary.

An assessment of different collective bargaining provisions on prohibited grounds of discrimination reveals the importance of social and historical context. Discrimination has varied according to national and local political, social and economic realities. For example, in many countries struggling to overcome the effects of colonialism, trade union movements were active in the national political struggle. In such contexts, discrimination on the basis of political beliefs and affiliation may have been critically important and is therefore included as a key aspect of non-discrimination clauses.

In other countries, gender-based discrimination may be the focus of non-discrimination clauses and initiatives. Trade union acknowledgement of other inequalities, such as that suffered by homosexual workers, may also vary significantly depending on the national context.

The inclusion of a general non-discrimination clause in a collective agreement is particularly important to ensure protection of human rights, since alleged problems of discrimination will then be subject to a grievance procedure and, potentially, to arbitration. Indeed, there is a burgeoning arbitral jurisprudence interpreting basic human rights guarantees in collective agreements. Workers may be more inclined to file a grievance regarding discrimination than to initiate a human rights complaint or to start a civil suit alleging discrimination. Thus, access to the grievance procedure can greatly enhance access to justice in the human rights area.

While grievance arbitration can help access to justice in the human rights area, it should not be the sole means of redress, for several important reasons. First, the individual who has experienced the discrimination does not always have direct control over whether a grievance procedure goes ahead. Sometimes, a union may decide not to pursue a human rights complaint, against the wishes of the individual concerned.

While legislated duties of fair representation may provide some measure of protection against arbitrary decision-making by the union, an individual should have the option of pursuing other avenues of redress (e.g. a human rights complaint). Second, arbitrators may not always have sufficient human rights expertise to solve some of the complex problems that arise in discrimination cases. More specialized human rights tribunals may be better equipped to deal with problems of inequality at work. Though the inclusion of non-discrimination and non-harassment clauses is important, such clauses often replicate a complaints-driven model of human rights enforcement. They are interpreted and applied in the face of an individual complaint or grievance regarding alleged discrimination or harassment. It is essential for individuals to have their rights affirmed in this way, yet more is needed. Collective bargaining can also be used to change identified problems of discrimination proactively and systematically. It should not be necessary for individuals to go through often long and arduous individual complaint channels or grievance procedures to see effective change in this area. Collective bargaining should be used to revise exclusionary or discriminatory workplace rules and policies, to promote fair compensation schemes, inclusive employee benefits, and equitable treatment.

Collective bargaining should also address proactive institutional mechanisms to accommodate group-based differences where it is not possible or desirable to change the broader rule or universal policy. "Accommodation" is the notion whereby workers have the right to be treated differently in order to enable their inclusion in the workplace despite their differences.

For example, an employee with a sight or hearing impairment may require special office equipment to palliate the effects of his/her disability. Though unions have sought to enhance employment opportunities and accommodation in the workplace, there has been resistance when this has involved deviations from traditional seniority or other workplace rules. Collective bargaining should ensure that accommodation policies are in place, so that individual accommodation measures are taken when necessary.

As noted in a report by the ILO-ICFTU, "[t]he current inadequacies of equality legislation and its enforcement in many countries underscore even more the potential of collective bargaining to address equality of opportunity and treatment within the terms and conditions of employment". Negotiating for equality with equality-seeking groups is bound to be more complicated and challenging than negotiations between habitual negotiating partners; it can, however, really enhance the effectiveness of the collective bargaining process.

STATE LABOUR REGULATORY INITIATIVES

Two regulatory initiatives that can help promote equality through collective bargaining are particularly important. First, enabling legislation is needed, to ensure that barriers to access to collective bargaining are minimized and that more facilitative measures are put in place. This reflects the need for broadly inclusive and democratic bargaining models as well as minimally decent working conditions and wage-setting procedures below which no group can settle, however limited their bargaining power.

Second, prohibitive legislation is needed, to ensure that collective agreements that would impede equality are not reinforced by the State. But equality demands more than blanket prohibitions on certain forms of action; legislation mandating reasonable workplace accommodation and proactive initiatives, such as pay equity and employment equity, helps to ensure that systemic discrimination against equality seeking groups is effectively eradicated.

Regulatory frameworks that encourage the equitable, democratic participation of all workers in workplace governance are essential to establishing a mutually reinforcing role for equality and collective bargaining across national, transnational and international levels of governance.

LEGISLATIVE ENGAGEMENT

Much has been written about the comparative advantages of particular national collective bargaining regimes, so a detailed discussion will not be presented here. Yet the assumption that equality and collective bargaining are each in some sense "private" matters may have stood in the way of more pointed analyses of the enabling role of the State in relation to equality.

But regulation on equality, secured in many countries through constitutional and international human rights forums and judicial enforcement leading ultimately to legislative change, should not be understood as the "public" dimension of a fundamentally "private" negotiating relationship. Collective bargaining on equality further complicates this dichotomy, because of the implication that there is an important role for private actors to play, within carefully crafted state regulatory frameworks, to ensure that equality is realised.

Civil society is not necessarily a preferred alternative to the State; rather, both need to be strengthened to "deepen democracy and undermine injustice, especially that deriving from private economic power". The choice of collective bargaining regime and of specific labour relations mechanisms within a given regime affects the extent and effectiveness of bargaining on equality issues.

For example, some labour relations scholars have affirmed that centralized wage bargaining, which is more prevalent in countries with citizenship-based, social partnership models of collective relations, plays a particularly significant role in narrowing wage differentials, notably those based on gender.

By contrast, decentralized wage bargaining systems, increasingly prevalent in voluntarist labour relations systems or in systems based on a democratic choice model of collective relations, tend to accentuate enterprise-specific productivity or efficiency concerns to the detriment of cost-of-living indexation of wages and broader "solidaristic" strategies.

They run the risk of exacerbating pay differentials, "since dominant groups are able to protect their differentials leaving other workers with less industrial muscle, including women, at the bottom of the wages hierarchy". Moreover, there has been a marked trend toward greater decentralization of pay determination, influenced largely by a wish to promote labour market flexibility. Potentially, this trend could exacerbate such differences.

Of course, the hybrid nature of many collective bargaining systems can mitigate the impact of some structures by superimposing others. For example, in systems that allow central bargaining to set wage minima and maxima, sectoral-level bargaining for wage increases may affect the resulting differential. Also, the hybrid nature of industrial relations systems includes the growing influence of transnational regulatory structures, international norms and comparative experience. So, on the issue of wage disparities, the development within European Union law of the proactive notion of equal pay for work of equal value has served as a counterbalancing force, offering another means with which to challenge the development of pay differentials in the European Union.

Similar developments within domestic jurisdictions such as those of Ontario and Quebec, which apply to both public and private sectors, can also counteract some of the wage effects of occupational segregation and limited bargaining power in traditionally decentralized systems of wage-bargaining.

Some collective bargaining mechanisms thought to enhance equality may actually prove to raise challenges for equality, too. Consider, for example, the legislative extension of collective agreements. By ensuring that the terms of a collective agreement extend to an entire industry, legislative extension has permitted the organization of a wide range of hitherto excluded categories of worker.

These workers are likely to be women or to belong to other historically disadvantaged groups. Certainly, this kind of negotiated "specific regulation" that is sensitive to the particular workplace context has a protective dimension. However, the extension itself can represent a real obstacle to the promotion of democratic participation. Legislative extension has been criticized for offering a "free ride" to workers thus covered, since it removes some of the material incentive for these workers to join a union.

Of comparable concern is the possibility that meaningful consultation with the workers in the particular industry may diminish, leading to a de facto representation gap despite the extended coverage, and a corresponding inability to understand and defend workers' equality concerns effectively. The equality-enhancing value of collective bargaining must therefore be considered in terms not only of its protective function but also of its capacity to foster meaningful dialogue by enfranchising workers. Carefully crafted approaches to legislative extension and more recent proposals to adopt broadly based bargaining schemes hold much promise for equality. For that potential to be harnessed, greater attention needs to be given to ways in which equality-seeking groups can participate actively in the construction of the regimes and in the elaboration of the extended contractual terms.

MINIMUM STANDARDS LEGISLATION

A crucial equality role is played by legislation setting a floor of decent working conditions, including a minimum wage, restrictions on hours of work, minimum rest periods, as well as occupational safety and health regulations. The existence of these laws and associated inspection and enforcement systems confirms that certain matters should not be left to bargains struck by the parties; those bargains are presumed to be inherently inequitable.

Legislation on minimum working conditions therefore remains important for the promotion of equality. It should be noted that challenges to its legitimacy in the 1980s and 1990s have been overtaken by the more contemporary recognition that dignity demands that all workers have access to decent work. There is sometimes an overlap between minimum standards and specific human rights legislation, for example, in the area of non-discrimination measures during pregnancy, and maternity leave. The role played by this type of legislation is not entirely captured by the term "prohibitive".

Certainly, at one level, labour standards and/or human rights legislation that offer privacy protection and as a result prohibit pre-employment and routine mandatory workplace testing for HIV/AIDS are effectively prohibitive in nature, and overlap in important ways with human rights prohibitions by reducing discriminatory reprisals. But legislation on working conditions has a broader, enabling role by raising the bargaining floor, which is particularly useful for those categories of workers whose bargaining power is most limited.

Legislated minima seek to ensure that they do not make "unconscionable" labour market bargains, or that bargains are not enforced against those workers who should not be permitted to enter into an employment contract (notably minors). Regarding HIV/AIDS, strong privacy rights protection may then enable the parties to put HIV/AIDS on the bargaining table, providing incentives for the parties to devise more effective, compassionate and dynamic approaches to the workplace dimensions of this epidemic.

The constructive legislative approach curtails punitive approaches to HIV/AIDS that further inhibit the productive capacity of the workplace actors; it seeks instead to mobilize tripartite-plus workplace actors to ensure they use collective bargaining to devise constructive policies and codes of conduct to deal creatively with this particularly pressing problem.

HUMAN RIGHTS LEGISLATION

Through its support for proactive equality measures to frame collective bargaining, the State recognizes that it supports collective bargaining at least partly because of its capacity to include all social groups. Human rights legislation that uses collective bargaining to promote equality goals validates the centrality of democratic participation, and marshals the specific insights that only local actors can bring to their workplace to the benefit of equality.

Previously excluded workers are thus able to develop their workplace governance capacity, since "a public is always better if more of its members have more developed capacities than fewer". Research suggests that a legal framework supporting equal rights is often a necessary precondition to getting social partners to address equality issues in bargaining. In turn, the effective enforcement and "implementation of legislative measures [in favour of human rights] may often depend on supporting institutions and policies which are derived from a collective framework".

GENERAL EQUALITY RIGHTS AND PROTECTION AGAINST DISCRIMINATION

Constitutional and international human rights guarantees against discrimination focus on the interventionist role of the State in promoting (or failing to promote) equality. Regarding explicit exclusions from collective bargaining regimes, the main issue is the inadequacy of state regulatory responses. In many countries, collective bargaining legislation is subject to constitutional scrutiny and must comply with constitutional guarantees on equality rights and freedom of association.

Statutory human rights provisions are the most prevalent means of protecting individuals and groups against discrimination at work. The most common legislative approach to outlaw discrimination accords individuals a right not to be discriminated against in employment and provides them with retroactive legal recourse should it occur. Human rights protection against discrimination at work is generally extended to social groups who in the past have been excluded in some way or subjected to discriminatory treatment.

Many human rights documents enumerate specific grounds of discrimination, such as race, national or ethnic origin, colour, sex, religion, age, civil status, and political affiliation. More recently, new grounds of discrimination have been recognized in some human rights laws, for example, physical and mental disability, and sexual orientation. Increasingly, general non-discrimination clauses are being included in collective agreements.

Statutory non-discrimination provisions also set important limits to collective bargaining and freedom of contract. Where individual collective agreement provisions deviate from human rights norms secured in legislation, the latter take precedence over the former. There are cases, for example, of seniority provisions being challenged as discriminatory pursuant to human rights legislative guarantees.

Certainly there are circumstances in which market forces alone can favour equality-enhancing collective agreements. For example, in countries with full employment, employers may be particularly keen to attract women and, as a result, include measures to foster women's access to the workforce, including anti-harassment policies, childcare facilities, and generous maternity leave provision. In other cases, market demand in certain niche areas, such as telecommunications services, may encourage employers to seek workers with excellent foreign language skills; this may lead those employers to adopt equality-affirming policies in order to attract and promote members of the ethnic or linguistic group concerned. While such initiatives should be encouraged, there are several risks associated with relying on these initiatives to the exclusion of broader regulatory frameworks.

First, they overlook the larger question of bargaining power, favouring those workers whose labour market position and skills enable them to exercise a certain amount of bargaining control. The equality gains are therefore distributed unevenly across economic sectors. Second, the durability of the gains in times of economic recession or crisis is increasingly being questioned.

The risk that disadvantaged groups are perceived as a reserve category of labour subject to less favourable treatment in times of high unemployment warrants attention. Third, certain historically disadvantaged groups have more difficulty than others in overcoming stereotypical assumptions about their workplace capacity. Finally, the need for proactive human rights legislation becomes particularly acute when private-sector actors do not voluntarily follow up these initiatives.

EMPLOYMENT EQUITY

Human rights advocates have long argued that implementing human rights on the basis of individual or group-based complaints of discrimination is insufficient to redress pervasive problems of inequality at work. In response, legislators have explored more proactive approaches to securing equality at work, mandating the establishment of employment equity and affirmative action programmes, and pay equity schemes.

These programmes require barriers to equality in the workplace to be assessed, discriminatory standards and practices to be revised and, in some cases, special group-based preferences (i.e. affirmative action) to be introduced in order to expedite the attainment of equality. Collective bargaining, where applicable, then takes place within a regulatory framework that requires positive action on equality in the workplace. This means that equality is a mandatory item on the workplace agenda. Most employment equity legislation institutionalizes some degree of worker participation in the pursuit of equality. Integrating proactive equity initiatives into the collective bargaining process permits a "bottom-up" approach to the institutional change required for equality to be achieved. The requirement that workers be consulted and included on employment equity committees is often written into the legislative framework.

Though such worker participation applies to both unionized and non-unionized workplaces, a trade union presence helps to ensure that worker participation is autonomous and escapes structural power imbalances in the employer-employee relationship.

PAY EQUITY

Pay equity legislative initiatives have been prompted by recognition that work traditionally done by women and other historically disadvantaged groups in the paid labour force has been systematically undervalued. These legislative schemes require a proactive approach to sex-based pay inequities to secure equal pay for work of equal value or work of comparable worth.

Collective bargaining has traditionally been concerned with pay levels. Does pay equity legislation enhance or conflict with unions' traditional role in securing better wages through collective bargaining? Pay equity has generally been endorsed by trade unions and legislative initiatives have been relied upon to bolster union bargaining power regarding securing pay equity.

As with legislation on minimum standards, pay equity legislation means that collective bargaining must consider how pay equity may be achieved, not whether it should be an objective. The complexities of pay equity are a challenge for law-makers and for employers and trade unions, for the notion of comparable worth contests a market-based determination of wages and challenges labour market inequities, which are often closely linked to social, religious and cultural norms.

The situation becomes even more complex where employers innovate with profit-sharing schemes to supplement traditional forms of employment remuneration. The limitations of pay equity initiatives have already been indicated. In general, they address horizontal but not vertical economic inequities. Pay equity has been used to address gender-based inequities, but has not been extended to other widespread inequities in pay.

Yet trade unions have criticized the effects of pay equity schemes on a number of grounds, notably, that workers risk seeing their historical gains undermined by complex arguments about the value of particular jobs. Even the task of ascertaining the worth of particular jobs has been criticized as an intrusion by management and human resources experts into workers' lives. The struggle for fair wages becomes sidetracked and overly technical because of the need for sophisticated job evaluation schemes and complex statistical analysis to ascertain whether pay levels are discriminatory.

Where job segregation occurs throughout an industry or a workplace, implementation of pay equity is rendered more difficult because of the lack of a (male) comparator. Large public-sector workplaces with a wide range of job categories appear to provide the best context for the implementation of pay equity.

Other problems are linked to the impact of structural adjustment in the economy, which erodes the wages and benefits of the male worker norm upon which pay equity schemes are based. Despite these challenges and in view of the regulatory initiatives in some countries, it remains critical for trade unions to play an active role, rather than leaving the determination of pay equity to employers. For, as in employment equity, the enforcement of pay equity norms is greatly enhanced by independent worker representation.

RETREAT OF THE STATE FROM LABOUR REGULATION

Despite the inherent pluralism of labour relations law, rooted in the ability of the parties to collective bargaining to make the laws that govern their workplace relations, state regulatory action is crucial to ensure the viability of both equality and collective bargaining. It is necessary to consider the impact of the retreat of the State from labour regulation on the effectiveness of collective bargaining in the promotion of equality.

With the unravelling of the welfare state in the 198Os and 1990s, and the associated emergence of a preference for minimal state intervention, has come a challenge to received wisdom about the role of the State in promoting equality. The "threat of exit" by footloose employers may prevent States from assuming a more proactive regulatory role, "re-regulating" instead to attract foreign direct investment and to encourage multinational enterprises to stay. If traditional labour relations law is increasingly ineffective, then reliance on it to promote equality is correspondingly ineffective.

That workforce changes are accompanied by "increasing concentrations of poverty and long-term unemployment, [yielding a] growing realization or ethnicisation of poverty and exclusion" further compounds the difficulties of pursuing equality. But the situation is not totally bleak. Labour law has always been in a state of flux in response to changing social, technological and economic conditions.

A result of questioning of the viability of the "minimal State", the emergence of a carefully tailored approach to target constructive state regulatory involvement on promoting an integrated approach to social policy and economic development. This approach includes promising possibilities - at the transnational level, too - for the interface between effective recognition of the right to collective bargaining and the promotion of equality.

The ILO has a crucial role to play in conceptualizing and operationalizing this shift. Given that the ILO Declaration reaffirms freedom of association and the effective recognition of the right to bargain collectively, the notion of collective labour relations is not directly challenged (at least not at a theoretical level); the issue is rather that its effectiveness in an increasingly transnational economic context is seriously called into question. Yet some of the recent empirical literature suggests that in some countries, when unions give high priority to equality-enhancing concessions and workplace changes, they advance those equality priorities relatively successfully through collective bargaining.

How far, then, does the promotion of equality enhance the effectiveness of traditional industrial relations law and practice, by broadening their representational base and strengthening their claims to democracy? Recently, some employment discrimination research has attempted to consider how dynamic regulatory approaches can help to eradicate systemic workplace bias, exclusionary employment practices (including "glass ceilings") and harassment notably in multi-skilled, teamwork contexts in which mentoring and other informal procedures are important for promotion. This research documents enterprise-level attempts to foster compliance by articulating policies and developing an interactive problem-solving culture.

Though controversial in that the approaches may replace hard rule enforcement through judicial or quasi-judicial mechanisms, they are nevertheless attracting growing interest because they bring to the workplace a range of newer, potentially constructive participants (such as specialized workplace diversity trainers) to help ensure compliance with non-discrimination principles.

Trade unions can lead by example with these more localized approaches to workplace governance and negotiate the terms of policies, assist with training and the choice of trainers, while ensuring that the mechanisms do actually both respond to the concerns of unionized workers and preserve their legal rights and recourses.

The future interface between collective bargaining and equality is also expected to involve opportunities for social dialogue at new levels of governance. If these complement collective bargaining, they should also be harnessed to promote equality. For example, the EU Directive 94/95 on works councils within the European Union and comparable forms of labour-management representation (e.g. in Japan and the Republic of Korea) may be harnessed to promote the representation of traditionally marginalized groups in workplace management.

These outcomes may increasingly be required by law, as the EU extends its equality of treatment provisions beyond sex discrimination to include all discrimination based on race, ethnic origin, religion or conviction, disability, age and sexual orientation. Yet trade liberalization has tended to place a premium on promoting greater market flexibility to foster economic competitiveness. The social dimensions of globalization need to infuse economic goals, to ensure that the growth in transnational regulatory regimes does not weaken negotiated equality protection.

Greater advances in collective bargaining and comparable approaches that promote equality through democratic workplace participation at different levels of governance may reduce reliance on unilateral initiatives, such as codes of corporate conduct. Government actors also play an important role in ensuring broad representation on various higher-level representational structures.

Worth mentioning is the importance of participation by representative organizations of workers and employers, and wider dialogue with other important social actors, including historically disenfranchised groups, in new regional integration initiatives to develop the social aspects of transnational governance constructs, which should be harnessed to promote equality.

Cease Surely, "[a] culture of democracy and dialogue cannot be improvised". Rather, if collective bargaining mechanisms are not equality-neutral, then proactive measures must be taken to tackle this inequality of access. The measures must involve all the tripartite actors, as well as a broader mix of civil society participants representing marginalized groups of workers and emerging employment relationships.

The measures entail thinking beyond old categories and traditional territorial boundaries. New, overlapping, or complementary approaches must be developed to ensure that the right to collective bargaining is effectively recognized through the promotion of equal access. Yet collective bargaining could do a lot to promote equality. Creative and context-sensitive agreements can greatly assist in promoting equality.

For collective bargaining has not always advanced equal rights: certain issues have not been raised or accorded sufficient priority at the bargaining table because they concern a minority of workers; and collective agreement provisions may conflict with the equal rights of women or minority groups. In a climate of economic uncertainty, there is a particular risk of protecting "insiders" at the expense of "outsiders" who have been and continue to be denied equal employment opportunities.

Finally, because the effectiveness of collective bargaining is affected by national and international legal regulatory frameworks and by labour market power, some of the most vulnerable unionized workers may not command sufficient bargaining power to advance equality objectives through the collective bargaining process.

Providing basic labour standards and equality rights in law buttresses the bargaining power of workers; in other words, if the law already recognizes equality principles in the workplace, then negotiations can focus on how to achieve equality at work.

The "retreat of the State" thesis on the interface between collective bargaining and equality is contested partly because it is argued that the ILO has an important role to play. Focused attention by the leading institution on international labour standards on how to support the social partners directly, and how to enhance governments' capacity to promote these activities would uniquely contribute to the promotion of equality and collective bargaining.

For example, some labour relations scholars have affirmed that centralized wage bargaining, which is more prevalent in countries with citizenship-based, social partnership models of collective relations, plays a particularly significant role in narrowing wage differentials, notably those based on gender. Support might include research and analysis, notably on emerging patterns of collective bargaining and broader social dialogue especially at emerging governance sites. The ILO also has a continuing normative role to play, notably in providing training and other forms of technical assistance to help the social partners effectively participate in and shape emerging workplace governance.

ILO action can help to shape the direction of globalization, by holding actors accountable to the requirements of a decent work agenda and by providing them with the capacity to meet them. Fundamental principles and rights at work are cardinal to this relationship. To be given their full meaning, they must be understood not only individually, but in their interaction. It has been contended that collective bargaining is effectively recognized when it responds to the challenge posed by unequal access.

It has also been argued that equality can enhance the effectiveness of collective bargaining, and that the ILO should continue to play a leading role in researching and strengthening the interface between these two rights, demonstrating their mutually reinforcing potential. In an increasingly integrated world, they promote a vision of both the social and the economic as central to sustainable development

13

Personnel Management and Industrial Relations

AN OVERVIEW

The relationship between the employers and employees and trade unions is called Industrial Relations. Harmonious relationship is necessary for both the employers and employees to safeguard the interests of both the parties of production. To maintain good relationship with the employees is the main function of every organization so as to ensure industrial peace and higher production. Personnel management is mainly concerned with the human relations in the industry because the main theme of personnel management is to get the work done by the human power and it fails in its objectives if good industrial Revelations are not maintained. In other words, good industrial relations means industrial peace which is necessary for better and higher production.

Definitions: Industrial relations have been defined by some of the thinkers a follows:

- "Industrial relations and personnel management are almost synonymous term with the only difference the former places emphasis on the aspect of employer relationship rather than on the executive policies and activities that are set up to foster good relations." - E.F.L. Brec
- "Industrial relations is that part of management which is concerned with the man power of the enterprise- whether machine operator, skilled worker or manager".

- 'Industrial relationship is the composite result of the attitudes and approaches the employers and employees towards each other with regard to planning, supervision, direction and coordination of the activities of an organization with a minimum of human efforts and friction, with an animating sprite of cooperation and with proper regard for the genuine well-being of all the members of the organization."

TEAD AND MATCAL

It is clear from the analysis of the definitions that employment relations are generally called industrial relations. It is a relationship between employer and employees employer and employee and trade unions and employees.

Impact of Industrial Relations on Industrial Peace

An economy organised for planned production and distribution, aiming at the realization of social justice and welfare of the masses, can function effectively only in an atmosphere of industrial peace.

If the twin objectives of rapid national development and increased social justice are to be achieved, there must be harmonious relationship between management and labour.

The impact of good industrial relations on production may be seen from the following facts:

- *Reduces Industrial disputes*: Good industrial relations reduce the industrial disputes. Disputes are reflections of the basic human urges or motivations to secure adequate satisfaction or expression which are fully cured by good industrial relations. Strikes, lock-outs, go slow tactics, gherao and grievances are some of the reflections of industrial unrest which do not spring up in an atmosphere of industrial peace. It helps promoting cooperations and increasing production.
- *High Morale*: Good industrial relations improve the morale of the employees. Employees work with great

zeal with the feeling in mind that the interest of employer and employees is one and the same i.e. to increase production. Every worker feels that he is a co-owner of the industry. The employer in his turn must realise that the gains of industry are not for him alone but they should be showed equally and generously with his workers. In other words, complete unity of the thought and action is the main achievement of industrial peace of workers into the society and their ego is satisfied. It naturally affects production, because a mighty cooperative efforts alone can produce great results.

- *Mental Revolution*: The main object of industrial relations ins a complete mental revolution of workers and employers. The industrial peace lies ultimately in a transformed outlook on the part of both. It is the business of leadership in the ranks of workers employees and government to work out a new relationship in consonance with a spirit of true democracy. Both should think themselves as a partners of the industry and the role of worker in such a partnership should be recognized. On the other hand, workers must recognize employer authority. It will naturally have impact on production because they recognize the interest of each other.
- *New Programmes*: New programmes for workers development are introduced in an atmosphere of peace such as training facilities, labour welfare facilities etc. It increases the efficiency of workers resulting in higher and better production at lower costs.
- *Reduced Wastage*: Good industrial relations are maintained on the basis of cooperation and recognition of each other. It will help increase production. Wastages of man material and machines and reduced to the minimum and thus national interest is protected.

Thus form the discussion it is evident that good industrial relations is the basis of higher production with minimum cost and higher profits. It also results in increased efficiency of workers. New and new projects are introduced for the welfare of he workers and to promote the morale of the people at work.

The conflicts and disputes between employer and employees on any industrial matter are known as industrial disputes.

Industrial Disputes

The disputes between employer and employer both and vitiate the industrial atmosphere and peace. Whether these tactics are successful or unsuccessful, unpleasantness is created between both the parties. The worst result ins the loss of production and decline in natural income. Industrial dispute is defined by *Section 2 (x)* of the *Industrial Disputes Act 1947* as follows:-

Industrial disputes is "Any dispute or difference between the employers and employees, or between employs workmen, or between workmen and workmen, which is connected with the employment or unemployment or the terms of employment or with the conditions of labour of any person:".

There must be following ingredients of an industrial dispute:

- There must be a relationship of employer and employee.
- The worker must be on the roll list of the industry.
- The demands of the workers must have been rejected by the employer.
- The dispute may be between two employers or between two employees.
- The dispute may be connected with employment or terms of employment or with labour conditions of any person.
- The industrial unit must be a going concern. It must not be dead.

The new industrial set-up has given birth to the capitalistic economy which divided the industrial society into two groups of labour and capitalists.

Causes of Industrial Disputes

The interests of these two groups are not common which created industrial disputes.

The main resources of industrial disputed may be classified into four groups:

(i) Economic

(ii) Managerial

(iii) Political

(iv) Others

ECONOMIC CAUSES OF INDUSTRIAL DISPUTES

Really, the most common causes of industrial disputes are economic causes.

These are follows:

- *Wages*: The wage-increase was the prime most cause of dispute both after the first and second world wars. A large number of strikes were organised during this time because of the rise in cost of living. The real wages of the workers declined faster and they were dissatisfied with their present wages and struggled for the improvement in wages. By having a cursory glance on the history of industrial dispute, it becomes clear that cause of most of the industrial disputes was wages.
- *Dearness Allowance and Bonus*: Increase in cost of living was the main cause of the demand of dearness allowance by the workers to equate their wages with the rise of prices. Bonus also play an important role as a cause of industrial dispute. Both the quantum and the method of bonus payment has led to a number of disputes.
- *High Industrial Profits*: During and after the world wars, prices of the commodities went up and the industrialists earned a huge profits. In order to get share in the prosperity of the industry, it naturally led to the resentment on their part. The increased profits also led to the demands of higher wage and

bonus. Now, in the changing world, concept of labour has changed considerably. They think themselves as a partner of the industry and demand their share in the profits.

- *Working Conditions and Working Horus*: The working conditions in Indian industries are not hygienic. There is not ample provision of water, heating, lighting, safety etc. Working hours are also greater. The demand of palatable working conditions and shorter hours of work led to labour disputes.
- *Modernization and Automation of Plant and Machinery*: The attempt at modernization and introduction of automatic machinery to replace labour has been the major cause of disputes of India. Workers go on strike, off and on, to resist rationalization. A strike in cotton textile industry in Kanpur in 1955 for 80 days long is an example of such disputes. Workers in life-insurance corporation went on strike recently against introducing computers in the corporation.
- *Weakness of Trade Unions*: Weaknesses of trade unions encourages the employers to deny certain basic needs of the workers such as medical, education and housing facilities etc. This led to resentment on the part of workers who resorted to direct action.

VISION FOR THE NATIONAL SKILL DEVELOPMENT INITIATIVE IN INDIA

At present the capacity of skill development in India is around 3.1 million persons per year. The 11th Five Year Plan envisions an increase in that capacity to 15 million annually. India has target of creating 500 million skilled workers by 2022. Thus, there is a need for increasing capacity and capability of skill development programmes.

High inclusivity: The skill development initiatives will harness inclusivity and reduce divisions such as male/female, rural/urban, organized/unorganized employment and traditional/contemporary workplace. Dynamic and demand-based system planning: The skill development initiatives support the supply of trained workers who are adjustable dynamically to the changing demands of employment and technologies. This policy will promote excellence and will meet the requirements of knowledge economy. Choice, competition and accountability: The skill development initiative does not discriminate between private or public delivery and places importance on outcomes, users? choice and competition among training providers and their accountability. Policy coordination and coherence: The skill development initiatives support employment generation, economic growth and social development processes.

Skill development policy will be an integral part of comprehensive economic, labour and social policies and programmes. A framework for better coordination among various Ministries, States, industry and other stakeholders will be established. The operational strategies will be adopted: Folding the future in: If we start from our current position, we are likely to extrapolate. Folding the future in allows us to innovate. Innovation is, therefore, an important element of the strategy.

Skills framework must move to a system of equivalence to diplomas and degrees: National Vocational Qualification Framework (NVQF) will be created with an open/flexible system which will permit individuals to accumulate their knowledge and skills, and convert them through testing and certification into higher diplomas and degrees. NVQF will provide quality assured various learning pathways having standards, comparable with any international qualification framework. NVQF will support lifelong learning, continuous upgradation of skills and knowledge.

Skills must be bankable: The process of skill acquisition especially for the poor and needy persons will be made bankable. The effort would be to complement public investment with institutional/ bank finance. Co-created solutions and forging partnerships: We have to accept a very asymmetric India as a starting point. Partnerships will be consciously promoted between Government, industry, local governments, civil society institutions and all potential skill providers. Institutional mechanism and standing platforms will be created to ensure sustainability. Game-changing delivery/innovation: Availability of public institutions above the high school level, after class hours for skill development by the Private Sector, without disturbing the normal working, will be explored. Necessary regulations would be brought in by the local management authority of the particular educational institution.

CORE OPERATING PRINCIPLES

Government financial support must complement private investment: The Central Ministries must focus on areas where private investment in skilled development is unlikely to be available or forthcoming. The Government would aim at useful public-private partnerships. States as key actors: The States being the key actors in Skill Development would set up over arching integrated framework for action for Skill Development through State level Skill Development Missions. Deployment of funds: The funds would be deployed more for activities than for buildings and other hard assets.

However, upgradation of machinery and equipment, teaching and learning aids will be a continuous process. Creation of infrastructure in latest technology, need-based new initiatives, creation of infrastructure in rural, remote and difficult areas will continue.

Focus of modular courses, open architecture and short term courses: With fast changing skills in the labour market, focus would be on short, relevant and effective courses that would get candidates into the workplace. They will be welded through NVQF to maintain dynamism and open to feedback. Separate financing from delivery: Today Government funds are only available for government delivery. National Skill Development Corporation will support private skill development initiatives. Following financing options will be explored:

(a) Link financing to outcomes: Today public and private training is financed largely on inputs viz., number of courses, number of students, faculty, etc. Efforts would be made to move towards Government financing linked to placement ratios and outcomes.

(b) *Focus funding on candidates:* The focus would be on funding the candidates rather than institutions to create choice. This could be structured as a scholarship, skill voucher, outcome based reimbursement, etc. Create infrastructure for on-the-job-training and encourage apprenticeships: The enabling infrastructure for large number of formal apprentices needs to be built that includes modification to the Apprentices Act, 1961. Publicise rating and outcome information on training institutions: A framework of accreditation and infrastructure for information dissemination around measurable criteria on institutions will be created. Ratings of public and private institutions would be put on public domain. Effective assessment and credible certification: Quality assured learning, credible assessment and certification will be developed. This will allow employers to use the certificate as a proxy to fast track job applicants.

Restructure employment exchanges as career guidance centres: Employment Exchanges will be restructured as career guidance centres to channelize candidates into jobs, apprenticeships and training. Expand formal employment: Formal employment is not only fiscally attractive but more amenable to financing innovations. This will require a review of existing State and Central legislations which encourage informal and unorganized employment.

Approach to Deliverables

Diversity of skills: There is a need to identify, catalog and project the range and depth of skills e.g. traditional, industrial-era and post-industrial era skills to understand and present the vast array of skills that individuals can choose from. Talent pool: The ultimate measure is the "500 Million" skilled people. Skill inventory along with its various levels and grades will be created. Employment outcomes Skill training must ensure a job for those who seek it. The placement ratio will be monitored and placed in the public domain by agencies involved in skill training.

THE MISSION STATEMENT, AIMS AND OBJECTIVES

MISSION

The policy envisions the establishment of a National Skill Development Initiative with the following mission: National Skill Development Initiative will empower all individuals through improved skills, knowledge, nationally and internationally recognized qualifications to gain access to decent employment and ensure India's competitiveness in the global market. Aims: The aim of skill development in the country is to support achieving rapid and inclusive growth through: a) Enhancing individuals? employability (wage/ self employment) and ability to adapt to changing technologies and labour market demands. b) Improving productivity and living standards of the people. c) Strengthening competitiveness of the country. d) Attracting investment in skill development. Objectives of National Policy on Skill Development:

The objectives of the national policy on skill development are to:

- Create opportunities for all to acquire skills throughout life, and especially for youth, women and disadvantaged groups.
- Promote commitment by all stakeholders to own skill development initiatives.
- Develop a high-quality skilled workforce/ entrepreneur relevant to current and emerging employment market needs.
- Enable the establishment of flexible delivery mechanisms that respond to the characteristics of a wide range of needs of stakeholders.
- Enable effective coordination between different ministries, the Centre and the States and public and private providers.

Scope of the National Skill Development Policy

The coverage of the National Policy on Skill Development includes the following:

- Institution-based skill development including ITIs/

ITCs/vocational schools/technical schools/ polytechnics/ professional colleges, etc.
- Learning initiatives of sectoral skill development organised by different ministries/departments.
- Formal and informal apprenticeships and other types of training by enterprises
- Training for self-employment/entrepreneurial development
- Adult learning, retraining of retired or retiring employees and lifelong learning
- Non-formal training including training by civil society organizations
- E-learning, web-based learning and distance learning.

Institutional Arrangements

Prime Minister's National Council on Skill Development, under the Chairmanship of Prime Minister has been set up as an apex institution for policy direction and review. The Ministers for Human Resource Development, Finance, Industries, Rural Development, Housing and Urban Poverty Alleviation, Labour and Employment and Micro Small & Medium Enterprises are members. Deputy Chairman, Planning Commission, Chairperson of the National Manufacturing Competitiveness Council, Chairperson of the National Skill Development Corporation and 6 experts in the area of skill development are other members.

Principal Secretary to the Prime Minister is the Member Secretary to the Council. National Skill Development Coordination Board: A National Skill Development Coordination Board has been set up under the Chairmanship of Deputy Chairman, Planning Commission. Secretaries of Ministries of Human Resource Development, Labour and Employment, Rural Development, Housing and Urban Poverty Alleviation and Finance are members.

Chairperson/Chief Executive Officer of the National Skill Development Corporation, Secretaries of four States by rotation, for a period of two years, and three distinguished Academicians/Subject Area Specialists are other members.

Secretary, Planning Commission is Member Secretary of the Board. National Skill Development Corporation: The National Skill Development Corporation is a non-profit company under the Companies Act 1956 with an appropriate governance structure. The head of the Corporation is a person of eminence/ reputed professional in the field of Skill Development.

The Corporation would constitute Sector Skills Councils with following functions:

- Identification of skill development needs including preparing a catalogue of types of skills, range and depth of skills to facilitate individuals to choose from them.
- Development of a sector skill development plan and maintain skill inventory.
- Determining skills/competency standards and qualifications.
- Standardization of affiliation and accreditation process.
- Participation in Affiliation, accreditation, examination and certification.
- Plan and execute Training of Trainers.
- Promotion of academies of excellence.
- Establishment of a well structured sector specific Labour Market Information System (LMIS) to assist planning and delivery of training.

National Council for Vocational Training

(NCVT) NCVT will be strengthened and re-engineered with a broader mandate and representation.

The main functions include:

a) Design, development and maintenance of NVQF which inter alia includes:
   - Setting up a framework for competency standards, structure of courses, credit structure, accumulation and certification.
   - Setting up a framework for affiliation and accreditation of institutions.
   - Quality control mechanism.

- Labour market information system and dissemination of information at the national level.
- Monitoring and evaluation on the effectiveness and efficiency of national skill development efforts through appropriate reporting and communication mechanism.

SOCIAL PARTNERS IN SKILL DEVELOPMENT

Partnerships will be consciously promoted between Government, industry, trade unions, local governments, civil society institutions and all skill providers. It will also include, training providers, professional societies, Self Help Groups, Cooperatives and NGOs/civil society institutions. Creation of an institutional mechanism and regular consultation with stake holders will form the corner stone of Skill Development Initiative.

Roles and Responsibilities of Stake Holders

Roles and Responsibilities of Government (Central /State or Local Level)

- Setting up priority and policy planning-statistics gathering
- Providing regulatory framework and enabling environment for stake holders.
- Devising financing mechanism, reward and promotional framework.
- Capacity building of social partners.
- Setting up of monitoring, evaluation and dissemination of information.
- Facilitating international cooperation.
- Setting up of a qualification framework and quality assurance mechanism.
- Preparation of work plans to meet sector specific skill sets.

Roles and Responsibilities of Employers/Industries

- Owning Skill Development activities.

- Identification of competencies and setting up of competency standards,
- Skill demand analysis and curriculum development.
- Facilitating training of trainers.
- Delivery of training, monitoring and evaluation.
- Participation in examination and certification.
- Participation in affiliation and accreditation process
- Sharing of work place experience, machinery and equipment.
- Support by way of physical, financial and human resources.
- Facilitating employment of trained graduates.
- Supporting skill development initiatives of other public and private agencies.
- Implementing apprenticeship schemes.
- Investing in skill development activities.

Roles and Responsibilities of Trade Unions

- Assist in developing competency standards.
- Assist in course designing, examination and certification.
- Raising awareness about the benefit of training, skill development plans and activities among the workers
- Promote skill upgradation and lifelong learning among the workers.
- Running special skill development institutes for skill development of workers.
- Promoting investment on skill development among the employers.
- Facilitate improving status of VET trained graduates.

Roles and Responsibilities of Civil Society Organizations

- Raising awareness about skill development plans and activities among the public.
- Facilitate improving status of VET trained graduates.
- Implementing skill development programmes of the Government.

- Assist in developing competency standards.
- Assist in course designing, examination and certification.
- Promote lifelong learning among the public.
- Promoting dignity of labour among the public.
- Sharing experience of learning with others.

EXPANSION OF OUTREACH, EQUITY AND ACCESS

The current capacity for skill development in the country is 3.1 million. India has set a target of skilling 500 million people by 2022 to meet the challenges of India @ 75.

Expansion of outreach Skill Development Initiative needs considerable amount of expansion of capacity and innovative delivery approaches and Public Private Partnerships.

A few of them are:

- Innovative approaches will be adopted to raise the capacity of the system extensively over a limited period.
- Incentive mechanisms will be developed to encourage the private sector to participate in skill development.
- The expansion of public training institutions will be promoted, particularly, in rural, border, hilly and difficult areas, where the private sector may find it difficult to invest.
- Innovative delivery models such decentralized delivery, mobile training, distance learning, e-learning and web-based learning will be used.
- Skill development centres at village and block level will be promoted to provide skill development opportunity as well as to act as one-stop kiosks with information

On the local labour market/employment, vocational learning opportunities and support schemes. f) Panchayats, municipalities and other local bodies will be involved in skill development and employment generation at the local level in collaboration with SHGs, cooperatives and NGOs. g) The coverage of vocations will be expanded. h) At present about

23,800 establishments are covered under the Apprenticeship Training Scheme imparting training to 2.58 lakh apprentices. Over the next five years, this will be increased to about 1 lakh establishments covering about 1 million apprentices. The existing Apprentices Act, 1961 will be revisited to meet desired target.

Equity and Access

- Equal access to skill development is essential for all social groups particularly women and disadvantaged part of society, to help them in securing decent employment and moving out of poverty. Removing barriers to access and addressing their specific needs are key elements in achieving inclusive growth.
- Entry barriers such as educational qualification, transportation, loss of wages, language etc. will be addressed. While enhancing the opportunity of skill development for all, entry assessments will be deployed to channelize people with different profiles and needs into appropriate skill development programmes.
- The effort will be combined with a major initiative in raising awareness among the target groups about the benefit of skill development, employment and learning opportunities and also about support schemes that enable them to participate in training.
- In addition to vocational skills, the provision of soft (or life) skills - including basic literacy, numerous, occupational safety and health, hygiene, basic labour rights, team work and confidence building - will be made as an integral component of the curricula. This will also help in empowerment of vulnerable groups.

Vocational Training for Women Skill development for employability will be used as an agent of change in promoting women's employment. Women face a multitude of barriers in accessing skills and productive employment, remaining on the job due to effect of globalization or otherwise and advancing to higher level jobs, as well as returning to the labour market after a period of absence spent, for example, in raising children.

- A policy of non-discrimination will be pursued vigourously to provide equal access for women to skill development and employment.
- This Policy will aim to raise women's participation to at least 30% by the end of the 11th Plan.
- Proactive measures that overcome barriers and facilitate participation, such as hostels for women, scholarships, transport, training materials and loans, will be made available on a large scale.
- The Women's Vocational Training Programme will be expanded and the institutional network providing training facilities exclusively for women, so that they can obtain skills with high wage and self-employment potential, will be greatly expanded.
- In order to promote skills and employability of women, the sectors which employ a large number of women will be identified. These may include construction, home-
  based traditional crafts or piece rate work, financial and health service as well as agricultural sectors.
- Gender stereotyping in vocational courses will be eliminated to encourage women's participation in non-traditional occupations, including existing and emerging technological fields.

REGIONAL IMBALANCE OPPORTUNITIES

- Infrastructure and programmes for skill development are particularly scarce in rural and difficult areas and thus the problem of access to training is most acute in these areas. Specially the women are increasingly the main workers in rural households, as their husbands migrate but often equipped with only traditional and outdated skills and knowledge.
- Skill development in rural areas contributes to improve productivity and working conditions in the agricultural sector while at the same time enabling

rural workers, particularly young people, to access emerging employment opportunities beyond the agricultural sector.

- The outreach and quality of skill development in rural areas will be improved so as to enable rural workers to acquire and upgrade technologies; improve linkages to value chains; increase agricultural production; expand access to market and engage in off-farm activities which can generate supplemental income.
- In view of the limited training infrastructure, a range of infrastructure facilities, including schools, community centres and local government buildings, will be utilized as training venues. Institutes for entrepreneurship training such as Rural Development & Self-employment Training Institutes (RUDSETI) will be further promoted. The Government itself will set up public institutions and will also promote the establishment of private sector training institutions through a package of suitably designed incentives such as provision of land and financial assistance. The convergence with national employment programmes, such as National Rural Employment Guaranteed Scheme (NREGS), will be promoted as an opportunity for imparting skills training in rural areas. Training facilities need to be updated regularly so as to meet changing demands.
- Village- or block-based skill development centres will be set up to serve the needs of local communities. Facilitated by the district offices and panchayats, these skill development centres will play a pivotal role in identifying local employment opportunities and providing, or organizing, adequate training and post-training support according to the specific needs of local areas. The centres will also function as information centres for training and employment opportunities as well as various support schemes. These efforts will be combined with the creation of

incentive mechanisms in motivating, particularly youth to participate in training and removal of other barriers in accessing training.

- Various mobile training arrangements will be deployed to reach out to remote and difficult areas.
- Skill development for self-employment will be an important component in these skill development efforts in rural areas. Post-training support, including mentoring for access to markets, credit and appropriate technologies, is an important part of skill development strategy for self-employment.
- Training modules will incorporate specific needs of target groups, e.g. literacy, the level of education and the local language. The delivery of training will be flexible in terms of hours and duration to encourage participation, particularly among women.
- In general, there is a regional imbalance in training opportunities and some parts of the country are quite deficient in skill development institutions. In order to provide more equitable access across the country, special efforts will be mounted to establish training facilities in deficient regions.

Disadvantaged Groups

- The reservations applicable to these groups will be strictly enforced, with appropriate gender composition.
- Existing schemes for benefiting these groups will be reviewed, strengthened and made more effective.
- Efforts will be made to mobilize capabilities and expertise of civil society organizations.
- New innovative schemes and measures will also be devised to ensure full and effective participation by these groups, as well as the accrual of real benefits from skill development initiatives.

Minorities

- Skill development opportunities for minority groups will be expanded, particularly in Minority

Concentrated Areas (MCAs).

- Existing schemes benefiting these groups will be reviewed, strengthened and made more effective.
- Efforts will be made to mobilize capabilities and expertise of civil society organizations.
- Formalization of non-formal skill acquisition and transfer will also be promoted in traditional art and craft sectors.

Persons with Disabilities

- The current level of participation of persons with disabilities in skill programmes is very low, despite guidelines of reserving 3% of the seats for them. The guidelines apply only to the government sector.
- People with varying degrees of physical and mental disabilities will be provided with appropriate adjustment training and skills training to bring them in the economic mainstream and make them productive citizens.
- This Policy aims to expand the facilities for people with disabilities and to provide reasonable accommodation that enables them to access the facilities through suitable transport and building designs.
- The number of Vocational Rehabilitation Centres will be doubled in the 11th Plan and expanded further in subsequent Plans. Similar efforts will also be made at the State level to improve access and outreach.
- Training will be integrated with efforts to secure appropriate employment opportunities. Programmes of public awareness and community participation will be strengthened to promote demand for vocational training by people with disabilities as well as to facilitate their inclusion in the labour market.

The School Drop-outs and Child Labour

- School education would be strengthened to reduce the school drop outs. The quality of school education will influence the effectiveness of skill development programme as a whole. This will lay solid foundation for young people to acquire employable skills and engage in continuous skill upgradation throughout their working life.

- School education will be used as a tool to increase vocational awareness among the young people.
- School drop-outs (leaving the schools before completing XII standard), child labour and out-of-school youth need to be given alternative education coupled with skill development opportunities to bring them into the economic and social mainstream.
- Short term, market oriented, demand-driven programmes will provide a flexible delivery framework suited to the characteristics and circumstances of the target group.
- Multi-skilling, multi-entry and exit, and linkages to skill upgradation opportunities in the future, will characterize such programmes. The scheme of Modular Employable Skills (i.e. short-term employable skills) will be expanded greatly to cater to the large size of the group.
- Formal educational requirements in accessing training will be reviewed in order to facilitate easy access.

Economically Challenged: Persons Below Poverty Line

- Skill development for employability is an important strategy in the fight against poverty. The poor will have a priority claim and easy access to opportunities for skill development.
- This Policy aims at mitigating the impact of these economic barriers at different stages, as well as actively promote access of the poor to educational and skill development opportunities through specially designed schemes and measures. Such measures as special coaching for competing in

admission tests, provision of non-formal skill development opportunities and the expanded provision of scholarships, books and soft-loans will be developed and implemented.

- Efforts will be made to better integrate skill development into broader poverty reduction programmes and to strengthen the existing skill development components of such programmes.

QUALITY AND RELEVANCE

Quality and relevance of skill development are key to India's global competitiveness as well as improving an individual's access to decent employment. For enterprises to compete in the global economy, the quality of training must reach world standards and be relevant to the needs of national and international markets. To increase the relevance with future employment market including promotion of self employment, soft skills and entrepreneurship skills will be made integral part of skill development. The demographic advantage that the country enjoys, coupled with prospects of global shortages in skills as the world population ages, means that the country could be supplying skills to the world.

Quality Assurance is Based on Five Key Functions

- Validation of Qualifications for ensuring that qualifications reflect market needs and workplace requirements and are expressed in the form of competencies with clear assessment criteria;
- Validation of Training Process for ensuring that proper tools, techniques, methodologies and material, as suggested in the curriculum/standards are used by the resource persons;
- Quality Assured Assessment of Learners for ensuring that assessment is based on national standards (competencies) and uses valid and reliable assessment methods;
- Accreditation of Training Providers and Training

Institutions for ensuring that training is delivered by competent and qualified trainers in well-resourced and managed institutions;

- Research and Information for linking the supply of skilled workers to trends in well-researched Labour Market Information (LMI) covering both the organised and unorganised sectors of the economy.

The objective of enforcing quality and relevance in skill development will be realised through improving infrastructure, improving quality of trainer and developing National Vocational Qualification Framework.

Quality of Infrastructure

- Extensive use of Information & Communication Technology will be promoted for learning or increasing the impact of learning.
- Optimum use of existing physical infrastructure will be ensured in multiple shifts or otherwise.
- Industries will be encouraged to provide their spare capacity to supplement skill development activities.
- Physical infrastructure will be created, expanded and upgraded according to skill requirement of specific sectors of economy.

Quality of Trainer

- Innovative ways of recruiting trainers will be adopted including the employment of former trainees who have gained workplace experience and of practitioners of a craft, trained as master craft persons.
- Innovative skill development schemes, in which trainees acquire theoretical learning at the institution while obtaining practical skills in the workplace, will be devised.
- Retired employees mainly from defence forces will be retrained to meet the requirement of trainers.
- Award and incentive mechanisms, including reward and career progression systems, will be reviewed and institutionalized to improve the status of trainers.

- A system of granting Accredited Trainer Status for a limited period, to all vocational trainers of programmes, leading to National Vocational Qualifications will be developed.
- Special efforts will be made to improve the gender balance among trainers.

NATIONAL VOCATIONAL QUALIFICATIONS FRAMEWORK

To stimulate and support reforms in skills development and to facilitate nationally standardised and acceptable, international comparability of qualifications, a "National Vocational Qualifications Framework" will be established. All the existing Institutions/Councils/Boards under different Ministries, involved in skill development will be encouraged to follow National Vocational Qualification Framework.

This framework will have the following features:

- Competency based qualifications and certification on the basis of nationally agreed standards and criteria;
- Certification for learning achievement and qualification;
- A range of national qualification levels - based on criteria with respect to responsibility, complexity of activities, and transferability of competencies;
- The avoidance of duplication and overlapping of qualifications while assuring the inclusion of all training needs;
- Modular character where achievement can be made in small steps and accumulated for gaining recognizable qualification;
- Quality Assurance regime that would promote the portability of skills and labour market mobility;
- Lifelong learning through an improved skill recognition system; recognition of prior learning whether in formal, non-formal or informal arrangements;
- Open and flexible system which will permit

competent individuals to accumulate their knowledge and skill through testing & certification into higher diploma and degree;

- Different learning pathways - academic and vocational - that integrate formal and non-formal learning, notably learning in the workplace, and that offer vertical mobility from vocational to academic learning;
- Guidance for individuals in their choice of training and career planning;
- Comparability of general educational and vocational qualifications at appropriate levels;
- Nationally agreed framework of affiliation and accreditation of institutions.
- Multiple certification agencies/institutions will be encouraged within NVQF.

LABOUR MARKET INFORMATION SYSTEMS

- Improving the relevance and reducing skill mismatch of skill development requires establishment of Labour Market Information System (LMIS) and Human Resource Planning (HRP) for the reliable and realistic assessment of economic trends and labour market needs.
- Sector specific LMIS will be established at national and state levels, and area specific ones at local levels with the help of Sector Skill Councils (under National Skill Development Corporation) to undertake labour market analysis.
- Human Resource Planning exercises will be undertaken to gauge the anticipated supply and demand of skilled workers by different skill levels, economic sectors and geographical areas, over different periods.
- The information so generated by the LMIS and HRP exercises will be collated and disseminated widely to government, employers, training providers, trainees and prospective trainees at national, state

and local levels, to enable them to take appropriate decisions.

- NCVT will be responsible for dissemination of information at the national level with inputs from SSCs and State Governments.
- Employment Exchanges will be strengthened and upgraded under the National Employment Service to provide counselling, guidance and placement services to the
employment seekers. They will also channel the candidates into jobs, apprenticeship and training. Efforts will be made to expand formal employment.

SKILL DEVELOPMENT FOR THE UNORGANISED SECTOR

Approximately 93 per cent of the country's workforce is in the unorganized sector. The sector cuts across all economic activities and includes rural and urban areas. It contributes to about 60 per cent of the country's GDP. Strengthening the skill base of the unorganized sector will improve productivity, working conditions, labour rights, social security and living standards.

Separate institutional mechanism will be explored which will interalia plan, implement and monitor the skill development efforts for the unorganised sector. The mode of informal apprenticeship and learning will be recognized and accommodated in the NVQF to help in horizontal and vertical mobility.

Target Groups The target groups in the unorganized sector include own-account workers, workers and apprentices in micro enterprises; unpaid family workers; casual labourers; home-based workers; peripatetic workers and migrant labourers; out of school youth and adults in need of skills; farmers and artisans in rural areas, among others.

In order to encourage participation in skill development, entry barriers such as educational qualification, transportation, loss of wages, problem of language, etc. will be suitably addressed.

- Various avenues/institutions including schools and public/private training institutions/civil society organizations/NGOs etc. will be encouraged to conduct skill development programmes for the unorganised sector.
- Mobile training vans will also be deployed in rural and remote areas where training infrastructure is awfully deficient.
- Skill development centres will conduct skill development programmes primarily to support services and unorganised sector.
- Public training institutions will be given greater managerial and academic autonomy to design and offer programmes that meet the requirements of local economy and specific target groups.
- Flexible delivery strategy and patterns that suit the needs of the target groups, such as part/full time and on/off site training, will be adopted.
- Training will be predominantly short-term to encourage participation.
- Arrangements will be made for the testing and certification of skills acquired in non-formal and informal arrangements. These certificates will be integrated with NVQF.

Informal Apprenticeship

- Skill development programmes will be devised in existing/traditional skills and knowledge. Mechanisms will be evolved to upgrade them into modern skill areas.
- Skills of local trainers will be upgraded in modern techniques, technologies and pedagogy. They will be trained and developed into master craftsmen. Opportunities for linking these arrangements to formal training institutions will be explored to extend expertise, pedagogical support and tools & equipment.
- Dual-type apprenticeships will be encouraged.

- Social protection mechanism for apprentices will be devised. Special efforts will be made to eliminate child labour, to improve access for girls, people with disabilities and other vulnerable groups.

Literacy and Soft Skills

Skill development initiatives for the unorganized sector will include a definite component on literacy, basic education and soft skills .

Skill Development for Self-employment

- The focus will be given to entrepreneurship skill development for the unorganized sector.
- Institutes for entrepreneurship development, technology incubation centres and other such institutional arrangements will be utilized to support successful adoption of entrepreneurship of unorganized sector workers.

Lifelong Learning and Recognition of Prior Learning

- Competency standards and certification systems will be developed for unorganized sector work and incorporated in the national testing and certification system.
- Mechanisms will be developed for vocational counselling and career guidance;
- Information regarding employment trends and training opportunities will also be provided to motivate young people and workers to acquire and continuously upgrade their skills and knowledge.

Replication of Successful Models

Various successful models have been tried in India and around the world.

In designing skill development strategies and programmes for the unorganised sector, successful models will be studied and adopted to suit local conditions.

FINANCING SKILL DEVELOPMENT

Skill development brings return to the individual, the employing enterprise and the economy as a whole. Therefore, all stakeholders, the Government both at Centre and States, the enterprise - public and private, and the direct beneficiary - the individual, would share the burden of mobilizing financial or in-kind resources for skill development.

To fulfil the mandate envisaged in this policy apart from adequate central outlay, the Planning Commission will also provide a specific budgetary provision for skill development in the State plans. In addition, private sector investment in skill development will be encouraged through innovative methods.

A National Skill Development Corporation (NSDC) has been established with Central Government commitment of Rs. 1,000 crore. Rs. 15,000 crore is envisaged to be generated from other Governments, public sector entities, private sector, bilateral and multilateral sources.

RESPONDING TO THE FUTURE

Occupational patterns are changing; new jobs and job titles, job enlargement, job enrichment, and new flexible work arrangements are emerging. Employment demands are shifting towards higher skill categories. 8.1.1 It is imperative, therefore, for India to move up the skill-ladder and produce a larger number of people with higher education and generic training for new types of knowledge work, both in high skill services and high technology industrial production. Knowledge professionals will need support from middle-skilled workers in new knowledge and technology areas. The skill development system will need to meet this challenge. The response time is limited as the rate of change is high and accelerating.

Promoting Excellence

To promote excellence, a significant number of well performing institutions will be assisted to develop into institutions of excellence. These institutions will be generously resourced, equipped with internationally comparable facilities and high quality faculty and able to offer high quality programmes in current and emerging technology areas. These institutions will be networked with a number of training institutions in their vicinity and serve as lead institutions in supporting their development.

EXPERIMENTATION, INNOVATION AND RESEARCH

- Policy encourages the creation of a National Skill Development Initiative that is highly dynamic and nimble-footed. This will always be extrapolating the future requirements.

  It will have to be constantly responsive to changes in the immediate as well as global environments, learn from them, and experiment with new approaches and structures. A culture of innovation will drive the future system.
- Research will be a key strategy for managing change and benefiting from it. Since experimentation and innovation flourishes in a vibrant and self-confident environment, flexibility and operational autonomy will be extended to deserving institutions.
- Research in international developments and in organizational practices and pedagogical approaches will be an on-going activity. Standing institutional arrangements will be established for the purpose and research will be funded both in these arrangements and in outside research institutions.

Policy Review

Skill development is placed in a highly dynamic environment and thus it is imperative that this Policy undergoes a periodic review and target revision to maintain its relevance. 8.4.2 The National Policy on Skill Development will be reviewed every five years and revised appropriately to take account of progress in implementation and emerging trends in the national and international environment. Research and the promotion of good practices are vital activities that will enable this Policy and the Skill Development Initiative to meet emerging needs.

The implementation of the Policy will be continuously monitored to provide the basis for review.

Outcomes of Skills Development Policy

- Demand driven system guided by labour market signals thereby reducing skills mismatch: Labour Market Information and Human Resource Planning
- Expansion of outreach using established as well as innovative approaches.
- National Vocational Qualifications Framework which will interalia include opportunities for horizontal and vertical mobility between general and technical education, Recognition and certification of competencies irrespective of mode of learning.
- System to deliver "competencies? In line with nationally and internationally recognised standards.
- Focus on new emerging occupations
- Life long learning- focus both on pre-service and in - service training
- Equity consideration - adequate participation of women, disabled persons and disadvantaged groups including economically backward & minorities- enhancing their access to training; improving employability and increasing employment opportunities
- Stress on research, planning and monitoring
- Involvement of social partners- responsibility for management and financing of the system would be shared with all stakeholders and provide greater space for Public Private Partnership.
- Promoting excellence
- Use of modern training technologies including distance learning, e-learning, web based learning etc.
- Skill upgradation of trainers, their quality assurance, and improvement of status.

GOVERNMENT OF INDIA

Ministry of Labour and Employment

National Policy On Safety, Health And Environment At Work Place

- Preamble
  - The Constitution of India provide detailed provisions for the rights of the citizens and also lays down the Directive Principles of State Policy which set an aim to which the activities of the state are to be guided.
  - These Directive Principles provide
    a. For securing the health and strength of employees, men and women;
    b. That the tender age of children are not abused;
    c. That citizens are not forced by economic necessity to enter avocations unsuited to their age or strength;
    d. Just and humane conditions of work and maternity relief are provided; and
    e. That the Government shall take steps, by suitable legislation or in any other way, to secure the participation of employee in the management of undertakings, establishments or other organisations engaged in any industry.
- On the basis of these Directive Principles as well as international instruments, Government is committed to regulate all economic activities for management of safety and health risks at workplaces and to provide measures so as to ensure safe and healthy working conditions for every working man and woman in the nation. Government recognizes that safety and health of workers has a positive impact on productivity and economic and social development. Prevention is an integral part of economic activities as high safety and health standard

at work is as important as good business performance for new as well as existing industries.

- The formulation of policy, priorities and strategies in occupational safety, health and environment at work places, is undertaken by national authorities in consultation with social partners for fulfilling such objectives. A critical role is played by the Government and the social partners, professional safety and health organizations in ensuring prevention and in also providing treatment, support and rehabilitation services. Government of India firmly believes that without safe, clean environment as well as healthy working conditions, social justice and economic growth cannot be achieved and that safe and healthy working environment is recognized as a fundamental human right. Education, training, consultation and exchange of information and good practices are essential for prevention and promotion of such measures.
- The changing job patterns and working relationships, the rise in self employment, greater sub-contracting, outsourcing of work, homework and the increasing number of employees working away from their establishment, pose problems to management of occupational safety and health risks at workplaces. New safety hazards and health risks will be appearing along with the transfer and adoption of new technologies. In addition, many of the well known conventional hazards will continue to be present at the workplace till the risks arising from exposure to these hazards are brought under adequate control. While advancements in technology have minimized or eliminated some hazards at workplace, new risks can emerge in their place which needs to be addressed.
- Particular attention needs to be paid to the hazardous operations and of employees in risk prone conditions such as migrant employees and various vulnerable

groups of employees arising out of greater mobility in the workforce with more people working for a number of employers, either consecutively or simultaneously.

- The increasing use of chemicals, exposure to physical, chemical and biological agents with hazard potential unknown to people; the indiscriminate use of agro-chemicals including pesticides, agricultural machineries and equipment; industries with major accident risks; effects of computer controlled technologies and alarming influence of stress at work in many modern jobs pose serious safety, health and environmental risks. The fundamental purpose of this National Policy on Safety, Health and Environment at workplace, is not only to eliminate the incidence of work related injuries, diseases, fatalities, disaster and loss of national assets and ensuring achievement of a high level of occupational safety, health and environment performance through proactive approaches but also to enhance the well-being of the employee and society, at large. The necessary changes in this area will be based on a coordinated national effort focused on clear national goals and objectives.
- Every Ministry or Department may work out their detailed policy relevant to their working environment as per the guidelines on the National Policy.

Goals

The Government firmly believes that building and maintaining national preventive safety and health culture is the need of the hour. With a view to develop such a culture and to improve the safety, health and environment at work place, it is essential to meet the following requirements:

Providing a statutory framework on Occupational Safety and Health in respect of all sectors of industrial activities including the construction sector, designing suitable control systems of compliance, enforcement and incentives for better compliance. Providing administrative and technical support services. Providing a system of incentives to employers and employees to achieve higher health and safety standards Providing for a system of non-financial incentives for improvement in safety and health.

Establishing and developing the research and development capability in emerging areas of risk and providing for effective control measures. Focusing on prevention strategies and monitoring performance through improved data collection system on work related injuries and diseases.

Developing and providing required technical manpower and knowledge in the areas of safety, health and environment at workplaces in different sectors. Promoting inclusion of safety, health and environment, improvement at workplaces as an important component in other relevant national policy documents. Including safety and occupational health as an integral part of every operation.

Objectives

The policy seeks to bring the national objectives into focus as a step towards improvement in safety, health and environment at workplace.

The objectives are to achieve:

- Continuous reduction in the incidence of work related injuries, fatalities, diseases, disasters and loss of national assets.
- Improved coverage of work related injuries, fatalities and diseases and provide for a more comprehensive data base for facilitating better performance and monitoring.
- Continuous enhancement of community awareness regarding safety, health and environment at workplace related areas.
- Continually increasing community expectation of workplace health and safety standards.
- Improving safety, health and environment at workplace by creation of "green jobs" contributing to sustainable enterprise development.

Action Programme

The following action programme is drawn up and where necessary time bound action programme would be initiated, namely:

Enforcement

- By providing an effective enforcement machinery as well as suitable provisions for compensation and rehabilitation of affected persons;
- By effectively enforcing all applicable laws and regulations concerning safety, health and environment at workplaces in all economic activities through an adequate and effective labour inspection system;
- By establishing suitable schemes for subsidy and provision of loans to enable effective implementation of the policy;
- By ensuring that employers, employees and others have separate but complementary responsibilities and rights with respect to achieving safe and healthy working conditions;
- By amending expeditiously existing laws relating to safety, health and environment and bring them in line with the relevant international instruments;
- By monitoring the adoption of national standards through regulatory authorities;
- By facilitating the sharing of best practices and experiences between national and international regulatory authorities;
- By developing new and innovative enforcement methods including financial incentives that encourage and ensure improved workplace performance;
- By making an enabling legislation on Safety, Health and Environment at Workplaces;
- By setting up safety and health committees wherever deemed appropriate;

National Standards

By developing appropriate standards, codes of practices and manuals on safety, health and environment for uniformity at the national level in all economic activities consistent with international standards and implementation by the stake holders in true spirit; By ensuring stakeholders awareness of and accessibility to applicable policy, documents, codes, regulations and standards;

Compliance

- By encouraging the appropriate Government to assume the fullest responsibility for the administration and enforcement of occupational safety, health and environment at workplace, provide assistance in identifying their needs and responsibilities in the area of safety, health and environment at workplace, to develop plans and programmes in accordance with the provisions of the applicable Acts and to conduct experimental and demonstration projects in connection therewith;
- By calling upon the cooperation of social partners in the supervision of application of legislations and regulations relating to safety, health and environment at work place;
- By continuous improvement of Occupational Safety and Health by systems approach to the management of Occupational Safety and Health including developing guidance on Occupational Safety and Health management systems, strengthening voluntary actions, including mechanisms for self-regulatory concept and establishing auditing mechanisms which can test and authenticate occupational safety and health management systems;
- By providing specific measures to prevent catastrophes, and to coordinate and specify the actions to be taken at different levels, particularly in the industrial zones with high potential risks;
- By recognising the best safety and health practices and providing facilitation for their adoption.

By providing adequate penal provisions as deterrent for violation of laws for the time being in force;

- By encouraging all concerned to adopt and commit to "Responsible Care" and / or "Corporate Social Responsibility" to improve safety, health and environment at workplace performance;
- By ensuring a suitable accreditation machinery to recognise institutions, professionals and services relating to safety, health and environment at workplace for uniformity and greater coverage as also authenticating safe management system;
- By encouraging employers to ensure occupational safety and health management systems, establish them in efficient manner to improve workplace safety and health;
- By specifically focusing on such occupational diseases like pneumoconiosis and silicosis; developing a framework for its prevention and control as well as develop technical standards and guidelines for the same;
- By promoting safe and clean technology and progressively replacing materials hazardous to human health and environment;

Awareness

- By increasing awareness on safety, health and environment at workplace through appropriate means;
- By providing forums for consultations with employers' representatives, employees representatives and community on matters of national concern relating to safety, health and environment at work place with the overall objective of creating awareness and enhancing national productivity;
- By encouraging joint labour-management efforts to preserve, protect and promote national assets and to eliminate injuries and diseases arising out of employment;
- By raising community awareness through structured, audience specific approach;

- By continuously evaluating the impact of such awareness and information initiatives;
- By maximizing gains from the substantial investment in awareness campaigns by sharing experience and learning;
- By suitably incorporating teaching inputs on safety, health and environment at work place in schools, technical, medical, professional and vocational courses and distance education programme;
- By securing good liaison arrangements with the International organisations;
- By providing medical criteria wherever necessary which will assure insofar as practicable that no employee will suffer diminished health, functional capacity, or life expectancy as a result of his work place activities and that in the event of such occupational diseases having been contracted, is suitably compensated;
- By providing practical guidance and encouraging employers and employees in their efforts to reduce the incidence of occupational safety and health risks at their places of employment and to impress upon employers and employees to institute new programmes and to improve existing programmes for providing safe and healthful working conditions, requiring employers to ensure that workers and their representatives are consulted, trained, informed and involved in all measures related to their safety and health at work;

Research and Development

- By providing for research in the field of safety, health and environment at workplace, including the social and psychological factors involved, and by developing innovative methods, techniques including computer aided Risk Assessment Tools, and approaches for dealing with safety, health and environment at workplace problems which will help in establishing standards;

- By exploring ways to discover latent diseases, establishing causal connections between diseases and work environmental conditions, updating list of occupational diseases and conducting other research relating to safety, health and environmental problems at workplace;
- By establishing research priorities as per national requirements; exploring partnerships and improving communications with various national and international research bodies;
- By ensuring a coordinated research approach and an optimal allocation of resources in Occupational Safety and Health sector for such purposes;

Occupational Safety and Health Skills Development

- By building upon advances already made through employer and employee initiative for providing safe and healthy working conditions;
- By providing for training programmes to increase the number and competence of personnel engaged in the field of occupational safety, health and environment at workplace;
- By providing information and advice, in an appropriate manner, to employers and employees organisations, with a view to eliminating hazards or reducing them as far as practicable;.
- By establishing occupational health services aimed at protection and promotion of health of employee and improvement of working conditions and by providing employee access to these services in different sectors of economic activities;
- By integrating health and safety into vocational, professional and labour related training programmes as also management training including small business practices;
- By adopting Occupational Safety and Health training curricula in workplace and industry programmes;

Data Collection

- By compiling statistics relating to safety, health and environment at work places, prioritising key issues for action, conducting national studies or surveys or projects through governmental and non-governmental organisations;
- By reinforcing and sharing of information and data on national occupational safety, health and environment at work place information amongst different stake holders through a national network system on Occupational Safety and Health;
- By extending data coverage relevant to work-related injury and disease, including measures of exposure, and occupational groups that are currently excluded, such as self-employed people;
- By extending data systems to allow timely reporting and provision of information;
- By developing the means for improved access to information;

Review

An initial review and analysis shall be carried out to ascertain the current status of safety, health and environment at workplace and building a national Occupational Safety and Health profile. National Policy and the action programme shall be reviewed at least once in five years or earlier if felt necessary to assess relevance of the national goals and objectives.

CEASE

There is a need to develop close involvement of social partners to meet the challenges ahead in the assessment and control of workplace risks by mobilising local resources and extending protection to such working population and vulnerable groups where social protection is not adequate. Government stands committed to review the National Policy on Safety, Health and Environment at Workplace and legislations through tripartite consultation, improve enforcement, compilation and analysis of statistics; develop special programmes for hazardous operations and other focus sectors, set up training mechanisms, create nationwide awareness, arrange for the mobilisation of available resources and expertise.

The National Policy and programme envisages total commitment and demonstration by all concerned stake holders such as Government and social partners. Our goals and objectives will be that through dedicated and concerted efforts consistent with the requirements of safety, health and environment at work place and thereby improving the quality of work and working life.

14

Employee Training and Development: Reasons and Benefit

EMPLOYMENT SCENARIO

APPROACH TO EMPLOYMENT IN ECONOMIC PLANNING

Planning in India focused at realising a high rate of growth of output in the long term. A basic assumption was that shortage of capital goods in relation to employable persons constituted a fundamental constraint on growth in the economy. Therefore the planning process made no attempt to define an independent employment strategy; the focus on economic growth was viewed as essential for improving the employment situation. Initially, labour force expansion was not seen as a problem to be contended with. Thus, in the Five Year Plans, the generation of employment was viewed as part of the process of development and not as a goal in conflict with, or to be pursued independently of economic development

Employment Planning in India

The approach to tackling the task of unemployment has varied from time to time. In the initial years of planning reliance was placed primarily on the expectations of a rapid industrial development and control of population. These expectations did not materialise and it was observed that the rate of growth of employment was generally much lower than the growth rate of GDP of the economy. Moreover the classical study of Dandekar and Rath (1969) showed a continuously increasing trend of people falling below the poverty line (BPL). Seasons of severe draught and failure of monsoons exposed large parts of population to extensive deprivations. Successive plans, strategies, policies and programmes were, therefore, redesigned to bring about a special focus on employment generation as a specific objective.

The seventies and eighties saw the emergence of special schemes like NREP, RLEGP to provide wage employment through public works programmes and schemes to promote self employment and entrepreneurship through provision of assets, skills and other support to the unemployed and the poor. While employment levels expanded steadily during the seventies and eighties, the rate of growth of employment continued to lag behind that of the labour force.

Unemployment among the educated showed a rising trend. Another feature of the employment situation is the sizeable proportion of the employed working at low levels of the productivity and income. The eighties exposed the weakness in the then ongoing strategies of expanding public sector irrespective of competition.

Employment and Unemployment Scenario in India

In India, due to the agrarian sector with seasonal operations time disposition and availability for work have been the criteria for measuring employment. The accepted method of measuring employment is the usual status. Reliable estimates of employment/unemployment are generated through National Sample Surveys conducted once in five years by National Sample Survey Organisation (NSSO).

In order to capture the complexities of the employment situation in India, the estimates of employment and unemployment by NSSO are derived on three concepts, Usual Status (US), Current Weekly Status (CWS) and Current Daily Status (CDS) as per the recommendation of "Dantwala Committee" set up by the Planning Commission in 1968. The three concepts are based on three different reference periods for ascertaining the activity status of a person. Under the Usual

Status concept, the reference period is one year and activity status of a person as employed, unemployed or out of labour force is determined on the basis of activity pursued by him during the year. On the CWS criterion, a person is considered as employed or unemployed if he has worked or has not worked though was available for work, respectively, even for one hour during the week.

Under the CDS approach, the unit of classification is half a day. In this approach the person days are distributed by activity category during an average week. Considering Principal as well as Subsidiary activities the concept of Usual Principal Status (UPS) and Usual Principal and Subsidiary Status (UPSS) within the Usual Status are worked out. All the concepts are on time utilisation only. Quality of work or income does not get reflected in these approaches.

National Sample Survey Organisation (NSSO) on the basis of the carries out detailed quinquennial surveys on employment, unemployment and labour force. The last survey for which results have been published relates to the year 1999-2000. As per the results of the National Sample Survey conducted in 1999-2000, total work force as on 1.1.2000, as per Usual Status approach (considering both principal and subsidiary activities) was of the order of 401 million. About 7% of the total work force is employed in the formal or organised sector (all public sector establishments and all non-agricultural establishments in private sector with 10 or more workers) while remaining 93% work in the informal or unorganised sector.

The size of the Organised Sector employment is estimated through the Employment Market Information Programme of DGE&T, Ministry of Labour. The capacity of the organised sector to absorb additional accretion to the labour force, taking into account the current accent on modernisation and automation, is limited. In other words, an overwhelming proportion of the increase in the labour force will have to be adjusted in the unorganised sector. About 373 million workers are placed today in unorganised/informal sector in India; agriculture workers account for the majority of this work force.

Total Labour Force as on 1.1.2000	410 million
Total employed labour force as on 1.1.2000	401 million
Growth of labour force during 1994-2000	1.10% p.a.
Growth of employment (1994-2000)	1.05% p.a.
Fully unemployed as on 1.1.2000	9 million

About 41 million jobs seekers (all of them not necessarily unemployed) are registered with the 938 Employment Exchanges located throughout the country. 72% of the job-seekers registered with the Employment Exchanges are less than 30 years of age. Educated job-seekers constitute about 69% of the total job-seekers registered with the employment exchanges.

Global Employment Scenario

The global employment and unemployment situation just as to the World Employment Report 1998-99, was as follows:

- Out of an estimated 6 billion population in the year 1997 around 3 billion was in the labour force.
- 160 million persons have been estimated to be fully unemployed.
- 25 to 30 per cent of the employed labour force were underemployed.
- A large number of young people in the age group of 15 and 24 (around 60 million in 1997) are continuously in search of work. i.e., unemployed.

A few important ceases which emerge from the report are:

Limited demand for unskilled and less skilled labour.

- Increase in demand for skilled labour on account of technological development and upgradation and changes in the organisation of work
- Problems in maintaining the continued employability of labour force

Demand for Multi Skilling

Some of the important strategies recommended in the World Employment Report are:

- Timely Investment in skill development and training at enhanced level.
- Enhancement of education and skill level of workers Responsive training system. Need for effective partnership of all stake holders.

Employment in the Eighth Plan

Labour force was projected to increase by about 35 million during eighth five year's plan period (1992-97) and by another 36 million during 1997-2002. Considering the backlog of unemployment of 17 million at the beginning of Eighth Plan the total number of persons requiring employment was estimated at 54 million during 1992-97 and 94 million during 1992-2002 . Employment growth was seen to result primarily from the growth of the economy and restructuring of output composition of growth. A GDP growth rate of 5.6% per annum was envisaged. This was projected to result an employment growth rate of 2.6 to 2.8% per annum or an average of about 8 to 9 million additional employment opportunities per annum.

Employment in the Ninth Plan

Growth of labour force was projected to be more during the Ninth Plan Period in comparison to the preceding decade. This required a commensurate increase in the pace of creation of additional work opportunities in the Ninth Plan. The growth target for Ninth Plan fixed is about 6.5% per annum on an average. The sectoral structure of growth corresponding to the target of 6.5% GDP growth along with the sectoral elasticities projected generation of 50 million work opportunities in the Ninth Plan Period (1997-2002).

The projected growth rate of employment was 2.44% in the Ninth Plan. The Ninth Plan envisaged a reduction in the unemployment rate from an average unemployment rate of 1.87% in the Eighth Plan to an average unemployment rate of 1.66% in the Ninth Plan as per Usual Status. Ninth Plan accorded priority to agriculture and rural development with a view to generating adequate productive employment and eradication of poverty. Productive employment is an important dimension of the state policy that seeks to achieve growth with equity. Greater productive employment was aimed in the growth process itself by concentrating on sectors, sub-sectors and technologies which are labour intensive, in region characterised by higher rates of unemployment and under employment.

Achievements During 1994-2000.

As has already been indicated the assessment of employment and unemployment situation is made through the National Sample Survey conducted by the National Sample Survey Organization on quinquennial basis. Therefore, the survey results of 1993-94 and 1999-2000 can only be used for assessing the employment generation took place in the economy. During the period 1994-2000 the labour force which was of the order of 384.29 million had gone up to 410.39 million resulting an annual increase of 1.10% during this period. This increase is considerably less than what was projected during 8th & 9th Plan.

Similarly, the total employment which was of the order 376.99 million in 1994 had gone up to 401.35 million resulting an annual average growth of 1.05% during this period. The growth rate of employment actually achieved is also substantially less than what was projected during the 8th and 9th Five Year Plan. The slow growth rate of the labour force may be due to reduction in the growth rate of population and other reasons like the more number of children may be joining the educational institutions instead of joining to the labour force. The slow growth of employment may be primarily due to (i) the fact that the GDP growth rate actually achieved had fallen short of what was expected during 8th & 9th Plan and (ii) growth of employment did not take place as per the employment projected during the Plan.

Employment Generation in India

- 7% of the total employed were in the organised sector i.e., unorganised sector dominated in the employment scenario.

- Additional employment generation in the organised sector is not significant i.e., scope for additional wage employment in the organised sector continued to be less.
- Significant employment generation took place in tertiary sector particularly in services industries.
- Substantial employment growth was observed in the small and unorganised sector, i.e., in small and tiny enterprises.
- Self-employment and casual continued to play a pivotal role in rehabilitation of unemployed .

Trends in Employment and Unemployment

The rate of growth of employment declined sharply from 2.37% per year in the period 1987-88 to 1993-94 to only 1.05% per year in the period 1993-94 to 1999-2000. There was sharp deceleration in the growth of labour force from 2.24% in the period 1987-88 to 1993-94 to only 1.10% in the period 1993-94 to 1999-2000. Growth rate of employment is less than the growth rate of the labour force indicating an increase in the unemployment rate. The open unemployment which is of the order of 9 million was not significant compared to the size of the population in the country.

Though, open unemployment was only 2.21% (9 million), the percentage of the population below the poverty line was as high as 26.1%. The fact of being employed is obviously no guarantee of escaping the poverty, which in our situation refers to a very basic level of subsistence.

Percentage of population below the poverty line which was of the order of 36% in 1993-94 has come down to 26.1% indicating that during the period 1994-2000 improvement in the income level of the employed had taken place. Organised sector employment is not growing and its share is only 7% of the total employment.

There was decline in self-employment whereas regular salaried and casual employment showed an increasing trend during 1993-94 to 1999-2000. There was substantial increase in the average daily wage earnings in the rural areas.

Poverty Alleviation and Employment Generation Programmes

Anti-poverty strategy comprises of a wide range of poverty alleviation and employment generation programmes, many of which have been in operation for several years and have been strengthened to generate more employment, create productive assets, impart technical and entrepreneurial skill and raise the income level of the poor. Under these schemes, both wage employment and self-employment are provided to people below the poverty line.

In 1998-99, various poverty alleviation and employment generation programmes are grouped under two broad categories of Self-Employment Schemes and Wage Employment Schemes. Funding and organisational patterns are also rationalised to achieve better impact. These programmes are primarily meant for poverty alleviation and have generally not been helpful in sustainable employment generation.

EMPLOYMENT ASSISTANCE TO SPECIAL CATEGORIES

Employment Service, as in the past, continued making efforts to cater to the special needs of vulnerable parts like Women, Scheduled Caste/ Scheduled Tribe, Persons with Disabilities and disabled Ex-servicemen job-seekers. The assistance and facilities extended to such job seekers by the Employment Service are outlined as follows:

WOMEN

- Separate counters have been provided at larger Employment Exchanges for women registrants.
- The State Governments/Union Territory Administrations have been advised to post women officers at such Employment Exchanges where two or more officers are in position.
- States/UTs have also been advised to consider inclusion of at least one woman representative in the

Advisory Committee attached to their Employment Exchanges, to ensure greater employment avenues for women job-seekers.

Table. Year-wise Performance of Employment Exchanges in Respect of Women job-seekers

Year	Registration	Placement	Live Register of Women	Total Live Register	% of Live Register of Women to Total Live Register
1991	1326.7	50.9	7307.7	36299.7	20.1
1992	1160.9	44.2	7652.9	36758.4	20.8
1993	1226.2	42.4	7865.3	36275.5	21.7
1994	1316.5	42.1	8044.5	36691.5	21.9
1995	1376.0	43.6	8020.3	36742.3	21.8
1996	1446.9	50.1	8379.5	37429.6	22.4
1997	1609.1	61.5	9032.7	39139.9	23.1
1998	1518.0	42.0	9526.1	40089.9	23.8
1999	1616.7	53.0	9932.7	40371.4	24.6
2000	1646.3	35.7	10457.3	41343.6	25.3
2001 (Jan-Aug.)	1107.0	21.8	10860.2	42272.1	25.7

Salient features in respect of women job-seekers are as under:

- Live Register of women job seekers has shown an increase of 48.6% from 1991 to 2001 (August).
- The placement effected through the Employment Exchanges continued to show a mixed trend. It was hovering between 36 thousand to 62 thousand per year.
- Among the major states Kerala has the maximum (24.1 lakh) women job seekers awaiting jobs, followed by Tamil Nadu (17.5 lakh) at the end of Aug. 2001.
- Among the major States lowest number of women job seekers are in Rajasthan (0.86 lakh) as at the end of August, 2001.
- The percentage of educated women job seekers among the total women job seekers has increased from 68.7.% in 1991 to 76.4% in 2001 (Aug.).

Scheduled Castes/Scheduled Tribes

Over the years, a number of special measures were adopted by the Employment Exchanges to safeguard the interest of the job seekers belonging to SC/ST communities.

It includes:

- Maintenance of separate registration cards,
- Ensuring that the vacancy notification from public sector establishments invariably indicate details regarding reservation,
- Providing vocational guidance and imparting pre-recruitment training,
- Sponsoring suitable candidates against unreserved vacancies,
- Enlisting the cooperation of SC and ST associations in locating suitable candidates.

Performance of Employment Exchanges in respect of Scheduled Caste/Scheduled

Table. Tribe and Other Backward Class job-seekers: (in lakh)

Scheduled Caste	• Registration	7.60
	• Placement	0.29
	• Live Register	59.48
Scheduled Tribe	• Registration	2.74
	• Placement	0.18
	• Live Register	17.62
Other Backward Class	• Registration	9.37
	• Placement	0.24
	• Live Register	68.38

Salient features in respect of SC/ST job-seekers are as under:

- Live Register of SC job seekers has increased from 44.5 lakh in 1990 to 59.5 lakh in 1999, amounting to an increase of 33.7%.
- Live Register of ST job seekers has increased from 11.49 lakh in 1990 to 17.62 lakh in 1999.

- SC & ST job seekers were 14.7% and 4.4% respectively of the total job seekers on the live register at the end of year 1999.
- Placement of SC job seekers has declined from 40.6 thousands in 1990 to 28.6 thousands in 1999.

Coaching-cum-guidance Centres

Twenty two Coaching-cum-Guidance Centres for SCs/STs have been set up, one each at Delhi, Jabalpur, Kanpur, Chennai, Hyderabad, Thiruvananthapuram, Kolkata, Jaipur, Ranchi, Surat, Aizawl, Bangalore, Imphal, Hissar, Nagpur, Bhubaneshwar, Guwahati, Mandi, Kohima, Jowai, Jammu and Jalandhar. Out of these, one centre at Jowai is still in the process of being made fully functional.

These Centres:

- Provide employment related coaching-cum-guidance to SC/ST applicants
- Provide information on job requirements and the type of tests/interviews they are likely to face when called by the employers
- Take up appropriate follow up action with the employers to ascertain the results of submission against reserved vacancies
- Undertake job development work besides providing occupational information/vocational guidance and counselling and organising Confidence Building Programme for job-seekers.
- Provide facilities to SC/ST job-seekers for practising shorthand and typing at the above centres except CGCs located at Aizawl, Hissar, Bhubaneshwar, Guwahati, Mandi, Kohima, Jowai, Jammu and Jalandhar.
- Arrange from time-to-time, Pre-recruitment Training Programmes for SC/ST candidates to improve their employability through competitive examinations conducted by the Staff Selection Commission, Banking Service Recruitment Boards, etc. for Group 'C' posts in collaboration with various employing authorities and recruiting agencies

Performance of various Coaching-cum-Guidance Centres during 2001 (upto September, 2001) is:

1	Registration Guidance	13800
2	Pre-Submission Guidance	3670
3	No. of candidates who attended Confidence Building Programmes	5263
4	No. of candidates who were trained under typing and shorthand scheme.	6557
5	No. of trainees who attended the Pre-Recruitment training Programmes.	227

Special Coaching Scheme For SCs/STs-

Salient features:

- A Special Coaching Scheme to prepare SC/ST candidates for competitive examinations/selection tests for Group 'C' posts is also being operated by DGE&T in Delhi and Ghaziabad.
- So far, 5719 SC/ST job-seekers have successfully completed coaching for clerical/stenographer posts in 18 phases. The 19th phase is in progress w.e.f. 1-7-2001.
- The course is of 11 months' duration and the trainees are given stipend @ Rs.175/- per month besides free course books and limited stationery.
- Guided by the benefits derived from the Special Coaching Scheme, the scheme has been extended to six more places at Kanpur, Kolkata, Bangalore, Hyderabad, Ranchi and Surat w.e.f. January, 1992.
- In seven phases of the extended scheme, 1588 SC/ST candidates have successfully completed the course. The 8th phase of this scheme has been launched w.e.f. 1-7-2001.
- The scheme has further been extended to six more Centres at Guwahati, Imphal, Hissar, Jabalpur, Chennai and Thiruvanathapuram w.e.f. July 1999 and 294 candidates have successfully completed the course in two phases. The 3rd phase is in progress w.e.f. 1.7.2001.

- In order to ensure the effectiveness of the services being provided by Coaching cum-Guidance Centres regular inspections are conducted. The inspection plan included technical as well as administrative and O & M inspections.

Persons with Disabilities

Employment Exchanges: The employment service, continued making efforts to cater to the special needs of disabled job seekers. Performance of Employment Exchanges in respect of Disabled job-seekers (in Thousands)

Year	Registration	Placement	Live Register
1993	49.3	4.5	337.6
1994	43.7	4.5	340.3
1995	48.3	3.7	352.7
1996	52.1	3.9	359.1
1997	51.6	4.5	392.6
1998	54.9	3.6	415.3
1999	62.7	4.2	455.9

- There has been consistent increase in the number of persons with disabilities on the Live Register.
- The number of disabled job-seekers placed in employment during 1999 was 4.2 thousand.

Special Employment Exchanges for Physically Handicapped: Although, Employment Exchanges under the National Employment Service are generally responsible for the placement of Physically Handicapped, Special Employment Exchanges were also set-up over three decades ago for their selective placement.

- These exchanges attempt at securing for the disabled the most satisfying form of employment suitable to their residual physical and mental potentialities.
- At present, 42 Special Exchanges are functioning in the country.

The performance of the Special Employment Exchanges during 1999 is given in the following table:

Registration	15085
Placement	1281
Live Register	96241

- In pursuance of the recommendations of the Working Group on Employment Service and the Task Force on the reorganisation of Special Employment Exchanges, it was decided to set up Special Cells in the Employment Exchanges for promoting employment of the handicapped.
- Forty one Special Cells for the physically handicapped with a Special Placement Officer attached to the normal Employment Exchanges and funded by the Central Government have so far been set up by the Ministry of Social Justice & Empowerment.
- These are in addition to the Special Cells/Units opened for the handicapped applicants at the Employment Exchanges by various State Governments.

Vocational Rehabilitation Centres for Handicapped:

- Ministry of Labour had been fully responsive and committed to the implementation the provisions of the Persons with Disabilities Act, 1995. The Directorate General of Employment and Training (DGE &T) has been regularly coordinating and supporting Ministry of Social Justice & Empowerment (Ministry of SJE), which is the nodal ministry for the welfare of people with disabilities.
- Seventeen Vocational Rehabilitation Centres (VRCs) for handicapped have been functioning in the country one each at Agartala, Ahmedabad, Bangalore, Chennai, Guwahati, Hyderabad, Jabalpur, Jaipur, Kanpur, Kolkata, Ludhaiana, Mumbai, New Delhi, Patna, Thiruvananthapuram, and Vadodara. Out of these, the Vocational Rehabilitation Centre at Vadodara has been set up exclusively for the disabled women.
- These Centres evaluate the residual capacities of persons with disabilities and provide them

adjustment training, facilitating them with early economic rehabilitation. Efforts are also made to assist them in obtaining other suitable rehabilitation services such as job placement, training for self-employment and in plant training.

- Rehabilitation services are also extended to the disabled living in rural areas through mobile camps and Rural Rehabilitation Extension Centres (RRECs) set up in 11 Blocks under 5 VRCs viz.; VRC Chennai, Kanpur, Kolkata, Ludhiana and Mumbai.
- Proposal to establish at least one VRC in each State/ UTs has been formulated.

Table. Performance Of Vocational Rehabilitation Centres For Physically Handicaped

1. No. of clients at the beginning of 2000	158
2. No. of clients admitted during 2000	35162
3. No. of clients evaluated during 2000	34274
4. No. of clients who left the centre without completing evaluation	341
5. No. of clients still under evaluation at the end of 2000	210
6. No. of clients rehabilitated during 2000	9502

Assistance to Disabled Ex-Servicemen and Dependents:

- In order to provide placement services to the disabled ex-servicemen/Border Security Force Personnel and the dependants of defence service personnel/Border Security Force personnel killed or severely disabled in action, against the vacancies reserved for ex-servicemen and earmarked for priority categories, an Ex-Servicemen Cell was set up in the Directorate General of Employment & Training in July, 1972. Subsequently, the scope of the special services was also extended for the benefit of ex-servicemen disabled during peace-time as well as dependants of the defence service personnel killed or severely disabled in peace time with death or disability attributable to military service with effect from February, 1991.

- At the end of October, 2001, there were 183 disabled soldiers and 2138 dependants awaiting employment assistance through the Ex-Service men cell.

Minorities

- In pursuance of the Prime Minister's directive for full integration of minorities in all aspects of national life, the State Governments have been advised to ensure that no discrimination is made against minority communities in matters of registration and in sponsoring names by Employment Exchanges.
- The State Governments have also been advised to create monitoring cells to watch the progress of minorities in the matter of their registration and placement and to instruct the Employment Exchanges to organise mobile Employment Exchange Registration Camps in minority concentration areas.
- In all there were 57.3 lakh job seekers on the Live Registers of Employment Exchanges belonging to the minority communities at the end of 1999. These account for 14.2% of total job seekers on the Live Register.

Plan Schemes

The major portion of the Plan outlay of the Directorate of Employment relates to:

- The schemes for setting up and strengthening of the Coaching-cum-Guidance Centres for practising shorthand and typing for Scheduled Caste and Scheduled Tribe candidates,
- Expansion in the Vocational Rehabilitation Programmes for the disabled,
- Improving Employment Market Information programme, and
- Construction of building of C.I.R.T.E.S. at Noida.
- Plan Programmes
- The total plan provision in the budget estimate for 2000-2001 for the programmes relating to both

Employment and Training Directorates of DGE&T was Rs. 24.37 crore.

- The budget estimate for implementation of training schemes "other than Vocational Training Project" for the year 2001-2002 was Rs. 13.28 crore. These funds were kept for modernisation and consolidation of the on-going training activities in the field institutes of Training Directorate namely, restructured pattern of training at four Model Industrial Training Institutes, restructuring of NVTS, training of industrial workers, apprentices and supervisors, development of instructional media packages; and for establishing of training facilities in emerging areas to meet the training needs of industry. A Centrally Sponsored schemes "Establishment of new ITIs in North-Eastern States and Sikkim" has been approved by the Cabinet on 20th March 2001. The other centrally sponsored scheme namely "modernization / strengthening of existing ITIs in the State of J&K" has also been proposed to be taken up in the revised form.
- To consolidate and streamline the existing training facilities for women and expand the network in new areas / regions, new schemes / proposals are being taken namely, setting up of three new Regional Vocational Training Institutes at Patna, Bhubaneshwar and one in Punjab; modernising the existing workshop equipment; introducing the concept of production-cum-training centres; diversification of non-formal training and focussing on promotion & publicity of vocational / skills training for women.
- The budget estimate for implementation of schemes under the "Vocational Training Project" for the year 2001-2002 was Rs. 6.83 crore for Central Sector Schemes and Rs. 0.75 crore for Centrally Sponsored Schemes. The World Bank assistance of the Project having 20 components in 28 States / UTs came to a close on 31.12.98. EFC approved continuation of

activities and incurring of expenditure from Plan funds during the remaining period of IX Plan in respect of schemes already approved by Cabinet Committee on Economic Affairs in May 1997. More than 500 ITI s in 28 States / UT s and central institutes under DGE&T have been upgraded under the project.

- For schemes of Employment Directorate, budget of Rs. 3.51 crore was kept. The important schemes are welfare of SC/ST, rehabilitation of handicapped, revision of National Qualification of Occupations (NCO) with a view to have compatibility with International Standard Classification of Occupations (ISCO) and strengthening of Employment Market Information Programme.

INFORMATION TECHNOLOGY INITIATIVES IN NATIONAL EMPLOYMENT SERVICE

World recognizes that India's capabilities in the field of Information Technology not only provide an opportunity to the country to emerge as an IT super power in the world but also a major vehicle for all round socio-economic development in the country. Numbers of steps have been taken to ensure that the benefits of an IT based economy not only reach the people at large but also grow at a fast pace in line with international trends. DGE&T, responsible for "National Employment Service" and "National Vocational Training" in the country, has taken initiatives to achieve wide spread applications of IT in all possible areas of employment service and vocational training.

IT INITIATIVE IN NATIONAL EMPLOYMENT SERVICE

With the advent of Information Technology, Directorate of Employment embarked upon prestigious project of converting its mechanical data processing unit into a full-fledged computer centre with the twin object of processing the data at higher speed and to produce tabulation of high quality. As a result of the efforts made, computer centre for the present has been equipped with two PC- AT/386 and one 486 (UNIX BASED) servers along with 32 terminals and 6 Pentiums machines besides having trained staff and qualified officers. As on date the computer centre is handling majority of the statistical data that is being collected through 14 returns through 938 employment exchanges.

In addition to this computer centre is also handling voluminous work being generated through the data collected on employment return I (on quarterly basis) and employment return II under the EE (CNV) Act 1959. On the basis of the tabulations of ER-I quarterly estimates of employment in the organized sector are worked out and on the basis of ER-II occupational profile of employees in the organized sector is reported.

Constant upgrading of the hardware and the development of required software have also resulted in undertaking the work relating to various ad hoc surveys and studies undertaken by D.G.E.&T., from time to time. Majority of the software has been developed in house. Periodic assistance from NIC is also sought in the matters relating to system up gradation etc. Keeping in view the importance and use of computers, it has also being decided to equip Vocational Rehabilitation Centres and Coaching - cum - Guidance Centres with computers so as to give sufficient exposure to the job seekers belonging to SC/ST and handicapped as these Centres work for increasing the employability of the job seekers belonging to under privileged part of the society.

Some of the Centres have already been provided with necessary hardware and software. In order to provide speedy and efficient service to the employers and the job seekers work relating to computerization of Central Employment Exchange is also in hand. Necessary software relating to vacancies advertised by Central Employment Exchange has been developed and all the advertisements issued by Central Employment Exchange are being processed on the computers. Action to provide connectivity through networking at the Headquarter of the D.G.E.&T., has also been receiving attention and work on this has also started.

IT Initiatives in National Vocational Training

A National Task Force on Information Technology and Software Development was setup on the directive of Prime Minister Office. The Task Force has made 108 recommendations for taking necessary action by various Ministries/departments of Government of India. Department of Electronics (Now Ministry of Information Technology) have also stressed that in order to make India, IT super power, it is essential to develop IT manpower at various levels ranging from Data Entry Operator to IT Technicians to IT Professional to Researchers.

Ministry of Labour has set up a Committee on IT Action Plan to suggest initiatives to be taken on various recommendations of the above National Task Force relating to Labour sector. The committee suggested that there should be promotion of IT related trades in training institutes to meet the skilled manpower requirement of IT sector. There should also be compulsory component of IT awareness in Vocational Training courses being offered in training institutes. The following initiatives have thus been taken by DGET.

- In order to spread awareness about information technology which is a compulsory for all trainees under CTS/ATS.
- A new trade "Information Technology & Electronics System Maintenance" (ITESM) has been brought under the purview of Craftsmen Training Scheme to meet the demand of IT technicians in the country.
- A scheme to introduce the trade ITESM in 100 ITIs has been jointly taken by DGET & Ministry of Information Technology. Rs. 11.70 crore are being provided by Ministry of Information Technology to upgrade the facilities in the identified ITIs, training of their instructors and development of necessary course wares.
- Action has been initiated to introduce the following new trades relating to IT areas under the craftsmen Training Scheme:
  - Computer Hardware

- Consumer Electronics
- Mechanic Industrial Electronics

- Training courses are being offered in the following trades under the craftsmen training Scheme and Apprenticeship Training Scheme:

Under Craftsmen Training Scheme

- Electronics Mechanic
- Mechanic Radio & TV
- Computer Operator & Programming Assistant
- Desk Top Publishing Operator

Under Apprenticeship training scheme:

- Programming & Systems Administration Assistant
- Desk Top Publishing Operator
- Mechanic Television Video
- Electronics mechanic
- Mechanic Radio, Radar, Aircraft.
- Advanced Training Institute for Electronics & Processes Instrumentation (ATIEPI) at Hyderabad & Deheradun conduct short term IT related courses of 1 to 6 weak duration to meet the growing demand of IT sector.

Some of the IT application courses offered at these institutes are as under:

- Repair and Maintenance of Electronic Telephone Instruments.
- Maintenance and servicing of Colour TV receiver.
- DOS and Windows
- Microprocessor and its application
- MS Office (Word and Power point)
- Computer ka parichay Avam Hindi Me Shabda Sanshodhak (Work Processing) Prashikshan.
- Internet and Web page Design.
- Internet and E-Commerce.
- Application course on Information Technology
- Computer Appreciation Course (for ITI Instructors)
- Assembling and Maintenance of Personal Computers
- UNIX & C

- OOPS in C++
- Basics of JAVA
- MS Office 2000 (Word & Excel)
- MS Office 2000 (Power Point and Access)
- Computer Engineering for Instructors
- Computer Application in Hospital Management
- A scheme on " Modernization & Expansion of Instructor Training Programme " at 5 Advanced Training Institutes (ATI) & Central Training Institute (CTI), Chennai under the administrative control of DGE&T, is being implemented keeping in view major development in the field of Information Technology and to cope with the demand for trained instructor .The total out lay of the scheme is Rs.200.00 Lakh during IX Five Year Plan. Under the scheme it is envisaged to introduce trade of Computer Operator & Programming Assistant and ITESM in central institute of DGET in the M/o Labour for the training of ITI instructor and craftsman: -
  - Introduction of trade "ITESM" in Advanced Training Institutes (ATIs) at Howrah, Mumbai, Hyderabad and Ludhiana under Craft Instructor Training Scheme (CITS) & Craftsmen Training Scheme (CTS).
  - Introduction of the trade of COPA in ATIs at Howrah, Mumbai, Hyderabad under CITS & in ATI Mumbai under CTS.
- The following instructions have been issued to the State Govt./UT administration dealing with Craftsmen Training Scheme relating to IT initiatives to be taken at the State level.
  - Wherever suitable space is available in Government ITIs in the second shift, the same may be made available to private educational institutes of repute imparting training in the area of information technology. In return, these private institutes would train a suitable number of staff of government ITIs.

   - To develop a website covering institutes under their control containing information in respect of various courses both long term and short term, prescribed application forms.
   - Efforts should also be made to declare the result of All India Trade Test for of various trade tests conducted at institute under their control on Internet from time to time so that the trainees who have appeared in the trade test should have easy access to it.
- For implementation of a separate central scheme for 'Establishment of Management Information System for NVTS' the following activities have been carried out:
   - Two Central Units (one for development and the other for implementation) are functioning for Application Softwares in identified MIS-Modules
   - The application software systems namely Affiliation System, Curriculum Development System, Certification System and Apprenticeship System have already been implemented at State Directorates of Delhi, Punjab, Haryana, Rajasthan and West Bengal. The implementation of these modules is being taken up in the remaining States. A separate software version of these module is also in use in concerned parts of DGET Hq.
   - The Training Statistics module, namely, Progress Monitoring & Information System (ProMISe) was developed to consolidate information relating to women training programmes and apprentices seats in Central establishments. As a part of ProMISe module, a wide database of central establishments covered under Apprentices Act has also been created indicating Trade wise seats located & seats utilized in the establishments. For updating the information using internet, the system is under enhancement to include user authorization for respective field offices.

- The ITI Admission and Information Management System (ITI-AIMS) have also been developed on pilot basis.
- A National Vocational Training Information Service (NVTIS) web site has been developed and can be accessed through DGET. The service provides statistics/information on Trades, Affiliated ITIs, Field Offices/Institutes, Trade Apprentices seats in the Central Establishments etc.

WOMEN'S VOCATIONAL TRAINING PROGRAMME

Genesis: The Women's Vocational Training Programme in Ministry of Labour, launched in 1974, aimed at the social development & economic growth of women through vocational/skill training. A separate Women's Cell was formed for the purpose, which has developed into the Women's Occupational Training Directorate. This Directorate is responsible for designing & pursuing long term policies related to Women's Vocational training in the country.

INSTITUTIONAL NETWORK

A network of Institutes, both under the Central & State Sector, have been set up for extending skill training facilities to women, which aim at stimulating employment among women of various socio- economic levels and different age groups.

Central Sector

Under the Central Sector, the Institutional Network includes:

- A National Vocational Training Institute (NVTI) for Women, the apex institute at NOIDA (1977); and
- 10 Regional Vocational Training Institutes (RVTIs) for Women at:

Mumbai	(1977)
Bangalore	(1977)
Trivandrum	(1983)
Hissar	(1986)
Calcutta	(1986)
Tura	(1986)
Allahabad	(1991)

Indore	(1992)
Vadodara	(1993)
Jaipur	(!994)

- The National/Regional Vocational Training Institutes for Women are the only women exclusive Institutes that provide facilities for structured, long-term regular advanced skill and post-advanced training to women.
- *Besides the regular courses, these institutes also organize:*
  - Short term/ad-hoc courses
  - Refresher Training Programmes in Advance Skills /Pedagogy for ITI instructors
  - Short term courses in preparation/use of Audio-Visual aids.
- The infrastructure development position is as follows:
  - The NVTI at NOIDA and RVTIs at Bangalore and Trivandrum are located in their own permanent premises;
  - RVTI Mumbai is operating from a permanent building provided by the State Government of Maharastra.
  - The NVTI- NOIDA has a furnished hostel for 200 trainees and the hostel at RVTI Bangalore and Trivananthapuram is likely to be made available shortly.
  - The building of RVTIs at Tura, Calcutta, Jaipur and Allahabad are nearing completion;
  - The construction of women hostel for RVTIs Calcutta, Allahabad, Jaipur are under progress.
  - Sanction for construction of the women hostel and staff quarters at RVTI Tura has been issued.
  - RVTI at Hissar is functioning from the temporary accommodation provided by the State Government. The State Government has provided land for construction of the Institute building at Panipat. CPWD has been requested to submit the building drawings and construction estimates.

– Action for obtaining land for construction of Institute building for RVTI at Indore is in progress.

TRAINING

Central Sector

Regular skill Training programmes are offered through three-tier system consisting of Basic, Advanced and Post advanced Skill courses.

Training areas presently covered are:

- Secretarial Practice,
- Electronics,
- Architectural Draughtsmanship,
- Computer Operation and Programming Assistant
- Dressmaking,
- Embroidery,
- Hair & Skin Care,
- Fruit and Vegetable Preservation
- Instrument mechanics
  - The training facilities for women have been steadily growing and, as on 1st November 2001, more than 2050 training seats had been introduced. Table reflects the seats sanctioned in the NVTI/RVTIs.
  - NVTI/RVTIs have, since inception, provided training to about 27000 women; roughly 9000 in short-term courses and more than 18000 in regular long-term skill training courses.
  - The growth in the number of trainees trained, since inception:

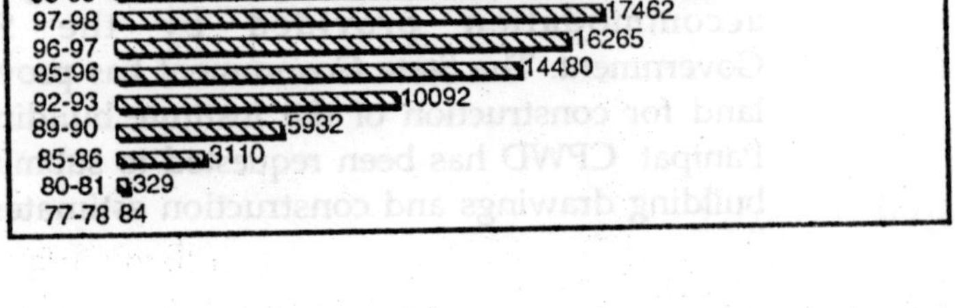

New Initiatives

- Continuous efforts are made to diversify, strengthen & modernize the existing training network.
- To assist in the placement of the passed out trainees and also monitor the movement of trained women in the employment market, Placement Cells are being set up in the Institutes. These cells, when established, would provide strong data-base and strengthen industry-institute linkages.
- The setting up of the Production -cum- Training centre in the NVTI/RVTIs has been approved by the Planning Commission. These centres are proposed to be made functional soon.

Project on 'Decent Employment for Women'

To extend the skill training to the poor women, the ILO have undertaken a project on `Decent Employment for Women in India', with the financial assistance from the US Labour Department. The Project is being implemented by ILO, and the Women Training Directorate, DGE&T would be the nodal agency from GOI.

The immediate objectives of the project are to:

- Improve the access of at least 2000 poor women in the informal sector to effective training for better employability and knowledge of their rights as workers;
- Ensure that at least 1500 women who are trained are organized and have the necessary structure and supports to translate training into decent employment and improved welfare for themselves and their families.

The programme will focus on enhancing productive employment and income earning opportunities for women as well as on promoting awareness of their rights at the workplace and as women workers in non-formal sector.

The programme is a pilot programme and will be implemented in mainly two metropolitans, namely New Delhi and Bangalore.

TRAINING METHODS

There are two broad types of training available to small businesses: on-the-job and off-the-job techniques. Individual circumstances and the "who," "what" and "why" of your training programme determine which method to use. On-the-job training is delivered to employees while they perform their regular jobs. In this way, they do not lose time while they are learning. After a plan is developed for what should be taught, employees should be informed of the details. A timetable should be established with periodic evaluations to inform employees about their progress. On-the-job techniques include orientations, job instruction training, apprenticeships, internships and assistantships, job rotation and coaching.

Off-the-job techniques include lectures, special study, films, television conferences or discussions, case studies, role playing, simulation, programmed instruction and laboratory training. Most of these techniques can be used by small businesses although, some may be too costly. Orientations are for new employees. The first several days on the job are crucial in the success of new employees. This point is illustrated by the fact that 60 per cent of all employees who quit do so in the first ten days.

Orientation training should emphasize the following topics:

- The company's history and mission.
- The key members in the organization.
- The key members in the department, and how the department helps fulfill the mission of the company.
- Personnel rules and regulations.

Some companies use verbal presentations while others have written presentations. Many small businesses convey these topics in one-on-one orientations. No matter what method is used, it is important that the newcomer understand his or her new place of employment.

Lectures present training material verbally and are used when the goal is to present a great deal of material to many people. It is more cost effective to lecture to a group than to train people individually. Lecturing is one-way communication and as such may not be the most effective way to train. Also, it is hard to ensure that the entire audience understands a topic on the same level; by targeting the average attendee you may undertrain some and lose others. Despite these drawbacks, lecturing is the most cost-effective way of reaching large audiences.

Role playing and simulation are training techniques that attempt to bring realistic decision making situations to the trainee. Likely problems and alternative solutions are presented for discussion. The adage there is no better trainer than experience is exemplified with this type of training. Experienced employees can describe real world experiences, and can help in and learn from developing the solutions to these simulations. This method is cost effective and is used in marketing and management training.

Audiovisual methods such as television, videotapes and films are the most effective means of providing real world conditions and situations in a short time. One advantage is that the presentation is the same no matter how many times it's played. This is not true with lectures, which can change as the speaker is changed or can be influenced by outside constraints. The major flaw with the audiovisual method is that it does not allow for questions and interactions with the speaker, nor does it allow for changes in the presentation for different audiences.

Job rotation involves moving an employee through a series of jobs so he or she can get a good feel for the tasks that are associated with different jobs. It is usually used in training for supervisory positions. The employee learns a little about everything. This is a good strategy for small businesses because of the many jobs an employee may be asked to do.

Apprenticeships develop employees who can do many different tasks. They usually involve several related groups of skills that allow the apprentice to practice a particular trade, and they take place over a long period of time in which the apprentice works for, and with, the senior skilled worker. Apprenticeships are especially appropriate for jobs requiring production skills. Internships and assistantships are usually a combination of classroom and on-the-job training. They are often used to train prospective managers or marketing personnel. Programmed learning, computer-aided instruction and interactive video all have one thing in common: they allow the trainee to learn at his or her own pace. Also, they allow material already learned to be bypassed in favour of material with which a trainee is having difficulty. After the introductory period, the instructor need not be present, and the trainee can learn as his or her time allows.

These methods sound good, but may be beyond the resources of some small businesses. Laboratory training is conducted for groups by skilled trainers. It usually is conducted at a neutral site and is used by upper- and middle management trainees to develop a spirit of teamwork and an increased ability to deal with management and peers. It can be costly and usually is offered by larger small businesses.

Trainers

Who actually conducts the training depends on the type of training needed and who will be receiving it. On-the-job training is conducted mostly by supervisors; off-the-job training, by either in-house personnel or outside instructors. In-house training is the daily responsibility of supervisors and employees. Supervisors are ultimately responsible for the productivity and, therefore, the training of their subordinates. These supervisors should be taught the techniques of good training.

They must be aware of the knowledge and skills necessary to make a productive employee. Trainers should be taught to establish goals and objectives for their training and to determine how these objectives can be used to influence the productivity of their departments. They also must be aware of how adults learn and how best to communicate with adults. Small businesses need to develop their supervisors' training capabilities by sending them to courses on training methods. The investment will pay off in increased productivity. There are several ways to select training personnel for off-the-job training programmes. Many small businesses use in-house personnel to develop formal training programmes to be delivered to employees off line from their normal work activities, during company meetings or individually at prearranged training sessions. There are many outside training sources, including consultants, technical and vocational schools, continuing education programmes, chambers of commerce and economic development groups.

Selecting an outside source for training has advantages and disadvantages. The biggest advantage is that these organizations are well versed in training techniques, which is often not the case with in-house personnel. The disadvantage of using outside training specialists is their limited knowledge of the company's product or service and customer needs.

These trainers have a more general knowledge of customer satisfaction and needs. In many cases, the outside trainer can develop this knowledge quickly by immersing himself or herself in the company prior to training the employees. Another disadvantage of using outside trainers is the relatively high cost compared to in-house training, although the higher cost may be offset by the increased effectiveness of the training.

Whoever is selected to conduct the training, either outside or in-house trainers, it is important that the company's goals and values be carefully explained.

Training Administration

Having planned the training programme properly, you must now administer the training to the selected employees. It is important to follow through to make sure the goals are being met.

Questions to consider before training begins include:

- Location.
- Facilities.
- Accessibility.
- Comfort.
- Equipment.
- Timing.

Careful attention to these operational details will contribute to the success of the training programme.

An effective training programme administrator should follow these steps:

- Define the organizational objectives.
- Determine the needs of the training programme.
- Define training goals.
- Develop training methods.
- Decide whom to train.
- Decide who should do the training.
- Administer the training.
- Evaluate the training programme.

Following these steps will help an administrator develop an effective training programme to ensure that the firm keeps qualified employees who are productive, happy workers. This will contribute positively to the bottom line.

EVALUATION OF TRAINING

Training should be evaluated several times during the process. Determine these milestones when you develop the training. Employees should be evaluated by comparing their newly acquired skills with the skills defined by the goals of the training programme. Any discrepancies should be noted and adjustments made to the training programme to enable it to meet specified goals. Many training programmes fall short of their expectations simply because the administrator failed to evaluate its progress until it was too late. Timely evaluation will prevent the training from straying from its goals.

Training and development managers and professional trainers today need all of the help they can get. With incessant organizational change, skills shortages and increased global competition, training employees on a cramped budget is getting harder. The training resources and learning tools in our training management part will help you create effective employee training and development programmes in your workplace.

Employee Training in Today's Workplace

Is your organization grappling with a constantly changing marketplace and internal reorganizations? As a training and development professional, are you increasingly expected to deliver real organizational benefits from your employee training programmes within shorter time frames and often with smaller training budgets? How are you meeting this challenge?

Larger organizations are continuing to adopt ever more comprehensive enterprise-wide Learning Management Systems (LMS) to deliver, track and report training programmes and expenditure. Small to medium-sized organizations on smaller budgets are also finding ways to identify, track and report employee skills.

Our inexpensive employee training tracking software can help you meet your tight training budget whilst delivering up to the minute automated reports on all aspects of your workplace training.

Training Programmes and Project Management

Also having an impact on the training industry is the increased attention being paid to the discipline of project management. "Projects" with unlimited budgets and never-ending timelines trying to satisfy fuzzy organizational objectives are becoming tolerated less and less in today's business world.

Hence, the demand for project management training has seen a dramatic rise in the last ten years. With this we have also seen an increased interest in project management tools and methodologies. Check out our project management software part for tools, templates and guides that can help your organization manage and deliver projects better.

How we manage training projects has also matured. As discretionary budgets have continued to shrink, rolling out expensive employee training programmes to satisfy ad hoc requests from department managers with no clear organizational rationale is no longer a viable option. More training projects are now being run using an Instructional Systems Design (ISD) model.

Using such a model guarantees that the learning objectives of the training programme tie in with a real organizational need. It also raises an organization's confidence that the training programme will be of high quality and satisfy the needs of all major stakeholders. Check out our guide on writing learning outcomes and our training projects template pack to help you deliver training projects more effectively.

Training Tools and Resources for Effective Training

Budget constraints and increased business competition have also led to a recent emphasis on the payback on training expenditure. Poor training needs analysis (TNA) and change management practices in the past have led to an extravagant wastage of training budgets, with experts estimating that only some 10 to 20 per cent of training dollars spent leads to some organizational benefit.

Donald Kirkpatrick's traditional four-level model remains as the most used model for evaluating the effectiveness of training. This, however, has been supplemented by Jack Phillips with a new fifth level, Return on Investment (ROI). Investigate our Training Evaluation Toolkit for a comprehensive guide and tools designed to help you evaluate the effectiveness of your training programmes.

How much are you using the new performance consulting approach in improving the effectiveness of your training programmes? With this approach, poor employee performance is diagnosed with an accurate and effective employee performance diagnostic tool before any action is taken.

Using a systems view, all workplace factors influencing employee performance are considered. The upshot is that training may not be the appropriate solution to a performance shortfall in every case. The eventual solution may be multifaceted, highlighting process deficiencies, irrelevant or inadequate rewards and recognition, ineffective goal setting, and so on.

Training Systems Best Practice

Is your training management system becoming more effective and efficient in delivering organizational capability?

Many training professionals have continued to move their organizations towards training best practice. Some do not know where to start.

Excellent human resource best practice models have been available for some time. Two prominent examples are the U.S. People Capability Maturity Model and the British Investors in People. As excellent as these models are, they are not specific to training systems. Our training best practice model, however, is specifically designed for training and development practitioners. Our Training Management Maturity Model features an evolutionary approach to achieving best practice. Coupled with an assessment, analysis and reporting tool, training managers are now able to take measured steps in improving the effectiveness of their training system.

Index

A

Absorbed 64
Aca 18, 21, 27, 58, 108, 119, 121, 170, 201, 290, 309
Accessibility 269, 305
Accomplish 3, 29, 35, 72, 76, 91, 138, 163, 213
Accountability 28, 69, 73, 169, 202
Accrual 251
Accumulation 196, 205, 244
Adequately 11, 27, 35, 73, 152, 154
Aggregating 153
Allocation 29, 36, 65, 89, 124, 184, 209, 210, 272
Alphabetical 75
Analytical 25, 31, 42, 97, 100
Applicability 97
Arithmetic 79
Assumptions 46, 61, 129, 168, 183, 205, 225
Audiovisual Methods 303
Autonomous 46, 104, 105, 163, 180, 184, 187, 190, 202, 215, 226

B

Barriers 33, 57, 97, 114, 122, 194, 219, 225, 248, 249, 251, 253, 258
Budgeted 15
Bureaucratic 21, 28, 29, 50, 51, 131
Burgeoning 70, 173, 217

C

Catastrophes, 269
Collaboration 52, 71, 80, 247, 285
Competencies 37, 38, 131, 176, 181, 246, 254, 256, 263
Conflicting 25, 29, 30, 33, 144
Criticism 42, 60, 62, 153, 185

D

Demonstrated 70, 131
Dilemmas 32
Diversification 10, 88, 291

E

Efficiency 8, 13, 28, 30, 38, 46, 51, 58, 60, 62, 93, 102, 103, 105, 117, 118, 173, 220, 235, 236, 245
Eligible 21, 32
Emphasis 8, 25, 27, 67, 71, 169, 174, 193, 199, 233, 308

Emphasized 207
Encourages 37, 101, 238, 262
Equilibrium 29
Equipment 95, 107, 108, 109, 135, 241, 246, 260, 266, 292, 306
Estimation 82, 83

F

Firefighters 30
Florida 18, 30
Fluctuations 27
Forecasting 21, 82, 83, 85, 86

H

Heterogeneous 22, 211
Hierarchy 44, 47, 50, 65, 90, 137, 174, 192, 220
Hybrid 220

I

Ideologies 66, 209
Implementation 4, 32, 36, 37, 43, 44, 45, 46, 59, 68, 78, 88, 104, 166, 168, 171, 173, 176, 177, 181, 183, 189, 215, 223, 227, 262, 263, 268, 269, 288, 291, 297
Implicit 32, 75, 156, 179, 200
Incumbents 20, 83, 95, 97, 102
Individualistic 66, 67

J

Jurisdictions 221

L

Legislation 9, 37, 63, 196, 197, 200, 207, 213, 216, 218, 219, 222, 223, 224, 225, 226, 241, 264, 268, 269, 273
Legislative Authority 28
Legitimate 33, 139
Liberalization 24, 230
LMM 44, 45, 46, 48, 49, 52, 54, 56, 57, 61, 62, 63

M

Managerial 7, 11, 16, 20, 21, 36, 45, 47, 49, 64, 65, 66, 67, 68, 70, 71, 87, 89, 97, 98, 143, 156, 168, 173, 210, 237, 259
Meredith 69
Mitigate 220

O

Obsolescence 49
Occurrence 97
Orientations 2, 68, 123, 302

P

Parameter 95, 194
Portfolio 73, 74, 76, 77, 78, 180
Predict 29, 34, 83, 114, 126, 127, 137, 142, 148, 149, 151, 152, 153, 154, 173
Preliminary 35, 112, 113, 187
Proactive 13, 24, 37, 38, 214, 218, 219, 221, 223, 225, 226, 228, 230, 249, 266
Probation 31
Procurement 2, 22, 206

R

Rationalization 61, 238

Reconciliation 26
Redundancies 89, 124

S

Scientific 8, 29, 46, 63, 138, 195, 198
Simultaneously 31, 162, 266
Sophisticated 189, 227
Speculative 78
Spiritual 65, 68
Statistical 108, 147, 151, 152, 154, 183, 215, 227, 293
Strategic 23, 35, 36, 38, 44, 45, 47, 49, 50, 51, 52, 54, 55, 73, 81, 90, 91, 94, 126, 129, 163, 167, 168, 173, 174, 175, 176, 177, 179, 180, 181
Subordinate 44, 88, 116, 146, 148, 304
Synonymous 167, 233

T

Territory 282

U

Unmanageable 84
Utilization 29, 38, 85, 88, 103, 107

V

Vergence 54, 61, 70, 174, 199, 250
Volunteers 18, 27, 30, 33